Ulli Waltinger

On Social Semantics In Information Retrieval

Ulli Waltinger

On Social Semantics In Information Retrieval

From Knowledge Discovery to Collective Web Intelligence in the Social Semantic Web

Südwestdeutscher Verlag für Hochschulschriften

Impressum/Imprint (nur für Deutschland/only for Germany)
Bibliografische Information der Deutschen Nationalbibliothek: Die Deutsche Nationalbibliothek verzeichnet diese Publikation in der Deutschen Nationalbibliografie; detaillierte bibliografische Daten sind im Internet über http://dnb.d-nb.de abrufbar.
Alle in diesem Buch genannten Marken und Produktnamen unterliegen warenzeichen-, marken- oder patentrechtlichem Schutz bzw. sind Warenzeichen oder eingetragene Warenzeichen der jeweiligen Inhaber. Die Wiedergabe von Marken, Produktnamen, Gebrauchsnamen, Handelsnamen, Warenbezeichnungen u.s.w. in diesem Werk berechtigt auch ohne besondere Kennzeichnung nicht zu der Annahme, dass solche Namen im Sinne der Warenzeichen- und Markenschutzgesetzgebung als frei zu betrachten wären und daher von jedermann benutzt werden dürften.

Coverbild: www.ingimage.com

Verlag: Südwestdeutscher Verlag für Hochschulschriften GmbH & Co. KG
Dudweiler Landstr. 99, 66123 Saarbrücken, Deutschland
Telefon +49 681 37 20 271-1, Telefax +49 681 37 20 271-0
Email: info@svh-verlag.de

Approved by: Bielefeld, University, Diss., 2010

Herstellung in Deutschland:
Schaltungsdienst Lange o.H.G., Berlin
Books on Demand GmbH, Norderstedt
Reha GmbH, Saarbrücken
Amazon Distribution GmbH, Leipzig
ISBN: 978-3-8381-2939-6

Imprint (only for USA, GB)
Bibliographic information published by the Deutsche Nationalbibliothek: The Deutsche Nationalbibliothek lists this publication in the Deutsche Nationalbibliografie; detailed bibliographic data are available in the Internet at http://dnb.d-nb.de.
Any brand names and product names mentioned in this book are subject to trademark, brand or patent protection and are trademarks or registered trademarks of their respective holders. The use of brand names, product names, common names, trade names, product descriptions etc. even without a particular marking in this works is in no way to be construed to mean that such names may be regarded as unrestricted in respect of trademark and brand protection legislation and could thus be used by anyone.

Cover image: www.ingimage.com

Publisher: Südwestdeutscher Verlag für Hochschulschriften GmbH & Co. KG
Dudweiler Landstr. 99, 66123 Saarbrücken, Germany
Phone +49 681 37 20 271-1, Fax +49 681 37 20 271-0
Email: info@svh-verlag.de

Printed in the U.S.A.
Printed in the U.K. by (see last page)
ISBN: 978-3-8381-2939-6

Copyright © 2011 by the author and Südwestdeutscher Verlag für Hochschulschriften GmbH & Co. KG and licensors
All rights reserved. Saarbrücken 2011

Acknowledgement

This work would not have been possible without the support of many people. I deeply thank Prof. Dr. Alexander Mehler for supervising this thesis and for supporting me for the past three years. He provided an inspiring and stimulating environment, resulting in many fruitful discussions that helped and improved my research ambitions. I am grateful and in dept not only for his guidance and mentorship, but also his patience and support. I want to express my gratitude to Prof. Dr. Ipke Wachsmuth who agreed to review this thesis in a very tight schedule and who provided useful comments and suggestions for further improvements. I would also like to thank the board of examiners: Dr.-Ing. Britta Wrede and PD Dr. Katharina J. Rohlfing. Many thanks are due to all of my colleagues at the Text Technology Department at Bielefeld University, in particular Dr. Armin Wegner for valuable discussions, not to mention Rüdiger Gleim, Alexandra Ernst, Olga Pustylnikov, Dietmar Esch and Tobias Feith. Finally, I would like to thank my family, Liese, Magdalena and Theresa - my beloved girls, for the enormous support and encouragement they offered me. Thanks for the endless patience over the past few years.

Ulli Waltinger

Abstract

In this thesis we analyze the performance of social semantics in textual information retrieval. By means of collaboratively constructed knowledge derived from web-based social networks, inducing both common-sense and domain-specific knowledge as constructed by a multitude of users, we will establish an improvement in performance of selected tasks within different areas of information retrieval. This work connects the concepts and the methods of social networks and the semantic web to support the analysis of a social semantic web that combines human intelligence with machine learning and natural language processing. In this context, social networks, as instances of the social web, are capable in delivering social network data and document collections on a tremendous scale, inducing thematic dynamics that cannot be achieved by traditional expert resources. The question of an automatic conversion, annotation and processing, however, is central to the debate of the benefits of the social semantic web. Which kind of technologies and methods are available, adequate and contribute to the processing of this rapidly rising flood of information and at the same time being capable of using the wealth of information in this large, but more importantly decentralized internet. The present work researches the performance of social semantic-induced categorization by means of different document models. We will shed light on the question, to which level social networks and social ontologies contribute to selected areas within the information retrieval area, such as automatically determining term- and text associations, identifying topics, text and web genre categorization, and also the domain of sentiment analysis. We will show in extensive evaluations, comparing the classical apparatus of text categorization – Vector Space Model, Latent Semantic Analysis and Support Vector Maschine – that significant improvements can be obtained by considering the collaborative knowledge derived from the social web.

Keywords: Social Semantics, Information Retrieval, Machine Learning, Text Technology, Text Categorization, Topic Identification, Text Clustering, Sentiment Analysis, Web Genre Classification

Contents

1 **Introduction**   1
    1.1 Moving from Text to the Web 2
    1.2 Classification, Categorization and Clustering 7
    1.3 About the Bag-of-Words 9
    1.4 Ontology vs. Knowledge Base 10
    1.5 Words, Concepts And Topics 11
    1.6 Open And Closed Content Models 12
    1.7 Thesis Contributions 15
    1.8 Thesis Outline 17

2 **Document Representation and Text Classification**   19
    2.1 Text Preprocessing 19
       2.1.1 Token vs. Words 19
       2.1.2 Sentence Segmentation 20
       2.1.3 PoS Tagging 23
       2.1.4 Lemmatization and Stemming 25
       2.1.5 Named Entity Recognition 26
       2.1.6 Document Structure Processing 28
    2.2 Text Representation 30
       2.2.1 Vector Space Models 30
       2.2.2 Feature Weighting 31
       2.2.3 Similarity Coefficients 33
       2.2.4 Index Term Selection 35
    2.3 Text Classification 38
       2.3.1 Naive Bayes Classifier 38
       2.3.2 K-Nearest Neighbor Classifier 39

	2.3.3	Support Vector Machine Classification	40
	2.3.4	Evaluation Metrics	42
2.4	Summary		43

3 Social Semantics in Information Retrieval — 45

3.1	Overview		45
	3.1.1	Information Retrieval	45
	3.1.2	Semantics	47
	3.1.3	Social Semantics	49
3.2	The Knowledge Acquisition Bottleneck		54
	3.2.1	Utilizing Feature Construction	55
	3.2.2	Towards the BOW by Topic Concepts	56
3.3	Social Semantic Concept Clouds		57
	3.3.1	Constructing Concept Knowledge	59
	3.3.2	Inducing the Concept Space	61
3.4	From Social Networks To Social Semantic Vectors		62
	3.4.1	Graph Structure of Social Networks	64
	3.4.2	Constructing Social Semantic Vectors	68
	3.4.3	Concluding Remarks	78

4 Evaluation of Social Network-induced Content Models — 79

4.1	Social Semantic Relatedness		80
	4.1.1	Related Work	81
	4.1.2	The Measure of Wiki Semantic Relatedness	84
	4.1.3	Experimental Evaluation	87
	4.1.4	Concluding Remarks	89
4.2	Social Network-induced Topic Identification		91
	4.2.1	Related Work	91
	4.2.2	A Method for Open Topic Identification	93
	4.2.3	Experimental Evaluation	97
	4.2.4	Concluding Remarks	101
4.3	On Social Semantics-induced Closed Topic Categorization		102
	4.3.1	Related Work	102
	4.3.2	Generalized Topic Concepts for Text Categorization	104
	4.3.3	Document-based Experimental Evaluation	104

		4.3.4	OAI-based Experimental Evaluation	109
	4.4	Concluding Remarks		114

5 Application Scenarios of Social Semantics   115

    5.1 Named Entity Instance Recognition 116

          5.1.1 The Algorithm to Named Entity Instance Recognition . 117

          5.1.2 Experimental Evaluation 121

          5.1.3 Concluding Remarks 123

    5.2 Social Semantics-induced Sentiment Analysis 124

          5.2.1 Related Work 126

          5.2.2 The Social Network-induced Polarity Enhancement . . . 128

          5.2.3 The German Polarities Clues 131

          5.2.4 Experimental Evaluation 133

          5.2.5 Concluding Remarks 138

    5.3 Web Genre Classification 138

          5.3.1 Related Work 140

          5.3.2 Hypertext Type Classification Algorithm 141

          5.3.3 Experimental Evaluation 146

          5.3.4 Remarks 151

6 Conclusion   155

    6.1 Outlook 159

List of Figures

1.1 The potential evolution scenario of web technology, moving from the Web 1.0 to a Web 4.0, by knowledge connectivity and social interaction after Mills [214] 3
1.2 Content intelligence by user interaction after Blumberg and Atre [30] 5
1.3 Outline of an RDF-graph connecting article contribution and authorship. (cf. Burleson [39]) 6
1.4 Different text classification methods by automation granularity (cf. Blumberg and Atre [30]). 8

2.1 Vector representation of document space as visualized by Salton et al. [273] 32
2.2 Cosine angle (α_1, α_2) between query and two document vectors. 35
2.3 SVM-hyperplane with maximal margin using linear and non-linear kernel constructed by the support vector machine algorithm. (a) linear separable, (b) non-linear separable, (c) schematic transformation of the input data (non-linear separable) in the higher dimensional feature space. 41

3.1 The three disciplines of semiotics after Morris [218, pp. 94]. . . . 48
3.2 Semantic relationships between the component of a lexical semantic model. 49
3.3 Application flow of an enhancement of a document representation by means of concepts derived from a reference ontology.
. . . . 59
3.4 Outline of the hyperlink structure of a *Wikipedia* article contributions and the associated category taxonomy. 62

3.5   Forced minimum spanning tree representation of the German *Wikipedia* collection. Orange edges denote article hyperlinks, green edges denote category hyperlinks, red edges denote the links to the main category. 65

3.6   Graph representation of the German *Wikipedia* collection with all comprised edges, article-to-article, category-to-category and redirects. White edges are those not needed for the spanning tree representation. 66

3.7   Graph representation of the German *Wikipedia* collection, setting the root-category *Hauptkategorie* at the center of the concept universe. 66

3.8   Extract of the German *Wikipedia* article graph using hyperlinks as edges starting from the article *Bielefeld* with a distance of one. 68

3.9   Overview of the construction of the *Social Semantic Vector* representation by means of the social network *Wikipedia* comprising article contributions and category taxonomy. 72

3.10 Enhancement-based document similarity model: Similarity (s) of document (1) and (2) by means of a feature enhancement of a shared concept cloud representation (3). (a) and (c) represent the links associated to enhanced (shared) concepts among individual texts and concepts derived from a social ontology. (b) denotes the initial overlap of textual features between (1) and (2) prior enhancement. (I) represents reference level (social ontology); (II) represents the document level. 76

3.11 Ontology-based document similarity model: Similarity (s) of documents (1) and (2) by means of mapped concept cloud representations (3) and (4). (a) and (b) denotes the mapping of the respective text onto associated concepts from a social ontology. (s) denotes the average similarity between each mapped concepts. (I) represents the reference level (social ontology); (II) represents the document level. 77

4.1 Graph representation of all category paths of the German Wikipedia social ontology, between the article concept *Bielefeld* and the root category *Hauptkategorie*. Edges comprise only category-to-category hyperlinks. 94

5.1 Hypertext Type – Conference Website: Type Segments marked by headlines 143

6.1 Screenshot of the eHumanities Desktop 160

List of Tables

1.1 Four cases of mapping categories and texts. (cf. Mehler and Waltinger [196]) 14

2.1 Outline of a JAPE rule as embedded in the ANNIE module of GATE. 27

2.2 Outline of the comprised TEI-P5 XML document representation. The attribute *'type'* of element *'w'* refers to the *Part-of-Speech-Tag* as used within the *Penn Treebank* project. [174]. The attribute *'subtype'* refers to a *Named Entity* category. The element *'s'* refers to the sentence structure of the document. . . 29

2.3 Document-Term matrix representation of document collection D and comprised term features T. 31

3.1 Knowledge repositories KB by comprised concept C and relation R information from a graph perspective. 61

3.2 Network topology of *Wikis* by language, nodes and edges. L denotes the average geodesic distance, C the cluster formation and CC denotes the cluster coefficient of the directed (d) and indirected (u) graph representation. (cf. [186, 191]) 67

4.1 Example WSR scores for different domains 86

4.2 Pearson correlations results of the net-based measures by term coverage and processing time using the *Cramer* test set (German). 88

4.3 Pearson correlations, coverage and processing time per pair of the distributional measures tested using the *Cramer* test set (German). 89

4.4 Pearson correlations of the *Wikipedia*-based measures by coverage and processing time using the *Cramer* test set (German). 89
4.5 Pearson correlations to human estimates utilizing the *GUR-65* dataset (German). 90
4.6 Spearman correlations to human estimates tested on the *Word-Similarity 353* dataset (English). 90
4.7 The number of considered subcategories of generalized topics by taxonomy level and category class. 99
4.8 Accuracy results of the topic identification experiments by means of OTM using the *Meyers Lexicon* corpus and ten topic labels. . 99
4.9 Accuracy results of the topic identification experiments by means of OTM using the *Meyers Lexicon* corpus and five topic labels. . 100
4.10 Accuracy results of the topic identification experiments by means of OTM using the *Wikipedia* corpus and ten topic labels. 100
4.11 Accuracy results of the topic identification experiments by means of OTM using the *Wikipedia* corpus and five topic labels. 101
4.12 SZ-based newspaper article corpus statistics by comprised categories and texts. 106
4.13 F1-Measure results of the different German-based SVM classification using the document-based benchmark collection. 106
4.14 Number of none unique features before and after topic generalization by reduction. 107
4.15 Results of SVM-Classification comparing Reduced-SVM and Generalized-SVM (Imp. 1) and Classical-SVM and Generalized-SVM (Imp. 2) by category. 108
4.16 Outline of the OAI meta data of Lossau [163]. Dots indicated omitted content. ([196, pp. 6]) 110
4.17 German meta data corpus by DDC classes and number of comprised OAI-PMH protocols. 111
4.18 Baseline results of traditional SVM classification on the basis of German OAI-Data using a reduced benchmark collection comprising 1000 OAI meta data records. 112

4.19 Results of traditional SVM classification on the basis of 7,473 meta data snippets. 113

4.20 Results of feature enhanced document representation using SVM on the basis of German OAI-Data. 113

5.1 Activity Ranking of Hubert Schwarz (H. S.) and Michael Krüger (M. K.) (cf. Waltinger and Mehler [340, pp. 3]) 120

5.2 Evaluation results of a named entity instance recognition by varying the foreknown knowledge. $e1$, $e2$ and *idf* refers to different edge weighting settings for ω. 123

5.3 Seed word and concept description as presented by the urban dictionary project. 130

5.4 Seed words enriched by urban dictionary based associated concepts. 130

5.5 The standard deviation (StdDevi) and arithmetic mean (AMean) of subjectivity features by English resource, text corpus (Text) and polarity category (Positive, Negative). 132

5.6 The standard deviation (StdDevi) and arithmetic mean (AMean) of subjectivity features by German resource, text corpus (Text) and polarity category (Positive, Negative). 133

5.7 *GermanPolarityClues* feature statistics by polarity and grammatical categories. 134

5.8 Overview of the *GermanPolarityClues* data schema by polarity feature, grammatical category (PoS using the *STTS*-Tagset [9]), positive (+), negative (−) and neutral (◦) polarity orientation. . 134

5.9 Accuracy results comparing four subjectivity resources and four baseline approaches. 135

5.10 F1-Measure valuation results of a English (E) subjectivity feature selection by resource, SVM-Kernel method (Linear and RBF), positive (F1-Pos) and negative (F1-Neg) polarity category. F1-Av denotes the average performance of the positive and negative results. 136

5.11 F1-Measure valuation results of a German (G) subjectivity feature selection by resource, SVM-Kernel method (Linear and RBF), positive (F1-Pos) and negative (F1-Neg) polarity category. F1-Av denotes the average performance of the positive and negative results. 137
5.12 Html-Tags used as features for the construction of the tag-matrix 146
5.13 Hypertext type with assigned segment types by corpus size . . . 148
5.14 Number of features by feature category and hypertext type. . . 148
5.15 Evaluation results for automatic segmentation experiment . . . 149
5.16 Results of SVM classification and included segments for the webgenre: conference website 150
5.17 Results of SVM classification and included segments for the webgenre: personal academic website 151
5.18 Results of SVM classification and included segments for the webgenre: project website 152
5.19 Results of hypertext type classification using stemmed token features using the hypertext stage grammar model 153
5.20 Results of hypertext type classification using bag-of-stages approach with stemmed token attributes and enhanced named entity recognition. 153

Acronyms

BOW	Bag-of-Words	9
CTM	Closed Topic Model	13
CGM	Closed Genre Model	13
DDC	Dewey Decimal Classification	13
FAQ	Frequently Asked Questions	7
idf	inverse document frequency	32
IR	Information Retrieval	1
kNN	k-nearest neighbors	7
KB	Knowledge Base	10
LDA	Latent Dirichlet Allocation	56
LDS	Logical Document Structure	14
LSA	Latent Semantic Analysis	9
NB	Naive Bayes	38
NE	Named Entity	4
NER	Named Entity Recognition	26
NEIR	Named Entity Instance Recognition	117
NLP	Natural Language Processing	2
OGM	Open Genre Model	14
OTM	Open Topic Model	13
ODP	Open Directory Project	11
OWL	Web Ontology Language	6

PDC	Polarity Difference Coefficient	136
PoS	Part-of-Speech	9
RDF	Resource Description Framework	6
SVM	Support Vector Machine	7
SSW	Social Semantic Web	1
SSV	Social Semantic Vector	75
SW	Semantic Web	5
TC	Text Categorization	7
TI	Topic Identification	2
tf	term frequency	33
UD	Urban Dictionary	129
VSM	Vector Space Model	9
WWW	World Wide Web	2
XML	Extensible Markup Language	6

Pre-Published Work

Much of the material presented in this thesis has been published in national and international peer-reviewed conferences and workshop proceedings, journal publications and given talks. The evaluations of the pre-processing and representation formats of documents, as described in Chapter 1, were published in Mehler et al. [204] and Waltinger and Mehler [342]. The preliminary studies of the proposed methodology on social semantics in Chapter 3 has been published in the journal contribution in Mehler and Waltinger [196] and also in selected conference proceedings: with respect to open topic models, the main contributions have been published in Waltinger et al. [343], Waltinger and Mehler [341] and Waltinger et al. [344], with respect to the definition of closed content models in extracts in Waltinger et al. [346]. An excerpt of the comparative study on semantic relatedness (Chapter 4) has been published in Waltinger et al. [345] and Waltinger and Mehler [341]. Content of Chapter 5 has been published in Waltinger [337], Waltinger [338] and Waltinger [339], particularly the polarity-enhancement method and the comparative study on sentiment analysis. In Waltinger and Mehler [340] the algorithm of the named entity instance recognition approach was published. With respect to the two-level approach to web genre classification, it is based on the conference contribution in Waltinger et al. [347]. The developed online software system, as outlined in Chapter 6, was published and presented in Gleim et al. [97, 98], Mehler et al. [205]. I wish to thank all of the anonymous reviewers of the publications for their beneficial comments and suggestions that helped to improve and shape this thesis.

Chapter 1

Introduction

> *"Web science is about more than modeling the current Web. It is about engineering new infrastructure protocols and understanding the society that uses them, and it is about the creation of beneficial new systems. It has its own ethos: decentralization to avoid social and technical bottlenecks, openness to the reuse of information in unexpected ways, and fairness. Web science is about making powerful new tools for humanity, and doing it with our eyes open."*
> Berners-Lee [19, pp. 4]

This thesis is about computational methods for the construction of document models and the automatic categorization of textual elements within the domain of Information Retrieval (IR). More precisely, we want to analyze at which level the *social factor* of the so-called Social Semantic Web (SSW) [28] can contribute to the performance of selected information retrieval tasks; what kind of technologies and methods are available, adequate and contribute to the processing of the rapidly rising flood of information while being at the same time capable of using the wealth of information in this large but more importantly decentralized internet.

We argue that the incorporation of collaborative constructed knowledge, derived from social networks, will help to overcome domain specific issues within the area of information retrieval and allows to improve the performance of information retrieval systems. In this context, this work will connect the concepts and methods of social networks and the semantic web to support the analysis of a social semantic web, which combines human intelligence with machine learning and natural language processing. This chapter introduces the aim and the motivation of this thesis. The end of this chapter provides an overview of the structure of the thesis.

1.1 Moving from Text to the Web

This thesis connects two research areas within the content-orientated IR [12], which has moved closer and closer in recent years. On the one hand, we discuss text categorization, text classification and Topic Identification (TI) within texts as the classical tasks within the field of text mining [114, 185, 197]. On the other hand, we deal with hypertext categorization and web genre classification, which contributes to the field of web mining [47, 198]. In both cases, we aim to discover and extract knowledge from natural language resources. Obviously, automatic (hyper-)text classification is of utmost interest in all areas of IR and Natural Language Processing (NLP) such as for search engines, digital libraries and knowledge discovering services.

Primarily, the exponential growth of the World Wide Web (WWW), enables us to retrieve and use a vast quantity of web-based documents to develop and test new computational methods. On the one hand, this might be due to the decrease in storage media costs, archiving an enormous amount of digital data. On the other hand, it is due to the rising popularity of participation and interaction within the online community. More precisely, we clearly moved from the so called *Web 1.0* to the *Web 2.0* (see Figure 1.1) by *harnessing collective intelligence* within the web community [228]. While we can consider that the *Web 1.0* was all about connecting information units via hyperlink structures, and getting people to participate, the phenomenon of the *Web 2.0* is about connecting people and user, *putting the 'I' in user interface, and the 'we' into webs of social participation* [214]. We can argue that a so-called *Web 3.0*, is currently on the point of its origin [20]. It can be expected that the main focus of the *Web 3.0* is set to an automatic identification and representation of the semantic meaning of information, connecting knowledge and putting them into a context.

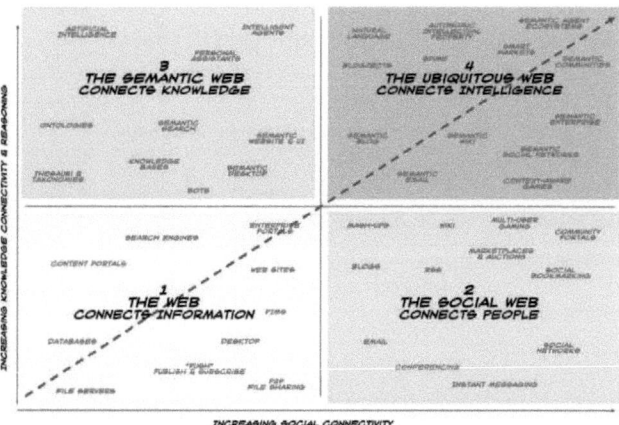

Figure 1.1: The potential evolution scenario of web technology, moving from the Web 1.0 to a Web 4.0, by knowledge connectivity and social interaction after Mills [214]

The expectations of a *Web 4.0* is that it might lead to connecting intelligences in a ubiquitous web, where both human and machines (content intelligence) communicate with each other [214]. As the main connector, again hyperlinks are building the foundation of the current definition of a *Web 2.0*. As users create and publish new content, it gets discovered through the task of connecting content elements, authoring hyperlinks. These associations allows the web to *organically grow*, which is *an output of the collective activity of all web users* [228]. On the other side, this phenomenon clearly indicates the need for intelligent methods of accessing the amount of available data. There is a need to induce semantic information in order to be able to extract only specific information that is relevant to the user.

As IR deals with accessing large collections of texts – the retrieval of query related documents per se – numerous sub-areas of IR attempts to offer detailed answers to a specific question:

- text categorization, as the task to assign documents to one or more (predefined) categories;
- hypertext type classification, as the task for identifying web-genre related information;
- information filtering, as the process of matching input documents to users interest profiles;
- question answering, which aims to extract specific answers, rather providing full documents.

Recent activities in the field of search engines emphasize this need by offering new services that try to deliver a more organized 'search experience', promoted as 'decision engines[1]' - promising to help users make better decisions when searching for specific information, or 'knowledge engines[2]' - comprising multiple sources to answer user queries directly. *Microsoft*'s semantic search initiative *Powerset*[3] thereby focuses on a single web-based document collection, using the online encyclopedia *Wikipedia*[4] as a resource for knowledge *retrieval*. Their focus is set on improving the way to find information by identifying the meaning encoded in ordinary human language, instantiated through keyword, phrase or question based search queries. By creating one of the biggest searchable web document index, the search engine *Cuil*[5] tries to provide a structure-enhanced search result presentation. This is done by analyzing pages not only by their content and relevance, but also offering Named Entity (NE) related categories for the exploration of the result set.

---

[1] www.bing.com
[2] www.wolframalpha.com
[3] www.powerset.com
[4] www.wikipedia.org
[5] www.cuil.com

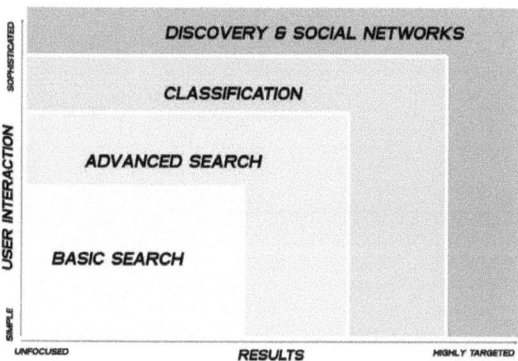

Figure 1.2: Content intelligence by user interaction after Blumberg and Atre [30]

All of these attempts and activities are heading towards the idea, converting the web into a distributed machine understandable data resource, subsequently improving the traditional web search by helping users to find specific information or answering detailed questions. In terms of *content intelligence*[6] (see Figure 1.2), we are moving from the simple unfocused services to more and more targeted and sophisticated solutions in the retrieval of documents. The task of enhancing semantic information by means of adding meaning to information fragments, should computers and humans assist to work in cooperation, reflecting the main idea of the so called Semantic Web (SW) [20, 102].

> *"The Semantic Web provides a common framework that allows data to be shared and reused across application, enterprise, and community boundaries. [...] It is about common formats for integration and combination of data drawn from diverse sources, where on the original Web mainly concentrated on the interchange of documents."* Herman [113, pp. 1]

---

[6]By means of a dynamic linkage of content units. Content intelligence *is enabled by metadata attached to the content, topic-specific ontology, resource ontology (to denote the real resource linked to nodes in ontology), and the methods (or programs) to handle them.* Sigel [291, pp. 13]

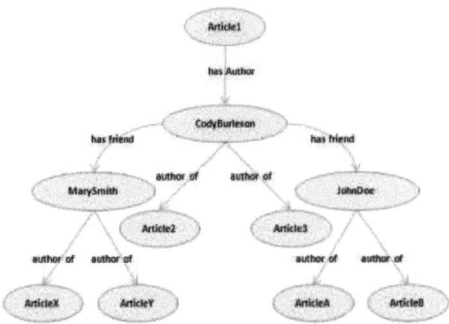

Figure 1.3: Outline of an RDF-graph connecting article contribution and authorship. (cf. Burleson [39])

In this sense, the SW is more about a web of relations *between* resources denoting real world objects e.g. such as people, countries or events rather than a web of accessible documents [102]. More formally, we can assume, following Chakrabarti [46, pp. 10], [294], that the data on the SW can be modelled as a directed labelled graph, that nodes represent resources or objects (e.g. Paris, France) and edges correspond to property types or relations (e.g. located in, is capital of). In terms of semantic annotation[7], there are numerous attempts at representing resources and their inter-relations on the SW. As the most widely accepted Extensible Markup Language (XML)-based interchange format, the Resource Description Framework (RDF) [110, 144] and its specification the Web Ontology Language (OWL) [235, 236] is used. Both are markup language recommendations for web resources by the W3C. The manual creation of semantic annotation is however an expensive and time-consuming task, which relates to the field of ontology management [297].

> "Ontologies are the vocabulary and the formal specification of the vocabulary only, which can be used for expressing a knowledge base [...] It should be stressed that one initial motivation for ontologies was achieving interoperability between multiple knowledge bases."
> Hepp et al. [111, pp. 6]

---

[7]In the sense of conceptualization: a body of formally represented knowledge [101, pp. 1]

Therefore, methods for automatic discovery, extraction and annotation of specific information and their inter-relation to other objects from natural language resources are of utmost interest in all areas of IR.

1.2 Classification, Categorization and Clustering

> *"Classification or categorization is the task of assigning objects from a universe to two or more classes or categories [...] The goal in text categorization is to classify the topic or theme of a document."* Manning and Schütze [172, pp. 575]

Text Categorization (TC) is one of the major tasks in the field of IR. In general, TC classifies texts into one (single-label) or more (multi-label) predefined categories. Categories themselves can refer, among others, to newspaper rubrics (i.e. politics sports or economics), email classification (i.e. spam, private, business), hypertext types (i.e. weblogs, Frequently Asked Questions (FAQ), private homepages, commercial online shops), emerging topics (i.e. presidential election, production of energy), but also to sentiment polarity categories (i.e. positive, neutral, negative sentiments). We can identify four different types of approaches to TC (see Figure 1.4) on the basis of their automation granularity.

- Manual subject tagging and annotation by experts is on the one side, one of the most costly methods, but also one of the most precise techniques within the field of TC.

- Rule-based approaches are based on manually - mostly also by experts - created classification rules that achieve a high accuracy but they take time and are restricted to one domain only.

- (Semi-)Supervised classifier involves machine learning techniques, such as Support Vector Machine (SVM) or k-nearest neighbors (kNN) algorithms [374].

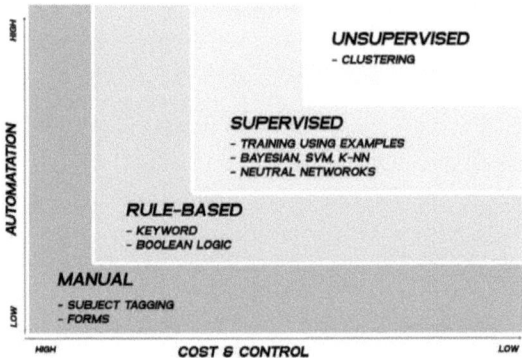

Figure 1.4: Different text classification methods by automation granularity (cf. Blumberg and Atre [30]).

The classification is based on the presence of pre-labelled text information for training, gaining automatically built classification rules. These methods involve only a limited amount of effort (preparation of positive texts only) and can be easily transferred to new domains.

- Unsupervised methods refer to clustering techniques excluding pre-defined categories or training material [171, ch. 14]. Thereby texts are automatically grouped together into a number of identified clusters. These approaches save costs and have the highest automation granularity since they do not require pre-existing taxonomy or category structure.

In general, we refer to text categorization when categories are known in advance and to text clustering when no category set is given. In this thesis, we adopt both (semi-)supervised machine learning and unsupervised clustering methods, because of their capability of being transferred to different domains within the IR. More precisely, we investigate how to improve the performance of supervised classifier by effective feature enhancement and reduction using unsupervised and semi-supervised methods.

1.3 About the Bag-of-Words

Whenever text categorization or text clustering is performed, a text representation format is needed. Most existing classification systems in NLP refer thereby to the Bag-of-Words (BOW) model, where a text is represented as an unordered collection of content elements. More precisely, to the Vector Space Model (VSM) [272], which is *the* popular text representation model in various fields of IR such as e. g. word sense discrimination [287], topic tracking [5] and TC [130]. The VSM makes use of linear algebra representing textual data as vectors, inducing a weighting scheme. While in general, the BOW method is very effective and easy to construct, it mainly focuses on words capable of being differentiated by their category affiliation. Hence, category-related documents share a similar vocabulary instantiated by their word appearances *explicitly* mentioned in the documents. However, this assumption has its limitations in two ways: First, dealing with short texts, and therefore with a very small set of textual data, delimits the possibility of sharing the same vocabulary. Second, dealing with large documents leads to a limitation in terms of effectiveness in the computation of the categorization process.

There are various attempts that have extended the BOW approach regarding additional lexical or non-lexical features[8]. Lexical motivated BOW extensions consider, for example, n-grams or entire phrases [42, 44, 240] for the task of TC. Others using syntax information such as Part-of-Speech (PoS) features [99, 270]. Additionally, various research studies have focused on the clustering of words for TC [13, 54, 76]. Several studies have researched the use of dimensionality reduction techniques such as the Latent Semantic Analysis (LSA) [45, 74, 121, 149, 168, 271, 287], by trying to measure indirect relations of texts. While the performance of these TC systems and their different notions of BOW have steadily improved since the introduction of machine learning techniques in the early 1990s [288], they are mainly limited to the vocabulary of the document collection used for TC.

---

[8]In this context, the extension of the traditional BOW, as a bag of *single* word features, focuses primarily on different notions of comprised lexical and non-lexical features - towards single word units.

These systems are only able to use those information snippets that are obtained and extracted from the text resources. Therefore, word generalizations or synonymous word resolutions (e. g. an instance of concept A is also an instance of concept B) [164] are ignored[9]. In addition, regarding the structure of documents and word order, the classical definition of BOW considers words as an unordered set of textual elements, and therefore ignores the actual context of the words themselves. This obviously leads to difficulty in the task of word sense disambiguation (e. g. polysemy) or structure-orientated classifications (e. g. web genre identification, functional document structure analysis). Even so, most of the TC approaches use pre-processing components (e. g. performing shallow parsing, lemmatization or stemming) in order to reduce multiple wordforms down to the common baseform (e. g. lemmata or stem). Features used for TC still remain those obtained out of the text collection.

> "... these [limitations of BOW approaches] shortcomings stem from the fact that the bag of words method has no access to the wealth of world knowledge possessed by humans ..." Gabrilovich [90, p.24]

1.4 Ontology vs. Knowledge Base

As consequence of the limitation of typical BOW approaches, features used for TC are only those that occur in the text, additional resources have to be processed in order to induce the existing text representation and its delimited vocabulary with domain-specific knowledge. Nevertheless, a central question arises when using external resources for the task of feature enhancement: what resource should be used in order to obtain common-sense and *domain-specific knowledge*[10]? In recent years, various approaches have been proposed regarding the domain of feature enhancement in TC. In general, we can distinguish between two different resources used as a Knowledge Base (KB) for TC-orientated feature enhancement.

---

[9]Certainly, these techniques could be processed prior the BOW construction (see next paragraph).

[10]Following the notion of [334, pp. 5], that domain-oriented knowledge is structured in a way oriented at the domain, and moreover, domain specificity is made the explicit target of structuring.

- Ontology-based KB are resources mostly based on external ontologies such as lexical-semantic networks *WordNet* [83] or *GermaNet* [154] involving expert knowledge. While these resources are highly structured, their coverage in terms of comprised vocabulary are rather low. Nevertheless, obtained background knowledge for feature enhancement does improve TC accuracy [8].

- Social network-based KB induces *world knowledge*[11] as constructed by various users such as at the Open Directory Project (ODP) [91], the online encyclopaedia *Wikipedia* [89, 165, 349, 370], or *Wiktionary* [372]. These user-generated content repositories can be a valuable resource of terminological knowledge comprising both common sense and domain-specific knowledge. As social network-based KB are authored by individual users, who contribute constantly new content, the coverage property of those KBs are rather high(e.g. the *Wikipedia* dataset[12]).

We analyze both KB with regards to TC accuracy and applicability in more detail in Section 5.1. Thus, we argue that collaborative constructed knowledge, used for the enhancement task, improves the effectiveness and accuracy of TC, and circumvents the data sparseness problem of traditional BOW approaches. Furthermore, we argue that within certain fields of IR, social network-based KB perform superior to lexical-semantic network-based KB.

1.5 Words, Concepts And Topics

Mapping an existing document, text fragment, query or single word onto specific concept entries of a KB (corpus-based or thesaurus-based model [239]), an association model[13] [123] is needed. This model spans the relationship between two or more concepts (e.g. synsets or text) on the basis of a defined relatedness or similarity score. With respect to the task of classifying topics, a topic probability or association is needed.

---

[11] World knowledge, following Gabrilovich and Markovitch [91], by means of collaborative constructed knowledge within one more more social networks.

[12] The online project *Wikipedia* is currently the largest online encyclopedia having more than 3.2 million articles in English online (1.4 million article in German).

[13] Association by means of word-concept mapping.

For example the words 'Microsoft', 'Windows', 'MSN' would have a higher topic probability to the concept 'Bill Gates' than to 'Steve Jobs'. Note, this probability is not able to define a specific semantic relation, but that one exists [353].

This issue relates to the domain of semantic relatedness and semantic similarity, which has become an important task in many NLP applications such as spelling error detection, automatic summarization, word sense disambiguation and information extraction [345]. In this thesis, we propose a method for determining the semantic relatedness between two single words (term-term association) or text fragments (term-group association) automatically. Moreover, we argue that with respect to the modelling of term-associations, KBs, which are based on world knowledge as constructed by a multitude of users within a social network, are superior to ontology resources that are constructed by expert knowledge.

1.6 Open And Closed Content Models

The traditional definition of text categorization can be expressed as the task of classifying documents by a fixed number of predefined categories. We want to refine this definition, however, by means of the changeability of content models. In general, regarding a classification scheme (e. g. categories or topics), we need to distinguish between either a closed or an open system of categories [196]. While closed classification systems use a fixed set of categories, open systems having categories or topics that change over time. Besides the fact that all systems change somehow in time, especially with the emergence of social ontologies [191, 209, 210] and their corresponding rate of change, a new reference point in the dynamic of a system has to be set. Consider, for example, TC systems that utilize the category taxonomy of the *Wikipedia* project as their topic categories. Users are constantly creating, deleting, merging and splitting categories within the online project. Therefore, open categorization systems need to be capable of reacting to this kind of system dynamics.

This follows Mehler and Waltinger [196], introducing a decision matrix (see Table 1.1) of content models with regards to their content categorization:

- Closed Topic Model (CTM): A fixed classification scheme (e.g. Dewey Decimal Classification (DDC)) or terminological ontology is given in advanced. CTMs relate to the traditional TC task, using (semi-)supervised methods, having a fixed scheme and a reliable training material.

- Open Topic Model (OTM): Topic categories are explored in an open ever-growing social ontology. New topics emerge by the collectively collaborated interaction and organization of constantly growing social ontologies (e.g. Wikipedia, Wiktionary) within the online community. OTM relates to a more sophisticated task within TC because no training material is involved. Furthermore, regarding unsupervised methods, the empirical data is constantly growing and there is, therefore, no fixed set of data for the clustering task. Thus, OTM relates to the task of topic identification with the extension of a human open topic universe.

In addition to the differentiation between the openness and closeness dynamic of topic-related classification, a second distinction should be drawn. We can identify a difference within text types as we deal with *news* or *journal articles*, *master* or *doctoral thesis* and so on. Therefore, there are texts sharing the same topic but varying in their text type or genre and vice versa [196].

In addition, regarding online media, we are also able to identify different hypertext types or genre [193, 198, 207, 258, 280, 281, 282]. Genre types on the Web are instantiated, for example, by *weblogs, personal homepages, academic project sites* or *search engine websites*. That is, genre defines *a particular style or category of work of art* within the off- or online universe [283]. By adapting the idea of openness and closeness character of topics towards the domain of (web-) genre, we can define two different genre models [196]:

- Closed Genre Model (CGM): genre categories are analogue to CTM enumerated in advance. CGM also refers to the traditional TC task, by having a fixed classification scheme. Approaches in genre classification, however, differ to topic-related categorization, we will analyze this issue in more detail in section 5.3.

	closed	open
topic	content classification scheme	emergent topics model
genre	genre palette	emergent genres model

Table 1.1: Four cases of mapping categories and texts. (cf. Mehler and Waltinger [196])

- Open Genre Model (OGM) within the dynamic of web communities: we can assume that fixed *genre palettes* [258] will also certainly change by *style, kind or sort of texts* [283]. Analog to OTM, OGM refer to the domain of an emergent web genre with regards to the dynamics of online communication.

This thesis focuses on computational methods for the categorization of open and closed topic and genre models. More precisely, we propose a method of incorporating the openness character of OTM within the classification task with respect to the dynamics of web-based communication. Furthermore, we investigate the use of OTM within the categorization process of CTM, by analyzing the performance of a feature-enhanced categorization of the CTM. Comprised features thereby refer to topic-related categories obtained through the categorization of OTM.

We will explore the categorization of CGM by means of document *and* genre-related structural components [199, 200, 203], seizing the notion of web genre subtype features [192, 347][14]. With respect to the actual categorization task within both fields, topic and genre categorization, a further fundamental differentiation has to be made. Performing a document classification or clustering, an exploration of relevant and most suited document features used for the task is needed. This analysis can be divided into two branches with regard to a documents structure. Observing a document by its lexical components, we will address the *micro structure* of a document. If we explore the document by its structure (e.g. functional or Logical Document Structure (LDS)), we will define it as a *macro structure* analysis [196]. While the majority of traditional TC methods focus on the lexical constitutes of documents, macro structure-

---
[14]Following Mehler et al. [203], the notion of *hypertext type* and *web genre* will be used interchangeably in this thesis.

related classification of texts [201, 202], graphs [190] or networks [187, 188] have recently drawn the attention of the research community. In this thesis we adopt both, micro and macro structure-related components, for the task of building topic and genre models. In addition, we analyze the profits of incorporating social ontologies as a resource for document-related semantic concepts and for the task of TC. By consolidating both the openness character of social interaction within the online community, and the *systematicity* [196] of traditional content models, we are heading towards our notion of *social semantics in information retrieval*[15], improving retrieval effectiveness.

1.7 Thesis Contributions

The contributions embodied in this thesis towards the field of information retrieval are as follows:

1. **Social Network-based Representation Model.** We propose a social network-based representation model as a two-fold Social Semantic Vector Space. We explore lexical and structural knowledge from texts and social ontologies, utilizing a repository of knowledge concepts as a source of feature enhancement and measuring direct/indirect similarities of textual elements.

2. **Term/Text Association.** We propose a method for determining the semantic relatedness of textual elements by integrating social ontologies and social tagging as repositories of natural language texts. We will evaluate our method in comparison to various current state-of-the-art algorithms, where significant improvements can be observed.

3. **Topic Association.** We propose a method of building open topic models by conducting a topic generalization technique, utilizing the social ontology of the online encyclopaedia *Wikipedia*. That is, we perform a topic-related text analysis for the task of topic identification and topic-orientated feature generation. Therefore, we extend the text representation model by means of topic related concepts, introducing the notion

---

[15]A detailed definition of the notion of *social semantics in information retrieval* will be given in Chapter 3.

of concept clouds. The task of topic identification is evaluated by using two different corpora.

4. **Topic Categorization.** We systematically evaluate the performance of topic-orientated feature enhancement to the task of text categorization by means of closed topic models. We show that feature enhancement contributes to classification accuracy, but more importantly that the topic feature prediction technique can act as a feature supplement, increasing accuracy and coverage. This assumption will be evaluated by means of an experimental setup using two different corpora.

5. **Sentiment Classification.** We formulate a method by using socially constructed definitions for the task of sentiment analysis. That is, we transfer our notion of social semantics to the domain of sentiment polarity analysis. We propose a method of enriching the delimited vocabulary of subjectivity dictionaries by means of a sentiment-concept enhancement. In addition, we propose a novel subjectivity resource for the German language, which is comprised in an extensive experimental setup

6. **Genre Categorization.** We propose a method of classifying closed genre models by resizing the notion of hypertext subtypes. We analyze the impact of textual, structural and subtype features for the task of web genre classification in a comprehensive evaluation setup.

1.8 Thesis Outline

This thesis is organized as follows. While Chapter 1 presented the motivation and summarized the contributions of this research, Chapter 2 will review the processing architecture of information retrieval systems. It will describe background perspectives of document representation and similarity, text categorization and machine learning algorithms, which are applied throughout this work. Chapter 3 presents the main contributions related to social semantics in information retrieval. In this chapter, we will define and instantiate the methodology of incorporating hierarchically organized collaborative knowledge to document models. After the definition of social semantics is motivated, algorithms and methods are presented on how to incorporate social networks and social ontologies into information retrieval systems. In Chapter 4 we will present the empirical evaluation of our model to social semantics. At first, a resource evaluation is performed on the basis of an automatic determination of the semantic relatedness of textual elements. Subsequently, two different evaluation scenarios are described and carried out with respect to the construction of social network-induced open- and closed content models. In each section, the related literature is surveyed and results are discussed. Chapter 5 presents three further application scenarios of the proposed methodology of a social semantics in information retrieval, covering named entity instance recognition, sentiment analysis and web genre classification. Finally, Chapter 6 will conclude this thesis and describe the focus for future research.

18

Chapter 2

Document Representation and Text Classification

This chapter's aim is to present a review of the processing architecture of information retrieval systems. We will describe the background perspectives of document representation, preprocessing and similarity, text categorization and machine learning algorithms, components that are used throughout this thesis. At the end of this chapter, the evaluation metrics that are used for the evaluation of the proposed algorithms are described.

2.1 Text Preprocessing

Words, phrases and sentences are important units in the processing of natural language texts. When building a text representation model, for example the BOW approach, we need to have access to these units despite its initial document format (e.g. html or plain text). Therefore, a document pre-processing is needed. Regarding structural information, the logic document structure must be considered, while with respect to linguistic information, the actual textual content must be processed.

2.1.1 Token vs. Words

In the most common form, machine-readable text is a stream of characters, which must first be segmented into words, then phrases and finally into sentences. Though, humans can intuitively assess what a word is from a computational perspective, it is rather hard to give a precise definition. Consider, for example, the sentence:

> *"We don't care," she remarked, "what a group of e.g. money-management experts say."*

How should the unit ⌐don't⌐ be processed? As one word, or as two parts ⌐do not⌐? Or should we split this unit into three parts as ⌐don⌐, ⌐'⌐, ⌐t⌐? What about the unit ⌐money-management⌐? Should it be split? As the most common principle, a given text is in first order not split into words but rather into tokens. Afterwards a word unit construction (e.g. abbreviation resolution, multi word reconnecting ...) is assimilated with respect to the actual computational task. The tokenization method carried out in this thesis is computed in four consecutive steps. First, we separate between structural and textual components. Hence, we identify structure-related characters that occur in the character stream. With respect to plain text, these characters are, for example, line-breaks such as \n or \r. With respect to hypertext, we extract the associated hypertext mark-up (e.g. division, paragraph or headings), in order to identify the document structure. In both cases, we are building a unified logical document structure (LDS) representation [249] on the basis of the XML-Standard *TEI-P5* [40, 122, 254, 313]. Second, the input stream of the textual components are normalized (multiple whitespace characters are reduced to one only) and split by a whitespace separator. Thus, we distinguish between whitespace and non-whitespace character - the initial tokens. Third, we additionally conduct a splitting for each non-whitespace character on the basis of punctuation marks or other than non-letter or number chars. Fourth, we reconnect tokens to word units following a rule-based method (e.g. reconnecting abbreviations, from ⌐e⌐, ⌐.⌐, ⌐g⌐, ⌐.⌐ to ⌐e.g.⌐, dates or web-address URL). The tokenized word representation is then added to the TEI-P5 representation, which is used for further processing.

2.1.2 Sentence Segmentation

Having detected the word boundaries of an input document, a sentence boundaries detection is conducted. Various computational linguistics methods (syntactic processing such as parsing) operate on individual sentences. The quality of a sentence-based segmentation, therefore, contributes to many linguistic phenomena such as text translation [255], part-of-speech tagging [310] or the computation of co-occurrence corpus statistics [25, 114]. On the lines of the tokenization process, the definition of a true sentence boundary varies diversely. Let's revisit the above example:

> *"We don't care," she remarked, "what a group of e. g. money-management experts say."*

The appearance of quoted text units produces in fact a nested sentence structure. Other characters also inherit this kind of boundary ambiguity such as:

⟨.⟩ ⟨!⟩ ⟨?⟩ ⟨:⟩ ⟨;⟩ ⟨…⟩

In this thesis, we treat the above example as one sentence. In general, it can be stated that approximately 90% of the appearances of a period refer to a true sentence boundary [230]. The majority of the leftover 10% refer to abbreviations. This determination leads to the proposal of Kiss and Strunk [143], which argue that the accuracy of a sentence boundary detection system can be improved by an enhanced abbreviation detection. In other words, having identified that a period is not an abbreviation, it must be a sentence boundary. Similar approaches were proposed by Grefenstette and Tapanainen [100], which presented a method concentrating primarily on the disambiguation of the period character. They followed the idea of the principle of exclusion for period characters by identifying numbers and alpha-numeric references, (e.g. 23.4, C-1.AT) but also using a list of frequent abbreviations. By that the precision evaluated on the *Brown Corpus* could be improved from 93.2% to 99.07%. The method proposed by Reynar and Ratnaparkhi [261] focused also on the disambiguation of ⟨.⟩ ⟨!⟩ and ⟨?⟩ character, but using a maximum entropy model. The classification focuses on a three token wide context window around the potential sentence boundary used for the training. Their evaluation was based on the *Wall Street Journal* (WSJ) corpus achieving a precision of 99.13%. Although both methods gain a high precision, we have implemented the *Punkt* sentence boundary system [141, 142, 143] for period disambiguation in our pre-processing architecture, since this method operates without any required training data or abbreviation lists – in an unsupervised mode. Nevertheless, their published precision results of 98.93% with the *WSJ* corpus are at the same level as the other two approaches. In principle, the algorithm of *Punkt* can be summarized as follows: The *Punkt* system assesses the log likelihood ration between two hypothesis: The first hypothesis H_0 argues that two consecutive words are independent of each other: $P(w_2|w_1) = p = P(w_2|\neg w_1)$. The second hypothesis H_A is that two sequenced words are depended: $P(w_2|w_1) = p_1 \neq p_2 = P(w_2|\neg w_1)$. p, p_1 and p_2 thereby refer to the maximum likelihood estimation. w_2 refers to the possible sentence boundary. The log likelihood ratio $log\lambda$ is defined by the binomial distribution to calculate the probabilities of both hypotheses:

$$log\lambda = -2log\frac{P_{binom}(H_0)}{P_{binom}(H_A)} \qquad (2.1)$$

so that:

$$log\lambda = 0 iff \frac{C(w_2)}{N} = \frac{C(w_1, w_2)}{C(w_1)} \qquad (2.2)$$

were $C(w_{1|2})$ is the number of occurrences of $w_{1|2}$, and $C(w_1, w_2)$ the number of times the bigram occurs in the N token long text. Furthermore, they argue that a period nearly always follows an abbreviation. Therefore, the probability of H_A is fixed to 0.99. In order to score candidate abbreviations, they additionally introduce three different characteristic properties.

- Strong collocational dependency: A final period occurs in abbreviations.
- Brevity: Abbreviations tend to be short.
- Internal periods: Additional internal periods occur in quite a few abbreviations.

Punkt combines these characteristics to a final scoring function $score(c)$ to detect possible abbreviations candidates c:

1. $log\lambda(c)$: collocation strength between c and the following period.
2. $f_{length}(c) = \frac{1}{e^n}$; where n is the number of non-period characters in the candidate.
3. $f_{periods}(c)$ = the number of internal periods +1.
4. $f_{penalty}(c) = \frac{1}{length(candidate)^n}$ where n is the number of occurrences of c not followed by a period in the text and $length(candidate)$ is the number of non-period characters in c.

The final scoring function is defined as:

$$score(c) = log\lambda(c) \cdot f_{length}(c) \cdot f_{periods}(c) \cdot f_{penalty}(c) \qquad (2.3)$$

where If $score(c) >= 0.3 \rightarrow c$ is an abbreviation. If $score(c) < 0.3 \rightarrow c$ is not an abbreviation. The remaining occurrences of a period refer to a true sentence boundary. Since *Punkt* uses statistics calculated out of an input text, this approach is language independent and does not require any training material. The performance can be expected to be better when using longer rather than shorter text. Thus, their published classification precision (German: 99.69, English: 99.13, Dutch: 99.25, Spanish: 99.66) shows their adaptability to other languages. These advantages led us to decide to implement the *Punkt* system in our pre-processing architecture.

2.1.3 PoS Tagging

Having detected word and sentence boundaries, we are conducting a *Part-of-Speech* (PoS) tagging [217] in order to detect the grammatical categories (e. g. noun, verb etc) of the lexical components (words) of a given text. This task contributes to the disambiguation between the grammatical functions of a specific word e. g.

- Give me my *robe*, put on my crown; [Antony and Cleopatra, W. Shakespeare] (used as a noun)

- I'll *robe* him, and make better lie on's back; [King John, W. Shakespeare] (used as a verb)

PoS tagging refers to the task of classification, identifying the Part-of-Speech information of the lexical component defined as *tags* on the basis of the word's syntactic context. The list of grammatical categories used for the classification task is manually constructed and defined as the tagset. The most popular tagset for the German language is the Stuttgart-Tübinger Tagset (STTS) [9]. In the line of text categorization, approaches of tagging systems vary [328] from look-up lists (accuracy: 90%) [50], rule-based (accuracy: >95%)[34, 35] implementations to machine learning methods (accuracy: >96%)[80, 176, 243]. See Witte and Mülle [361, pp 59-82] for an evaluation of state-of-the-art PoS-Taggers. In our pre-processing architecture we have implemented the method of the Trigram'n'Tags (TnT) tagger following Brants [32]. TnT uses second order Markov Models [50, 253] for the tagging task. That is, the probabilities of the possible values (PoS-tags of a word) of a state depend upon the two previous states. Therefore, states represent tags and the output represents words. The transition probabilities depend on the states, the pairs of tags. The output probabilities only depend on the most recent category. Brants [32] calculates this model by:

$$\arg\max_{t_1...tT} \left[\prod_{i=1}^{T} P(t_i|t_{i-1}, t_{i-2}) P(w_i|t_i) \right] P(t_{T+1}|t_T) \qquad (2.4)$$

where $w_1...w_T$ refers to a given sequence of words of length T, and $t_1...t_T$ to the elements of the tagset. t_{-1}, t_0 and t_{T+1} determine the markers of the beginning and the end of a sequence. This method needs a training corpus (tag annotated text) for estimating the transition probabilities between tags and words. TnT makes use of the maximum likelihood probabilities $\hat{P}$ derived from the relative frequency defined as:

- Unigrams: $\hat{P}(t_3) = \frac{f(t_3)}{N}$
- Bigrams: $\hat{P}(t_3|t_2) = \frac{f(t_2,t_3)}{f(t_2)}$
- Trigram: $\hat{P}(t_3|t_2,t_1) = \frac{f(t_1,t_2,t_3)}{f(t_1,t_2)}$
- Lexical: $\hat{P}(w_3|t_3) = \frac{f(w_3,t_3)}{f(t_2)}$

where t_1,t_2 and t_3 refer to the tags in the tagset and w_3 to the word occurrence within the lexicon. N refers to the total number of words in the training corpus. In addition, TnT introduces a smoothing calculation due to the problem of sparse data. Since in most training corpora not enough instances of certain trigrams occur to be able to predict a reliable probability, a linear interpolation for trigrams of unigram, bigram and trigam is estimated by:

$$P(t_3|t_2,t_1) = \lambda_1 \hat{P}(t_3) + \lambda_2 \hat{P}(t_3|t_2) + \lambda_3 \hat{P}(t_3|t_2,t_1) \qquad (2.5)$$

where $\hat{P}$ are the maximum likelihood estimates of the probabilities. $\lambda_1 + \lambda_2 + \lambda_3 = 1$ represents the context-independent linear interpolation where: $\lambda_1 = \frac{f(t_3)-1}{N-1}$, $\lambda_2 = \frac{f(t_2,t_3)-1}{f(t_2)-1}$ and $\lambda_3 = \frac{f(t_1,t_2,t_3)-1}{f(t_1,t_2)-1}$. All λ parameters are incrementally built for each trigram t_1, t_2, t_3 with $f(t_1, t_2, t_3) > 0$. P defines the probability distribution. The most critical point in PoS-tagging is the handling of unknown words. That is, words that never occur in the training corpus, and therefore no tag probability exists. In this context TnT follows a suffix analysis (term suffix as a final sequence of characters) as proposed by Samuelsson [278]:

$$P(t|l_{n-m+1},...l_n) \tag{2.6}$$

The probability of tag t for given m characters l_i of an n long word. The maximum likelihood estimation for a suffix of length i is defined as:

$$\hat{P}(t|l_{n-i+1},...l_n) = \frac{f(t,l_{n-i+1},...l_n)}{f(l_{n-i+1},...l_n)} \tag{2.7}$$

by corpus frequencies. Our implementation extends the approach of TnT for handling unknown words by additionally using a prefix analysis with the suffix method as described above. Suffix and prefix probabilities are then combined and normalized within the tagging process. In order to detect the sequence of states with the highest probability, we have implemented the *Viterbi* algorithm [253], which has proven to be adequate for this task. The evaluation of our extended implementation of the TnT-Tagger was performed using two different corpora. For the German Negra corpus [320] we evaluated 3,000 sentences gaining an F1-Measure of 0.975. For the English language, we used 5,000 sentences of the Penn corpus [174] for the evaluation, achieving an F1-Measure of 0.956.

2.1.4 Lemmatization and Stemming

The process of determining the tense (e. g. in verbs) or the nominative (e. g. nouns) infinitive of a word form is called lemmatization. As for example:

am, are, is → be

This task is needed not only to reduce the number of textual features (multiple word forms are reduced to one lemma representation) but also in order to retrieve information out of a lexical type network. We have developed an interoperable lemmatization module in our pre-processing architecture by building an extensive full-form lexicon (German/English), combining word-, lemma-form and PoS-information. The size of this lexicon could be extended through other systems (Morphy [124], Treetagger [286], TextMiner [182]) to the number of 3,5 million entries (German language). In addition, a rule-based noun-composition detection is integrated in order to predict the singular form of complex nouns. The stemming module focuses on the normalization of words to their roots by stripping inflectional suffixes, affixes and progressive forms (e. g. ing, s). After the stemming process each word is represented through its stem (e.g the word *predicts*, *prediction* and *predicted* are reduced to *predict*). The majority of existing stemming algorithms are rule-based, for example:

sses → ss
ies → i
ss → ss
s →

The most popular stemming algorithm (initially for the English language) has been proposed by Porter [248] defining a set of production rules for the normalization. We have implemented an adaptation of the Porter stemming algorithm using the *Oleander Stemming Library*[1] for eleven languages.

2.1.5 Named Entity Recognition

Named Entity Recognition (NER) refers to an information extraction task for the identification and classification of proper names and entities in texts. In the line of PoS-tagging a pre-known list of entity categories such as person, location, organization, city, country, weapon, etc. is given and single word forms or phrases are mapped/classified to them. In recent years, this task has been quite successfully studied [66, 134] using different approaches such as list-based, rule-based, machine learning techniques but also hybrid methods [1]. In general, all methods form their basis on the internal/external evidence method as proposed by McDonald [180]:

- Internal evidence: Derived from within the sequence of words that comprise the name (e. g. GmbH - follows after a company name).

---

[1] http://www.oleandersolutions.com/stemming/

- External evidence: Criteria provided by the context in which a name appears (e. g. Paris Hilton - in this context Paris refers to the name but not the city).

Strictly list-based approaches are rather limited in the disambiguation of external evidence (e. g. Apple [company|fruit]) or complex entities (e. g. Microsoft Office Software | MS Office), due to the fact that named entities refer to an open class. In addition, a constructed list or gazetteer will in no case be sufficient enough to cover all known variations of proper names. The majority of published NER approaches propose either SVM-based multi-classification techniques [125, 173] or conduct Hidden Markov Models [79, 373] for the task of named entity recognition. Other approaches combined statistical models (e. g. maximum entropy) and rule-based bootstrapping methods in order to construct extensive gazetteer dictionaries by automatic means [24, 56, 211, 220, 252]. In recent years, the ANNIE module for NER within the GATE framework [68] gained some popularity in the research community. It uses a hybrid approach, combining gazetteer of different domains with hand-crafted JAPE rules (see Table 2.1). We have implemented the majority of

```
1   Rule: Company1
2     Priority: 25
3     (
4         {Token.orthography == upperInitial} //Token heuristic
5       + {Lookup.kind      == companyDesignator} //Gazetteer
6     )
7     :match
8     -->
9     :match.NamedEntity = { kind=company, rule="Company1" }
10    //Return
```

Table 2.1: Outline of a JAPE rule as embedded in the ANNIE module of GATE.

JAPE rules in our pre-processing architecture, since it is one of the few freely-available tools that constantly continue toward further development within the research community. However, all these methods are not capable of predicting the proper instance of a named entity within its context. That is, we are currently able to classify the expression e. g. *George Bush* as a person, but identify the right instance (e. g. is it *George W. Bush* or *George Bush Sr.*) is left out. The task of named entity disambiguation therefore assumes to us the next step to be taken. A method in the context-sensitive named entity recognition will be proposed in a later chapter.

2.1.6 Document Structure Processing

Document structure processing focuses on the identification and extraction of the *Logical Document Structure* (LDS). A fundamental requirement of our pre-processing module is thereby to be able to process a wide range of input documents (Plaintext, PDF- Open Office, Word- and (X)Html documents) by automatic means. We therefore developed different mapping routines, extracting textual and structural information out of the documents. All text documents (regardless if plain-text or web documents) form their basis by their structural components. More formally, *a text document is spanned by the constituents of its text structure* (e.g paragraphs, sections, headers, etc.) Mehler et al. [204, p. 4]. Our mapping routines annotate the internal structure of documents by means of a LDS representation on the basis of *TEI-P5* [40, 122, 254, 313]. From the point of view of hypertext, we argue that content is structured by a systematic usage of recurrent structure tags (e. g. breaks, span, div, h1, etc.). At first glace, the usage of all structure tags is an appropriate indicator for the document structure. However, *tag abuse* [15] is a common problem when analyzing a source code of web documents in more detail [347]. We evaluate each document, therefore, by its tag usage and compute a valid mapping following the *TEI-P5* definition. With respect to the cleaning and validation of the rebuilt mark-up representation, the program *Tidy*[2] is used. However, dealing with Plain-Text, no structural information (e. g. html-tags) is given. We therefore developed a rule-based method on the basis of sentence length and line break occurrences in order to rebuild/annotate the internal structure. In all cases, we gain a valid *TEI-P5* representation of the LDS, which is further combined with the lexical representation of the input document (see Table 2.2).

---

[2]http://tidy.sourceforge.net/

```
 1  Input:
 2  Germany
 3  Bush and Kohl Discuss the Fall of the Berlin Wall
 4
 5  Output:
 6  ...
 7  <text>
 8   <body>
 9    <div>
10     <p>
11      <s>
12       <w type="#NE" subtype="#Location" lemma="Germany">Germany</w>
13      </s>
14     </p>
15     <p>
16      <s>
17       <w type="#NE" subtype="#Person" lemma="Bush">Bush</w>
18       <w type="#CC" lemma="and">and</w>
19       <w type="#NE" subtype="#Person" lemma="Kohl">Kohl</w>
20       <w type="#VBD" lemma="discuss">Discuss</w>
21       <w type="#DT" lemma="the">the</w>
22       <w type="#NNP" lemma="Fall">Fall</w>
23       <w type="#IN" lemma="of">of</w>
24       <w type="#DT" lemma="the">the</w>
25       <w type="#NE" subtype="#Location" lemma="Berlin">Berlin</w>
26       <w type="#NE" subtype="#Location" lemma="Wall">Wall</w>
27      </s>
28     </p>
29    </div>
30   </body>
31  </text>
32  ...
```

Table 2.2: Outline of the comprised TEI-P5 XML document representation. The attribute *'type'* of element *'w'* refers to the *Part-of-Speech-Tag* as used within the *Penn Treebank* project. [174]. The attribute *'subtype'* refers to a *Named Entity* category. The element *'s'* refers to the sentence structure of the document.

2.2 Text Representation

The majority of text mining approaches are based on the idea that a text document can be represented by a – mostly unordered – set of words (*bag-of-words* representation). Let $D = \{d_1, d_2, ..., d_n\}$ be a document collection, and let $T = \{t_1, t_2, ..., t_m\}$ be the set of terms – the dictionary – of D, the n-dimensional vector $d \in D$ and $d \in R^n$, where R is a set of real numbers. In order to define the importance of a term within a given document, most commonly a vector representation is used, that is, each document term a is represented through a feature value (e. g. frequency information) of importance – feature weight – inducing a *Term Document Model* or through Boolean values – quantifying the existence of a term in a document or not, inducing the *Boolean Model*. Other approaches are the *Probabilistic Model* [65, 88, 264] and the *Logical Model* [61, 62, 322]. As a generalization of the Boolean model, the *Vector Space Model* (VSM) [275] represents one of the most widely used representation model in the research community. In the following section we describe, in more detail, the VSM and the most prominent feature weighting methods. Furthermore, we describe various text similarity measures in order to determine the resemblance between documents.

2.2.1 Vector Space Models

The procedure of the *Vector Space Model* (VSM) [275] can be divided into a three stage model. At first, document-feature extracting and indexing are processed. Therefore, content-relevant features (e. g. terms, stems or phrases) are extracted from the document collection. Second, a weighting of the indexed feature is computed, in order to enhance the retrieval of relevant documents. Finally, a document ranking is performed. In this regard, documents are ranked with respect to the query on the basis of a distinctive similarity measure. In general, the VSM represents texts as elements of a vector space. Each component of a vector thereby corresponds to a term or feature. A collection of n-documents can be represented by a document-term matrix (see Table 2.3), where the rows indicate documents and columns represent term features. Each vector has a direction and a magnitude. The correlation between feature vectors implies a similarity between documents. The importance

$$\begin{pmatrix} & T_1 & T_2 & ... & T_t \\ D_1 & w_{11} & w_{21} & ... & w_{t1} \\ D_2 & w_{12} & w_{22} & ... & w_{t2} \\ \vdots & \vdots & \vdots & & \vdots \\ \vdots & \vdots & \vdots & & \vdots \\ D_n & w_{1n} & w_{2n} & ... & w_{tn} \end{pmatrix}$$

Table 2.3: Document-Term matrix representation of document collection D and comprised term features T.

or significance of a component is defined through a numerical value, the larger the value, the more important the feature is to the document. These values can be weighted, reflecting the distribution of the features over all texts in a corpus (frequency information) or as binary features, whether a word occurs in the text or not (boolean information). A basis vector of the vector space is defined as a text that has only one term [275]. Let D_i be a vector space of a number of i texts. Let T_j be the index terms weighted by their importance and restricted to 0 and 1. Each document is represented by a t-dimensional vector, where t defines the number of terms: $D_i = (d_{i1}, d_{is}, ..., d_{it})$, and d_{it} represents the weight of the jth term [273]. See Figure 2.1 for a vector representation of a three-dimensional document space. Note that the standard VSM representation does not capture information about the actual order of feature occurrences.

2.2.2 Feature Weighting

Feature weighting is used to discriminate the importance of individual features of one document with respect to the document itself (all comprised term features) or with respect to the entire document collection. In general, there are three main factors of feature weighting: Feature document frequency, corpus collection frequency and feature length normalization [321].

> "... the frequency of word occurrence in an article furnishes a useful measurement of word significance [...] the relative position within a sentence of words having given values of significance furnish a

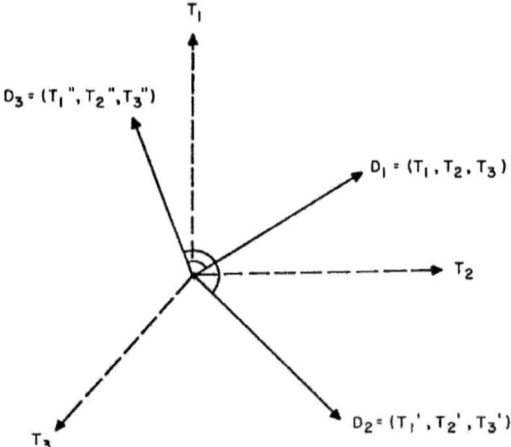

Figure 2.1: Vector representation of document space as visualized by Salton et al. [273]

> *useful measurement for determining the significance of sentences. The significance factor of a sentence will therefore be based on a combination of these two measurements."* Luhn [167, pp. 160]

Most of the proposed feature weighting methods assume that the importance of a feature (e. g. document frequency) is inversely proportionate to the number of documents the feature appears to have (e. g. collection frequency) [274, 276]. In order to consider the individual length of a document, following the notion that longer documents have usually a larger feature set than shorter one, a document length normalization is often performed. This follows the idea that a feature, which occurs in many documents tends not to be a good document discriminator, and therefore should be given less weight than the one that occur only in a few documents [265]. Let t be the number of terms in the collection, N be the number of documents in the collection, and $tf(ij)$ be the normalized term frequency of term t_i in the document d_j, which is defined as

$$tf(ij) = \frac{freq_{i,j}}{max_l freq_{l,j}}. \qquad (2.8)$$

$max_l freq_{l,j}$ denotes the frequency of the most frequent term in d_j. df_i be the number of documents that contain the term t_i. Then the inverse document frequency (idf), with

$$idf(t_i) = \log \frac{N}{df_i}. \tag{2.9}$$

as the function, which measures the distribution of the term t_i over the document collection N. Hence, a term that occurs only in one document of the collection has a high *idf* value. In the context of term discrimination, a high value of $tf_{i,j}$, the term frequency (tf), tends to be useful to enhance the recall value. High-frequency terms that occur in the whole collection, however, are not concentrated in a few documents, *affect negatively the precision*[3] (Salton and Buckley [276, pp. 516]). One of the most popular feature weighting function is hence the combination of term-frequency (tf) and inverse document frequency (idf) information as described in Salton and Buckley [276, pp. 516] with

$$tfidf_{i,j} = tf_{i,j} \cdot idf_i = \frac{freq_{i,j}}{max_l freq_{l,j}} \cdot \log \frac{N}{df_i} \tag{2.10}$$

The product of tf and idf ensures a delimited influence of very common and very rare term features in the computation of document similarity [276].

2.2.3 Similarity Coefficients

The comparison of documents, text vectors, in the VSM is determined by means of a similarity coefficient [274, 277]. In general, a function δ defines the similarity of two document representations d_1 and d_2, where $\delta(d_1, d_2) \in [0, 1]$. A high value of $\delta(d_1, d_2)$ corresponds to a high degree of similarity between document d_1 and d_2, where a low value indicates a dissimilarity between both. More formally [326, ch. 2] [352, pp. 47], a function δ is defined as a similarity function if it fulfills at least

$$\delta(d_i, d_j) > 0 \tag{2.11}$$

Furthermore, we assume that a similarity function to satisfy the following

$$\delta(d_i, d_j) \geq 0 (non - negative) \tag{2.12}$$

$$\delta(d_i, d_j) = \delta(d_j, d_i)(symmetry) \tag{2.13}$$

---

[3] Search precision, in terms of all documents would be retrieved in an information retrieval system.

$$\delta(d_i, d_j) \in [0,1] (normalization) \tag{2.14}$$

if it further fulfils

$$\delta(d_i, d_j) = 1 \iff d_i = d_y (identical) \tag{2.15}$$

$$\delta(d_i, d_j) + \delta(d_j, d_t) \geq (d_i, d_t)(triangle inequality) \tag{2.16}$$

it is defined as a metric ([326, ch. 4.1], [329, pp. 15]). In addition, a similarity function that is positively definite is called a *kernel function* ([329, pp. 16]). The similarity function δ can be used to perform a document ranking on the basis of an input query, or to transform a document collection into a similarity graph representation, used for document clustering. Most commonly, the similarity of two documents $d_i, d_j \in D$ represented as sets of terms, can be measured by a set intersection ratio. These *set-based* similarity measures [321] are for instance the *Dice coefficient* δ_{Dice}, the *Jaccard coefficient* δ_{Jacc} or the *Overlap coefficient* δ_{Over} [321, pp. 25].

$$\delta_{Dice}(D_i, D_j) = \frac{|D_i \cap D_j|}{|D_i| + |D_j|} \tag{2.17}$$

$$\delta_{Jacc}(D_i, D_j) = \frac{|D_i \cap D_j|}{|D_i \cup D_j|} \tag{2.18}$$

$$\delta_{Over}(D_i, D_j) = |\frac{|D_i \cap D_j|}{\max(|D_i|, |D_j|)}| \tag{2.19}$$

The most popular used *geometric-based* similarity measure is the *cosine coefficient*, which measures the angle between two document vectors. Let $\vec{d_i} = (w_{i1}, w_{i2}, ..., w_{it})$ and $\vec{d_j} = (w_{j1}, w_{j2}, ..., w_{jt})$ denote the vector representation of the documents D_i and D_j respectively, where $w = 0$ if a term is absent. The cosine of the angle between $\vec{d_i}$ and $\vec{d_j}$ is defined as

$$\delta_{Cos}(\vec{d_i}, \vec{d_j}) = \frac{\vec{d_i} \cdot \vec{d_j}}{\|\vec{d_i}\| \|\vec{d_j}\|} \tag{2.20}$$

where $\vec{d_i} \cdot \vec{d_j}$ denotes the dot product and $\|\vec{d_i}\| \|\vec{d_j}\|$ denotes the Euclidean norm ([171, pp. 121]). The *un-normalized* similarity between $\vec{d_i}, \vec{d_j}$ is defined as

$$\delta_{UnCos}(\vec{d_i}, \vec{d_j}) = \sum_{k=1}^{t} w_{ik} \cdot w_{jk} \tag{2.21}$$

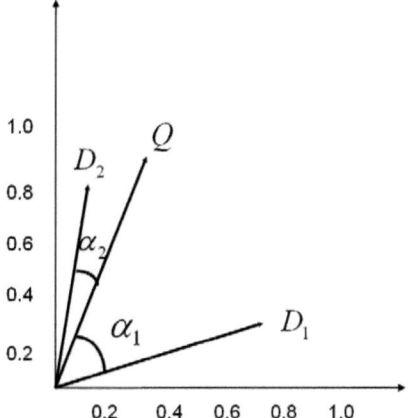

Figure 2.2: Cosine angle (α_1, α_2) between query and two document vectors.

The *normalized* inner product cosine is defined as

$$\delta_{NormCos}(\vec{d_i}, \vec{d_j}) = \frac{\sum_{k=1}^{t} w_{ik} \cdot w_{jk}}{\sqrt{\sum_{k=1}^{t} (w_{ik})^2 \cdot \sum_{k=1}^{t} (w_{jk})^2}} \quad (2.22)$$

Since term-weights cannot be negative, $\delta_{NormCos}$ will range between $[0, 1]$, where the angel between two term vectors cannot be greater than 90 degree.

2.2.4 Index Term Selection

A central problem in the construction of document models is the size of the term dictionary, associated to the processed document collection. Since these dictionaries (defined as T) can contain several thousands of word features, a tailored term dictionary contributes to the problem of complexity reduction for the computation of similarity scores, classifications of documents and, in general, the processing of feature-matrices [206, pp. 20]. Consequently, the processing of a tailored term index T' contributes to the computational performance and the classification accuracy [27]. In general, the task of term index reduction correlates to the task of feature selection [14, 127, 146, 367]. In this regard, the index reduction is enabled by mapping a set of term features to a limited document representation $T \mapsto T'$. The construction of T' can be treated by using feature selection methods or by feature modification by means of re-weighting of feature values. On the other side, feature enrichment methods also contribute to an increase of classification accuracy.

Feature index selection: One of the most common term selection methods is the removal of terms that add more or less 'topical noise' into T [292, pp. 1662]. Thereby, common or non-informative words (e. g. certain PoS category), defined as *stopwords*, such as articles, prepositions or conjunctions (e. g. he, she, and, is, or ...) are excluded in the construction of T [171, pp. 86]. Although most of those terms would already have a very low $tfidf$ score, it is most common to eliminate stopwords in the pre-processing phase and thereby increase the computation of document representation and similarity [206, pp. 21]. In contrast to a simple stopword-dictionary look-up approaches, the computation of term-based *ranking score methods* are used. Most commonly, the *information gain* [151] [216, pp 57-58], the *mutual information* approach [317, 241] or the *GSS coefficient* [93] are applied in order to select only those features of T of high discriminative power with respect to the computational task.

Feature index modification: In contrast to term selection approaches, most term modification models focus on the morphological constraints of word forms. In this context, various word form variants are reduced to their baseform or stem-information. Through the reduction of canonical forms of inflected or derived words, declined nouns or conjugated verbs, the actual size of T will also be reduced. A detailed analysis of these approaches can be found in the previous Section 2.1.4.

Feature index transformation operates mostly on an entire term-document matrix. A popular index transformation method is *Latent Semantic Analysis* (LSA) [74]. LSA has obtained particular attention, due to its success in a large variety of tasks including Information Retrieval. LSA is based on a term×context matrix X, displaying the occurrences of each term in each context[4] [45, 74, 149, 287]. The decisive step in the LSA process is then a *singular value decomposition* (SVD), which enhances the contrast between reliable and unreliable relations[5]. In this regard [74, pp. 11], any rectangular matrix, such

---

[4]This context mostly refers to documents as in the case of the VSM.

[5]According to Deerwester et al. [74, pp. 2], the LSA tries to overcome the deficiencies of term-matching retrieval by treating the unreliability of observed term-document association data as a statistical problem. The applied technique (SVD) poses to estimate the so called

as a Term-Document-Matrix (txd), X, is decomposed into the product of three matrices:

$$X = T_0 S_0 D_0', \qquad (2.23)$$

where T_0 and D_0 have orthonormal columns, and S_0 is diagonal. This decomposition is called the *singular value decomposition* of X. The columns of T_0 are called *left singular vectors*. The columns of D_0 are called *right singular vectors*. The diagonal elements of S_0 are called *singular values*. If the *singular values* of S_0 are ordered descending by their size, the first and largest k values are kept, the remaining are set to zero. The product of the resulting matrices is a reduced model with a matrix $Xhihat$, which is only approximately equal to X, and is of rank k.[74, pp. 13]:

$$X \approx Xhihat = TSD' \qquad (2.24)$$

Therefore, the high-dimensional input matrix X is reduced to a subspace of k singular values (e.g. $k \approx 100$ to 300). After applying SVD, each term feature is represented as a k-dimensional vector. A similar technique to LSA is the *random projection* method proposed by Widdows and Ferraro [356]. Widdows and Ferraro [356] states that this method does not rely on complex procedures such as SVD. The important advantage of these approaches is that they are better able to capture paradigmatic relations such as synonymy or hyponymy between term features, since paradigmatically similar words tend to occur in similar contexts [74, 149][6], [194, pp. 4] [262, 345, 348]. However, they are also at a disadvantage with respect to direct co-occurrence measures, because the matrix computations are computationally demanding.

Feature index enrichment methods focus on the introduction of concepts and terms that are not found in T. A central point in the document representation enhancement builds the semantically motivated knowledge, obtained by other resources. Most commonly $t \in T$ will be enriched by synonym and hyponomy terms or using only sense-numbers extracted from a lexical resource such as *WordNet* [83] or *GermaNet* [154]. Nevertheless, these resources have mostly a very limited dictionary to query and are very costly to build and maintain. The concept-enhancement approach by means of *open-topic-concepts*

---

latent structure. The description of terms and documents, by means of their latent semantic structure, is used for indexing and retrieval purposes.

[6]In terms of measuring indirect content based similarity relations.

[341, 346] will contribute right here. Collaboratively constructed resources form thereby the basis of generating semantically related topic-concepts. It should be noted, that there is no direct linguistic expert knowledge involved in building these resources used for a social semantic driven feature enhancement.

2.3 Text Classification

In this section, we describe the most frequently used methods of text categorization, which are further applied throughout this thesis. As described in the previous chapter, we define text categorization as the task in which texts are classified into one or more predefined categories using information from labelled texts (supervised or semi-supervised classification). In contrast to text categorization, text clustering deals with the classification with the absence of predefined category labels or training material (semi-supervised or un-supervised classification).

2.3.1 Naive Bayes Classifier

The Naive Bayes (NB) method belongs to the area of supervised probabilistic classifier. The method is based on *Bayes' Theorem*, where the maximum likelihood is used for the estimation of the naive Bayes models. In general, this classifier relies on the assumption that the presence or absence of a specific feature within a class is independent of other feature items. Because of its simplicity, NB is often used within the classification domain, sometimes outperforming even more sophisticated methods [96, 148, 216]. According to the *Bayes' Theorem*, the posterior probability for the class C_j can be defined as:

$$p(C_j|t_1,\ldots,t_n) = \frac{p(C_j)\, p(t_1,\ldots,t_n|C_j)}{p(t_1,\ldots,t_n)} \qquad (2.25)$$

where $T = \{t_1, \ldots, \ldots, t_n\}$ is a set of term features and $C = \{C_1, \ldots, \ldots, C_j\}$ a set of categories. It has to be noted that it is implied that each document belongs to exactly one class in C only. Combining the *Bayes' formula* with the (*naive*) assumption of feature independence will lead to the conditional probability of word features for a given class C_j by

$$p(t_1,\ldots,t_n|C_j) = \prod_{j=1}^{n} p(t_j|C_j) \qquad (2.26)$$

It defines the probability that a set of features belong to C_j. NB assumes a statistical independency of the conditional probabilities, so that the likelihood is decomposed into a product of term features [116]. The *Naive Bayes classifier* operates in two steps: First, a learning step for the estimation of the probabilities of term features for each class by its, for example, relative frequency values, which are labelled in the training corpus. Second, the actual classification of the unknown input stream uses the predicted probabilities of the Bayes rule. We will utilize *Naive Bayes* Classifier in this thesis with respect to a sentiment analysis classification (in terms of the calculation of a lower-bound reference baseline and for the construction of a English-based subjectivity dictionary).

2.3.2 K-Nearest Neighbor Classifier

One of the most widely used classification methods, the k-nearest neighbor classifier [366] is outlined now. In general, this classifier selects k documents of the training data that have the highest similarity score to a given input stream [289]. While there are various measures for the determination of document similarity, a common approach among others is thereby to apply the cosine metric for the calculation of the similarity matrix (see previous section). In order to be able to determine whether a document d_i belongs to class C_m, the similarity between $\delta(d_i, d_j)^7$ has to be computed for all documents d_j in the training set [118]. Then, the k most similar documents, defined as neighbors, are selected. That is, a subset of the closest neighbors having the same class are used as a 'class fingerprint' – an estimator of the probability of the membership to the specific class [118]. The central parameter of this classifier is the optimal number of k neighbors. There are many proposals for estimating the best neighbor parameter. As a commonality, most of them propose to use additional training data combined with a cross-validation for the prediction of the parameter k. Overall the k-nearest neighbor method has shown a good classification performance [118, 127]. However, since the similarity score needs to be computed with respect to all documents in the training corpus, this method is computationally demanding. We will apply this classification method in the field of traditional text categorization (Section 4). Hence, we utilize the k-nearest

---

[7]Hence, the best neighbor strategy could alternatively be approached, by a search for the best neighboring (candidate) centroids among the centroids of all training categories [311].

neighbor approach for a document-based feature construction.

2.3.3 Support Vector Machine Classification

In terms of *machine learning*[8] methods applied to text categorization, *Support Vector Machine* (SVM) is the most successfully applied supervised linear and non-linear binary classification algorithm [129, 130]. The basic concepts of SVMs are the *maximal margin separation*, which are induced from the *statistical learning theory* [323]. Analog to other classifiers, documents are represented by a weighted vector representation $D_i = (t_{i1}, t_{i2}, ..., t_{iN})$. A single SVM tries to separate two different classes, a positive class C_{pos} (indicated by $y = +1$) and a negative class C_{neg} (indicated by $y = -1$). Within the feature space, a hyperplane is introduced initially defined by $y = 0$. Following Hotho et al. [118, pp. 34] the linear separation can be expressed by

$$y = f(\vec{t_i}) = b_1 + \sum_{j=1}^{N} b_j t_{ij} \in \{-1, +1\} \qquad (2.27)$$

Thus, the SVM tries to determine a hyperplane between the positive and negative training example, by predicting the best b_j parameter that maximizes the distance, defined as the margin ξ of the hyperplane, between the closest positive and negative training examples (see Figure 2.3). The linear kernel method operates on a constrained quadratic optimization problem, and can therefore handle even a large number of documents and their associated feature sets efficiently [129]. The actual *support vectors* correspond to those documents that have the distance ξ to the hyperplane, and therefore mark the actual hyperplane. Unknown documents are initially converted to a vector representation, and afterwards either classified as a member of C_{pos} if $f(t_d) > 0$ or otherwise as a member of C_{neg}. In order to construct a non-linear hyperplane or decision surface, the input stream is mapped into a high-dimensional feature space or map and a prediction of the non-linear decision boundary is computed [323]. Therefore, input features are projected into a higher dimension feature space

---

[8] *"A computer program [e. g. classifier] is said to learn from experience E [e. g. pre-labled data] with respect to some class of tasks T [e. g. comprised categories] and performance measure P (e. g. evaluation metric], if its performance at tasks in T, as measured by P, improves with experience E."* Mitchell [216, pp. 2]

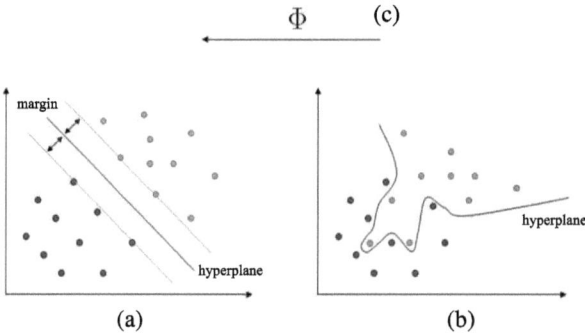

Figure 2.3: SVM-hyperplane with maximal margin using linear and non-linear kernel constructed by the support vector machine algorithm. (a) linear separable, (b) non-linear separable, (c) schematic transformation of the input data (non-linear separable) in the higher dimensional feature space.

(see Figure 2.3 (c)). Following Hotho et al. [118, pp. 35] the feature space can be defined by

$$\Phi(t_1,\ldots,t_N) = (t_1,\ldots,t_N, t_1^2, t_1 t_2, \ldots, t_N t_{N-1}, t_N^2) \qquad (2.28)$$

The introduction of the kernel function, sometimes referred to as the kernel trick $K(x,y)$, is subsequently used in order to be able to use a linear operating classifier algorithm to solve a non-linear problem. The kernel function can be expressed by

$$K(x_i, x_j) = \Phi(x_i \dot\Phi(x_j)) \qquad (2.29)$$

and can be regarded as the proximity function, which measures the distance between two input vectors in a non-linearly feature space. As a special case of kernel function, the Gaussian radial basis function (RBF) kernel is sometimes used, defined as

$$K(x_i, x_j) = \exp(-\gamma ||x_i - x_j||^2) \qquad (2.30)$$

The advantage of the RBF-kernel compared to other kernel functions is that the output values of Gaussian function range between zero and one, while others (e.g. linear kernel) range between zero and infinity [58, 155]. There are two important parameters to be determined in conducting a classification task using SVM. First, there is the regularisation parameter, mostly referred to by C. This parameter regulates the trade-off between margin maximization and error rate during the classification of the training set. Second, there is the γ parameter, which regulates the sensitivity of the distance function. When using an RBF-Kernel this refers to the prediction of the width of the Gaussian function. In most cases, these parameters are tuned by an empirical evaluation following a brute force (grid-search) approach, that combines different value settings of C and γ [177]. In this thesis, we primarily utilize the SVM implementation SVM^{light9} of Joachims [126].

2.3.4 Evaluation Metrics

In order to evaluate the performance of text categorization or clustering a two-way contingency table (confusion matrix) is introduced following Kohavi and Provost [145, pp 271].

	Class-Positive	Class-Negative
Prediction-Positive	TP (true positive)	FP (false positive)
Prediction-Negative	FN (false negative)	TN (true negative)

where

- precision: $P = TP/(TP + FP)$
- recall: $R = TP/(TP + FN)$
- fallout: $F = FP/(FP + TN)$
- error: $Err = (FN + FP)/(TP + TN + FP + FN)$
- accuracy: $Acc = (TP + TN)/(TP + TN + FP + FN)$

Selecting a subset D' of the overall document set D, the values of *precision*, *recall* and *accuracy* reflect the performance of the *true set* of *relevant documents* with respect to D [366]. The *precision* value denotes thereby the fraction of relevant documents to the retrieved documents; the *recall* value denotes the fraction of retrieved relevant documents with respect the all other relevant document of D. While in most machine learning and classification experiments,

---

[9]Version 6.02

accuracy is used as the standard evaluation metric, sometimes the F-Measure [321, c 7] is used, defined as:

$$F_\beta(P, R) = \frac{(\beta^2 + 1)PR}{\beta^2 P + R} \qquad (2.31)$$

where P and R denote precision and recall. The β is used as a tuning parameter between P and R. In general, both, P and R, are set as equally important, defined as the F_1 measure

$$F_1 = \frac{2PR}{P + R} \qquad (2.32)$$

Therefore, the F-Measure reflects the weighted harmonic mean between precision and recall, where an increase of the intersection of both scales correlates to an increase of the F-Measure. The computational task of categorization or classification is therefore to maximize both precision and recall in order to gain a high classification accuracy and F-Measure.

2.4 Summary

This chapter has presented the research background of this thesis. We will build upon this research in the following chapters. With the increase amount of digital and machine readable documents available on the Internet, IR systems aim to improve the retrieval quality by providing a structured access to document collections [12], [118, pp. 30]. In general, document representation models (e.g. BOW/VSM) pose for both, the retrieval task (in terms of document classification and ranking) and as the actual information content (in terms of document indexing) [206]. Pre-processing pipelines [171] such as a tokenization, stemming, lemmatizing (see Section 2.1), but also feature weighting and selection methods (see Section 2.2.2) play in this context, prior to the actual construction of the document representation model (see Section 2.2) an essential role [132]. Since data on the web is usually noisy and ambiguous, a comprehensive pre-processing is an important process before applying text and web mining, or machine learning techniques (see Section 2.3) [245]. It has a mutual influence on the components of IR systems (e.g. feature space reduction). Precisely because of its simple data structure (in terms of no explicit semantic information required for the construction process [118, pp. 27]), the

VSM [277] enables an efficient text analysis even handling large document collections. Since it was first introduced in 1975 by Salton et al. [277], it (the VSM and its modifications) is, nevertheless, still an important component of a majority of current state-of-the-art IR systems[10]. Within the area of traditional text categorization, SVMs (see Section 2.3.3) have proven to be an efficient and accurate technique, which are applied to this domain [77, 129, 130]. On the contrary, most existing classification systems in NLP refer thereby again to the BOW model for document representation[11]. That is, classification features are primarily those extracted from the actual document collection (positive/negative examples). In this thesis, we investigate how to improve the performance of the supervised machine learning technique (SVM) by an effective feature enhancement through collaborative constructed knowledge concepts. Therefore, we aim to combine human intelligence (in terms of collaborative constructed knowledge derived from social networks) with machine learning and NLP (in terms of traditional classification techniques) to overcome domain specific issues (in terms of the limitations of the BOW model) within the area of IR and to improve the performance (in terms of accuracy) of IR systems.

---

[10]Such as within the *Apache Lucene* project, a Java-based full-featured text search engine, which is used for the index of the Wikipedia document collection [166].

[11]However, various attempts have been made to expand or enhance the local context of texts with additional term features. We will discuss these approaches in Section 4.3 in more detail.

Chapter 3

Social Semantics in Information Retrieval

3.1 Overview

In Chapter 2 we discussed the background perspectives of document representation and similarity, text categorization and machine learning algorithms, which are further applied throughout this thesis. We will now proceed in developing the methodology of a *Social Semantics in Information Retrieval*. At first, we will provide the definitions of the key concepts with respect to *Information Retrieval* and our notion of *Social Semantics*. In Section 3.3 we will instantiate the methodology by developing the method for the construction of a social semantic concept space, inducing hierarchically organized collaborative knowledge from social networks. Consequently, Chapter 4 presents the evaluation of the developed model to *Social Semantics*.

3.1.1 Information Retrieval

The definition of Information Retrieval (IR) specifies the *representation, storage, organization of, and the access to information items* [12, pp. 1]. More precisely, it deals with the representation and presentation of information or content items with a strong focus on the user's perception and interest. Therefore, it strongly relies on identifying the user's information needs [206]. While data retrieval consists mainly of determining documents of a collection that contain a certain keyword with respect to the user query, IR sets the focus on the actual retrieval task of specific information about a certain subject. This follows the notion of document content *interpretation, extracting syntactic and semantic information* out of a document [12, pp. 2], while the *relevance* to the user is at the center. More formally, Baeza-Yates and Ribeiro-Neto [12, pp. 23] define an IR model as a quadruple:

1. D, is a set of representations of the documents of a collection.

2. Q, is a set of composed user queries.

3. F, is the framework for modelling document representations, queries and associated relationships.

4. $R(q_i, d_j)$, is a ranking function that associates a real number with a query $q_i \in Q$ and a document representation $d_j \in D$ (think of document similarity coefficients).

Therefore, IR models consider documents as a set of representative keywords defined as index features, describing the documents main subject within a given context (e.g. category-, topic-, genre or sentiment-based). The ranking function (e.g. document similarity, relatedness or association function) spans the reference plane between an input query and the respective documents. With respect to the context, these queries can imply a quite diverse topic universe such as:

- *"What is the best camera for less than 400 dollars?"*
  This question embodies the task of identifying user-generated review polarities with respect to certain objects in ranking manner (sentiment analysis).

- *"When was Helmut Kohl, the soccer referee, born?"*
  Named entity recognition, disambiguation and information extraction are needed here in order to tackle this kind of issue (named instance recognition analysis).

- *"Where can I find the official contact website of a certain company webpage?"*

  This query embodies the task of web genre identification (web genre segment analysis).

- *"Find me the latest documents concerning the coal mining stock exchange?"*

  Consider the scenario that the query term *stock exchange* might not actually occur within the content of the comprised text collection (but for instance the terms *financial market, shares, equity, dept...*), therefore a topic-based query interpretation needs to be established (topic identification) in order to continue recalling relevant documents.

These examples illustrate very clearly the diverse context universe, ranking functions that need to be established, in order to model the actual users need. Therefore, a *semantic* interpretation of the user query/need has to be set in the center of attention.

3.1.2 Semantics

> *"The Internet is a giant semiotic system. It is a massive collection of Peirce's [238] three kinds of signs: icons, which show the form of something; indices, which point to something; and symbols, which represent something according to some convention."*
>
> Sowa [295, pp. 1]

Semantics[1] is a branch of linguistics dealing with the meaning of language and (linguistic) expressions, belonging to the domain of semiotics[2]. In general, the discipline of *semiotics* – the study of sign processes [218, 237] – can be divided into three different branches (see Figure 3.1): *semantics, syntactics* and *pragmatics* [218].

---

[1] Semantics: Greek *semaino* - *to signify*.

[2] *"Most semioticians accept Morris's [218] definition of semantics as a branch of general semiotics, which was also adopted within logic. A minor trend in semiotics defines both fields as mutually exclusive."* Noth [225, pp. 104]

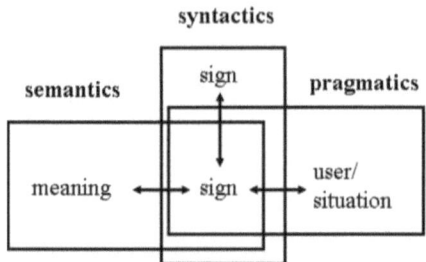

Figure 3.1: The three disciplines of semiotics after Morris [218, pp. 94].

The term semantics [112, pp. 14], – from a linguistic perspective deals with the theory of the meaning of individual units of natural language [227]. These units can be expressed through spoken or written characters or signals. Allan [6] defines the term semantics, from a natural language perspective, as follows:

> "Semantics is the study of meaning in human languages. More precisely, it is the study and representation of the meaning of every kind of constituent and expression in language, and also of the meaning relationships between them." Allan [6, pp. 5]

Pragmatics defines, in this regard, the *context-dependent assignment of meaning to language expressions used in acts of speaking and writing* [6, pp. 4]. Our notion of semantics refers therefore to the meaning of lexical constituents and their relationships in natural language. Within the domain of semantics various subfields of linguistics exit. While formal semantics focuses on the logical aspects of meaning such as sense and implication, conceptual semantics studies the cognitive structure of meaning. This thesis focuses on the third field of semantics, the lexical semantics, the study of word meaning and word relations [112, pp. 21] [244, pp. 5] (see Figure 3.2). In this context, natural language documents represent more than the occurrences of words. We can identify complex word relations between them. These relations are at the bottom of word meaning on a semantic level. In the line of Andreas and Hotho [8], we argue that considering semantic relations and meaning within IR models, an improvement of the quality of information search can be fulfilled, which goes beyond the approaches operating on *simple* term occurrences [170, 330].

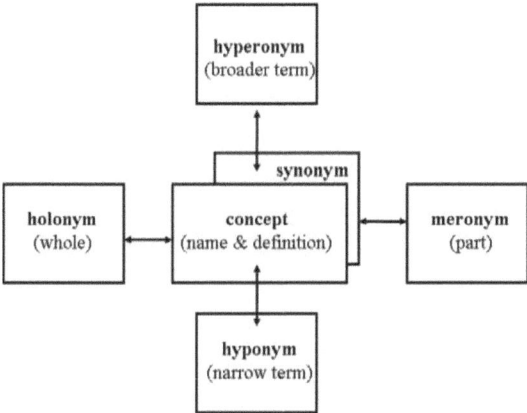

Figure 3.2: Semantic relationships between the component of a lexical semantic model.

3.1.3 Social Semantics

With the emergence of the so-called *Web 2.0* [228] on the Internet, a large variety of *social resource sharing systems* [43] (e.g. *Wikis*[3], *Blogs*[4], *YouTube*[5], *Furl*[6], *Flickr*[7], *del.icio.us*[8]) have been introduced. These mainly user-centric publishing and knowledge management platforms have acquired a large number of users in recent years. In addition, a huge amount of information and data was compiled within a very short period of time. One of the main reasons for the success of these platforms is that there is not a specific competence needed in order to participate. Built-in tools enable even non-technicians to engage in the social community, such as creating, editing or revising online content (e.g. within the *Wikipedia*-Project). Moreover, most of these resource systems induce a so-called lightweight knowledge representation. This *user-created bottom-up categorical structure development of an emergent thesaurus* became popular as the terms *social ontology* [191], *folk classification* [43] or

---
[3] http://www.wikimedia.org/
[4] https://www.blogger.com/
[5] http://www.youtube.com/
[6] http://www.furl.net/
[7] http://www.flickr.com/
[8] http://delicious.com/

folksonomy[9]. The term *folksonomy* is thereby a combination of 'taxonomy' and 'folk' and reflects the *conceptual structures created by user* [43]. The term *social ontology* refers to the formal and conceptual representation of knowledge (ontology), which is constructed within a (social) community. A detailed definition can be found in Mehler [191]:

> "*Typically, social ontologies tend to evolve in an unsupervised, uncontrolled, unplanned and unmoderated manner. They miss an overall architecture or blueprint as they are built by large, heterogeneous communities of interacting agents, who participate in social tagging without explicit mutual negotiation and complete knowledge of the underlying ontology. [...] Social ontologies share with folksonomies a kind of implicit constitution. However, unlike folksonomies (though like both terminological and formal ontologies) they span hierarchical structures.*" Mehler [191, pp. 3]

We can infer that these socially created terms, concepts and thesauri convey a certain semantic information and interpretation of texts, even though not authored by experts but rather by a huge amount of volunteers in a collaborative manner. It is precisely this phenomenon that lets us hypothesize that the connection between computational methods derived from web-mining and the collaboratively constructed knowledge derived from social communities will assist us in improving the interpretation and analysis of words and texts in IR [299]. Moreover, it lets us extract the associated meaning from a user perspective and makes explicit the semantics behind the tag and word space in IR systems [296]. By the unification of both, the community-driven social interaction and knowledge creation, and the systematicity of traditional IR models, we are moving towards a direction of IR models – comprising the social components of semantic-driven retrieval systems – a *Social Semantics in Information Retrieval*.

The perception of a combination of collaborative constructed knowledge structures with traditional content models follows, in principle, the idea of the arising phenomenon of the so called *Social Semantic Web* (SSW) [28]. The

---

[9]There is no official reference to the term *folksonomy*. However, various scientific articles [303, 178] refer to the online contribution of Wal [336].

SSW reflects in this sense the convergence of two closely related fields – the *Web 2.0* and the *Semantic Web*. We can identify a progressive rapprochement of both web phenomenon. The notion of the Web 2.0, with its community-driven dynamics, and the Semantic Web, with its main idea of a machine-readable WWW. Blumauer and Pellegrini [29] describe this phenomenon as follows:

> *"Die wachsende Adaption semantischer Technologien zu Zwecken der strukturierten Erschließung von 'Web 2.0 Content', aber auch der Einsatz von Social Software zur kollaborativen Anreicherung von Web Content mit maschinenlesbaren Metadaten sind Ausdruck eines Trends in Richtung 'Social Semantic Web'."* Blumauer and Pellegrini [29, pp. 6]

From a technological perspective, they differentiate both branches in the sense of content analysis [29, pp. 7]. The so-called Web 2.0 put the user into the fore. That is, the content is created and structured by large number of volunteers – in terms of community-driven collaboration (by means of social software). The idea of the Semantic Web sets the focus primarily on a machine-readable metadata enrichment of web content. The transformation and convergence of both phenomena may also describe the idea of what a possible Web 3.0 could stand for [29, pp. 19]. In this context, the application of *Semantic Wikis* [284] has drawn some attention in the research community lately. These software tools aim to combine the strengths of the *Semantic Web* (with a focus on the key concepts: machine processable, data integration, enabling complex search queries) and the famous *MediaWiki*[10] technologies (with its focus on: easy to use and contribute, strongly interconnected, enabling collaboration). The basic concept behind this is, that users are not only allowed to contribute web content, such as in the *Wikipedia* project, but to be able to specify individual entities and concepts (e.g. single words or phrases) that occur in the contributed article. These specifications can be made by predefined or newly created relation types (e.g. the relation "is born at" to connect a proper name with a geographic reference). A related approach is the so called *Social Semantic Bookmarking* [33]. These online-based bookmarking systems [119] aim to allow the (collaboratively) annotation of resources with tags[11] that are

---
[10]mediawiki.org
[11]Tags in terms of text-based description labels.

extended by semantic definitions and descriptions. By the collaborative constructed annotation of metadata expressions of web content, an improvement within the information retrieval may be achieved for both sides, the traditional web user (e. g. submit complex search queries[12] such as in the *DBpedia* project [11]) and for the automatic content analysis of machine processing.

Related to this, the field of a so-called *Emergent Semantics* [2], refers to the representation of semantics and their discovery as a result of a self-organizing process of distributed agents (say users). The basic idea is that there is no centralized coordination or reference for the annotation or representation of semantics, but rather an ad-hoc approach, that evolves over time. At the center, so-called *microformats*[13] are used, which are defined by the user within the existing (X)Html markup structures (e. g. <div *class="org"*>IBM</div>, where *class="org"* marks the relation 'is a organization'). The introduced semantic definitions should in this context be understandable for human *and* the machine-processing domain. Cudré-Mauroux [67] brings this to the point:

> *"Emergent semantics refers to a set of principles and techniques analyzing the evolution of decentralized semantic structures in large scale distributed information systems. Emergent semantics approaches model the semantics of a distributed system as an ensemble of relationships between syntactic structures."* Cudré-Mauroux [67, pp. 1]

In this sense, information agents/users should *interoperate irrespective of their initial vocabularies* [67]. Each agent has to map its vocabulary (e. g. defined in its base schema or ontology) to the vocabulary of other agents/user with which it wants to interoperate. He refers to this phenomenon as a *Agreements as a Semantic Handshake Protocol*. With respect to our perception of a Social Semantics in IR, the described approaches focus in most cases on the annotation of semantic meaning within natural language texts. The actual annotation task should be fulfilled by users, as a user-driven process of giving semantics to items through the use of tags [67, pp. 1]. In contrast to this, we are focusing on an *automatic* identification and representation of the meaning within natural language texts. Moreover, there are a multitude of different approaches

---
[12]Using as for example the SPARQL Query Language for RDF
[13]microformats.org

towards *Social Semantics*, such as *Live Social Semantics* [4, pp. 15], which aims to semantically interlink personal data from several different sources to enhance real-world interactions[14], the *Social Semantic Desktop* [18] as a collaborative environment for sharing and deployment of data and metadata, or *Social Semantics for Agent Communication* [293, pp.1], which focuses on communication languages for multiagent systems. Contrary to them, our point of view on *Social Semantics*, which is applied in this thesis, primarily follows the definition of the so-called *Ontological Semantics*, a field of research that is concerned with the reasoning behind knowledge derived from texts using ontologies as knowledge bases.

> *"Ontological semantics is a theory of meaning in natural language and an approach to NLP that uses a constructed world model, or ontology, as the central resource for extracting and representing the meaning of natural language texts and for reasoning about knowledge derived from texts."* Nirenburg and Raskin [224, pp. 6]

Following Nirenburg and Raskin [224, pp. 10], ontological semantics focuses on the meaning representation of text, establishing the lexical meaning of individual words and phrases, disambiguating these meaning, and filling gaps in the structure by means of ontological knowledge. Ontologies contain in this context the knowledge about type of things, such as objects, processes, properties and about their combinations. Moreover, they argue that the final result of this process of text understanding may include some information *not* overtly present in, or directly obtainable from the source text. These central aspects of the theory of ontological semantics, connecting text elements to chunks of meaning representation using knowledge bases [224, pp. 13], applies also to the field of social ontologies, and describe very well the main principle of a social semantics in IR that we are focusing on. It is precisely the access of collaborative world knowledge [91], derived from online communities and networks, and the incorporation of traditional content models, that let us improve the retrieval effectiveness and accuracy in the domain of IR.

---

[14]Real-world interaction by means of RFID-Tags (Radio Frequency Identification Transponders)

This thesis investigates the effect of social semantics for different tasks in IR as a contribution to the text- and web mining community. The main research questions examined in this thesis are thereby:

- How can we identify and extract concepts out of socially-constructed knowledge resources?
- What kind of lexical semantics can be identified?
- Which community-driven resources fit best to the respective content model task?
- How do socially constructed concepts increase the effectiveness and accuracy of text- and web categorization?

We hypothesize that social semantics contributes to a more user-centered notion of information retrieval, and significantly improves current state-of-the-art approaches to IR. We will explore this hypothesis within various directions, which are currently of high interest in the IR community: *term-associations, topic identification, text categorization*, as well as *named entity recognition, web genre classification* and *sentiment polarity identification*. In the following sections, we systematically analyze, propose and evaluate the *social semantic factor* of IR components and document models.

3.2 The Knowledge Acquisition Bottleneck

A focal point, when building content models for classification is the so-called knowledge acquisition bottleneck [21, 89, 346]. That is, word features that occur only in the test set but not in the training set of a supervised classification are entirely ignored when using the BOW approach. Therefore, trained classifiers are not capable of analyzing such words, which might have an important meaning for a proper classification. On the other side, we could have term features that occur very frequently in the test set, but infrequently in the training set. These features might be underestimated for the representation of certain categories.

Consider for example the following three news headlines from the New York Times:

(a) The Knicks open a four-game homestand Saturday against the Philadelphia 76ers.
(b)The Boston Market is developing its franchise program.
(c) The Bobcats had set an ignominious franchise record with 59 points in their season-opening loss to Boston.

With respect to the BOW approach, (b) and (c) have a higher similarity due to the overlap of term features (franchise, Boston). However, since (a) and (c) are both about the next challenges of the national basketball association (NBA), the BOW approach would lead us to a spurious classification. As a result, introducing unjustified associations between the distinctive category and the falsely interpreted word features. This example clearly shows that text categorization is not only about the words occurring in texts, but also about common (topic) concepts texts represent. Using the BOW, the connection between words remain implicit, and might not be learned or comprised (e. g. due to infrequent occurrences) in the training phase of a classifier, without inducing external knowledge. Thus, the BOW approach does not account for "... *the contextual adjacency words on a linguistically plausible level"* [90, pp. 23].

3.2.1 Utilizing Feature Construction

In order to overcome the issue of a bottleneck of knowledge acquisition – the limitations of a BOW document representation – a topical or conceptual feature interpretation and knowledge enhancement needs to be established. In recent years, various studies of the NLP community addressed the issue of relying on differently distributed feature data that could learn to predict categories. While, some of them used probabilistic models inducing feature smoothing [327] to avoid zero probabilities in the training phase, an enhancement of new knowledge was not applied. Therefore, utilized features still remain those obtained from the BOW approach.

Others induced additional information of external corpora, proposing a generalized vector space model [363], using a transfer learning technique of NB-driven classification [69], or introducing a layered abstraction-based method, targeting the predicted membership toward topic models of other corpora [17]. Machine learning techniques address the problem among others by using SVMs [128], or the combination of SVM and LSA, introducing Latent Semantic Kernels [64]. Consequently, considering an additional test set after the initial training phase, in order to minimize the error-rate (in terms of misclassifications). With respect to computational methods comprising external resources, we can identify three different branches by the resources they used. Corpus-based methods use inter alia collocations for building associations to semantically-related words in texts [23, 263, 165]. Approaches comprising semantic relations (e.g. synonym, hyperonym) use lexical-semantic word-nets such as *WordNet* [83], *GermaNet* [154] or *EuroWordNet* [332] to address the data sparseness problem [244, 8]. Network-driven methods combine typically user-generated content such as from the *Open Directory Project* (ODP) or *Wikipedia* with machine learning techniques on basis of SVM [90, 91, 349, 370] or building a Latent Dirichlet Allocation (LDA) [26].

3.2.2 Towards the BOW by Topic Concepts

As a commonality, most of these attempts enhance their existing data set using direct word relationships (e.g. semantic relations such as 'word a' is a hyperonym of 'word b'), significant co-occurrence neighbors (e.g. immediate to the left, right or sentence based), or article titles of the *Wikipedia* (e.g. /Barack Obama/) as additional term features. On the other side, there are approaches, which induce topic-oriented concepts [8, 196, 290, 341, 346] for a feature enhancement, following the idea that text categorization is about the (topical) concepts that texts represent. Lexical semantic word nets, which are evidently widely used and accepted in the NLP community, offer, on the one side a rich structured data resource, since they are built and provided by linguistic experts, and on the other side they lack in terms of word coverage. None of the above stated lexical word nets contain significantly more than $100,000$ lemmata of one language, whereas more than ten-times the amount of lexemes can be found in (web-based) corpora and resources of a decent size.

In addition, the hierarchy of these resources (e. g. connected lexemes by their semantic relations) are more or less static (in terms of expandable), as defined by linguistic experts (which are expensive in both time and money). In this context, the dynamic aspects of social ontologies will help to overcome the static property of word net taxonomies and their delimited word coverage. Therefore, enabling information retrieval systems to access the rich knowledge of social networks and social ontologies, as a source of terminological knowledge, will help to overcome the bottleneck of knowledge acquisition, and improve the performance of text categorization. As a note to the commonly used terminology, even though dictionaries, directories or taxonomies most commonly use 'category' as their initial term for nodes, the usage refers mostly to topical labels of individual documents. In this thesis, we refer to those topical entries as concepts, such as the definition of concepts of attributes in a vector space.

3.3 Social Semantic Concept Clouds

The methodology that we propose for the improvement of traditional document models for text categorization integrates external knowledge and data structures to enhance existing representation formats. Aggregated concepts are thereby used for the construction of topic- and context-related *concept clouds* (see Definition 3.3.2), which are subsequently either added to the prior constructed document representation model (e. g. BOW) of the classified text or used as an entry point to the comprised social ontology (see Definition 3.3.1) structure.

Definition 3.3.1. *Social Ontology (Mehler [191, pp. 3]):*

Let S be a social ontology given as an empirical system $S = (C, R, \top)$ such that C is a set of empirical categories and $R \subseteq C^2$ is the empirical relation over C where for all $(C_i, C_j) \in R$ it holds that C_i is the supertype of its subtype C_j or C_i is a holonym of C_j or C_i is otherwise superordinate to C_j. Further, $\top \in C$ is the unique main category of S.

Figuratively speaking, for a given text fragment, we are taking a '*knowledge breath*[15]' to either enrich the initial feature set with semantically-related topic concepts as textual features, or map the input text onto the ontology structure (e. g. category taxonomy) for a further graph-related processing. In this way we are heading towards an increase of the expressiveness of the latent topics in texts.

Definition 3.3.2. *Concept Cloud:*
A set of semantically-related (e. g. semantic relation, semantic relatedness) concepts C (e. g. topic) as a conceptual representation (e. g. token, categories or phrases) of a given object T (e. g. input text fragment).

We argue that with the semantic extension of traditional document models, a possibly better understanding of the actual document content and context may be achieved, thus improving the effectiveness of text categorization. From a computational point of view, the idea of feature enhancement follows in principle, the notion of mapping a given text fragment onto the structural components (e. g. taxonomy) of a reference knowledge repository (e. g. social ontology). The actual ontology descriptors (e. g. category labels) and also the associated content information (e. g. article collection) may then be used as a set of topic-related concepts. In short, the proposed notion of feature enhancement can be subdivided into four different phases (see Figure 3.3):

a) The input document is converted into an initial document representation model (e. g. BOW).

b) The document representation is subsequently mapped/classified onto/by the concept structure of a given knowledge base (e.g social ontology).

c) The concept descriptors derived from the knowledge base are used as an additional feature set (e. g. category label).

d) The constructed feature set is added to the initial document representation, which in itself is then used for further processing (e. g. text categorization).

---

[15]In this context, knowledge breath refers to the task of enhancing the existing document representation with additional features.

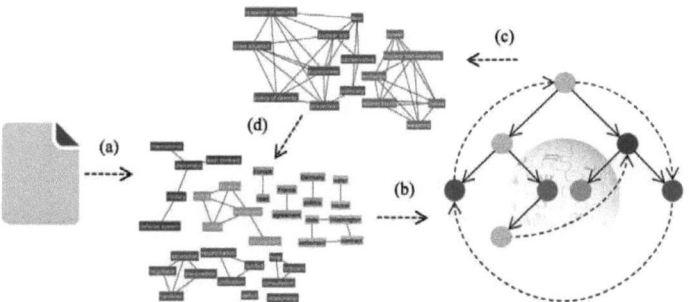

Figure 3.3: Application flow of an enhancement of a document representation by means of concepts derived from a reference ontology.

3.3.1 Constructing Concept Knowledge

We use external resources to provide background knowledge about a document contents. In principle, any comprised knowledge repository must comply with the following requirements [90, pp. 31]:

1. Let the knowledge base be a collection of concepts $C = \{c_1, ..., c_n\}$. For example, such concepts can be category or article labels from social networks, but also *synset*[16] labels from lexical word net databases or single terms derived from a corpus using statistical methods.

2. Furthermore, let there be a collection of texts that are associated to each concept. These textual objects serve as reference points instantiating individual concepts referred to as entire article text collections, example sentences or associated tokens. We refer to these objects as $T_i = \{t_{i,1}, ..., t_{i,m}\}$ as a set of textual objects associated with $c_i, i \in \{1, ..., n\}$.

3. Further, let $R = \{r_1, ..., r_p\}$ be a collection of relations, where each relation is a set of pairs of concepts $r_k = (c_i, c_j)$. Such relations can be appointed by lexical relations such as *hyponomy* and *synonymy* spanning a hierarchical structure or more generally spoken by an *"is-a"* relation.

---

[16] A synset represents a concept in lexical-semantic nets such as *WordNet* or *GermaNet*, and contains a set of words, each of which has a sense that names that concept.

The task of concept cloud construction maps a given text fragment defined as a set of words W onto a number of associated concepts C on the basis of their reference to comprised textual objects T. In particular, we need to build a mapping $f : W \to C$, which is capable in mapping individual documents, text fragments or single tokens onto a open set of concepts. This task reflects a classical text categorization scenario, where documents are classified to predefined categories (in our case collaboratively constructed concepts).

Previous approaches already introduced different repositories for feature construction such as the *Medical Subject Headings* (MeSH) taxonomy [140, 368], the *Yahoo Web Directory* (YWD) [72, 162], or the *Open Directory Project* (ODP/DMOZ) [95, 103, 301]. In this work we comprise three different knowledge repositories (Table 3.1) for the task of concept cloud generation:

1. **Co-occurrence networks:** A concept may be typified through attributes (words and multi-word units) that significantly co-occur in a given context (e.g. sentence occurrences). Co-occurrence relations are labelled by their significance value. In this work, we utilize the dataset of the *Leipziger Wortschatz Projekt* [22, 114, 251] in order to obtain the co-occurrence statistics.

2. **Terminological ontologies:** Lexical networks such as *WordNet* offer a powerful resource of expert knowledge. Hence, as described in the previous section, they evolve within a much longer timescale. Concepts are instantiated thereby through *synset* and *lemmata* information, which are connected through different lexical relations such as *synonymy* and *hyperonymy*. We will utilize as a reference line, *GermaNet* as the German pendant to *WordNet* as our source of terminological knowledge.

3. **Social ontologies:** Social networks such as the *Wikipedia* offer a wide range of domain-specific knowledge through their partly high-quality article collection. Concepts reflect in this sense the category taxonomy, where the article collection is associated to. As the most prominent example of social networks we utilize the category taxonomy of the *Wikipedia* dataset for feature construction.

KB	Concepts	Relation	$|C|$	Edges	$|R|$
GermaNet	words, synsets	+	≈ 0.1 million	word & sense	≈ 0.3 million
Wikipedia	article titles, categories	+	≈ 1.5 million	hyperlinks	≈ 19.0 million
Leipzig	words	+	≈ 10.0 million	co-occurrence	≈ 60.0 million

Table 3.1: Knowledge repositories KB by comprised concept C and relation R information from a graph perspective.

3.3.2 Inducing the Concept Space

Regardless of the actual purpose of application of feature construction, in terms of inducing domain-specific knowledge (DSK) or general purpose knowledge (DPK), our definition of a *Concept Enhancement System* (CES) is as follows (see Algorithm 1). Given a resource of DSK or DPK, the CES operates similar to a text classifier, representing concepts as vectors of the most characteristic attribute features (e. g. words). In general, first a conversion of the ordinary knowledge repository in the vector space of concept attributes is conducted. Second, the identification of the most appropriate attributes for a given concept needs to be established. This task follows the notion of feature selection with respect to classical text categorization systems. In consideration of social networks, the attribute selection can be based upon textual constraints (e. g. tf, df or tfidf), but also on the network hyperlink-topology [184, 187] (e. g. importance weighting by the number of incoming or outgoing hyperlinks [229]). Thus, only those attributes are kept in the vector representation that best describes the individual concept definition. Based on the attribute reduction, a concept reduction is deployed. This step is needed, since there might be concept vectors, which comprise an insufficient number of attributes, and thereby mislead the concept representation (e. g. concepts that contain only two attributes). On the other hand, building a CES out of a large knowledge repository may lead to millions of induced concepts and attributes. In order to handle such a KB efficiently in a vector space representation - ensuring a reasonable classification flow – a convergence toward the most suitable concepts needs to be assimilated.

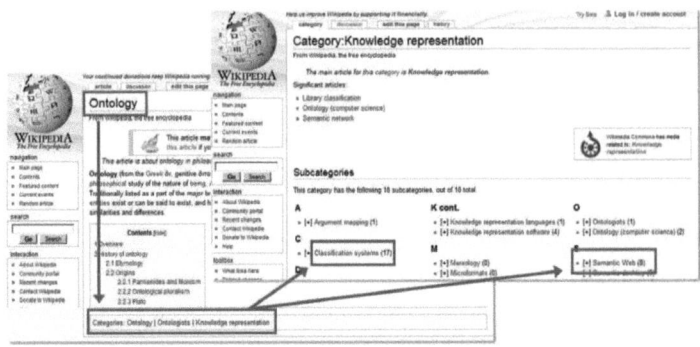

Figure 3.4: Outline of the hyperlink structure of a *Wikipedia* article contributions and the associated category taxonomy.

Once we have built the CES, any given input stream can be mapped onto the vector space, extracting a number of appropriate concept definitions (e.g. topically related), by using a similarity metric or classifier (e.g. NB [240], *Rocchio* relevance feedback [266], cosine similarity [321], or centroid-classifiers [312]).

3.4 From Social Networks To Social Semantic Vectors

At the center of our approach of concept construction, we make use of the most distinctive knowledge repository of social networks, instantiated by the electronic encyclopedia *Wikipedia*[17]. This resource offers not only one of the biggest human created document collection[18] that is publicly available, but also induces a comprehensive category taxonomy (social ontology), which is

---

[17] http://www.wikipedia.org/
[18] October 2009: The *Wikipedia* project is available for currently 264 different languages. The German pendant comprises a number of 975, 494 articles (3, 083, 391 articles in English).

Algorithm 1 Building SocialConceptClouds.

Concept Space Construction

Require: C, T, V_{ces}

    for each $c \in C$ do

        Attribute mapping - set of documents associated to c

        $V_{ces}(c) \leftarrow T(c)$

        Attribute weighting - term features are weighted by $tfidf$

        $V_{ces}(c) \leftarrow aw(V_{ces}(c))$

        Attribute selection - remove attributes with deficient concept affiliation

        $V_{ces}(c) \leftarrow as(V_{ces}(c))$

        Concept selection - remove concepts with deficient attribute affiliation

        $V_{ces}(c) \leftarrow cs(V_{ces}(c))$

    end for

Concept Cloud Construction

Require: V_{ces}, $V_{input}(text)$.

    Attribute weighting - term features of input text are weighted by $tfidf$

    $V_{input}(text) \leftarrow aw(V_{input}(text))$

    for each $c \in C$ do

        $Score(c) \leftarrow sim(V_{input}(text), V_{ces}W(c))$

    end for

    Let $SocialConceptCloud$ be the set of concepts with highest $Score(c)$

    return $SocialConceptCloud$

---

constructed in a hierarchical manner[19]. Even further, users do not only create new articles, but also manually categorize/tag the respective content through already established or newly introduced category labels, which are connected to the social ontology (e.g. *Ontology* → *Knowledge representation* → *Information science*) (see Figure 3.3.2). Additionally, individual words or phrases within an article, are interlinked (inducing hyperlinks) to other related contributions within the corpus (e.g. *Ontology* → *Hierarchy*). Obviously, this hyperlink

---

[19]The *Wikipedia* category taxonomy does not actually induce a classical tree-based taxonomy, but more an acyclic graph structure. We will analyze this issue in more detail in a later section.

structure formation - above the level of a single article contribution - can be described by means of graph analysis [183].

3.4.1 Graph Structure of Social Networks

With respect to the types of hyperlinks induced by the social software[20], we can identify among others[21] the following:

- CategoryUp links: associates category nodes of the hierarchy, in terms of superordination.

- CategoryDown links: associates category nodes of the hierarchy, in terms of subordination.

- Category2Category links: associates category nodes to category nodes, in terms of co-subordination.

- Page2Category links: associates document nodes to category nodes.

- PageAnchor links: associates different sections within a single contribution node.

- Page2PageIncoming links: associates a directed edge between another document node (start node) to the observed document node (target node).

- Page2PageOutgoing links: associates a directed edge between two document nodes, starting from the observed document node.

- Page2Ref links: associates document nodes to external reference nodes.

---

[20]The used software, called MediaWiki (http://www.mediawiki.org/), allows a collaborative writing, editing and revising of pages and hyperlinks, a wiki-website consists of.

[21]The software allows a multitude of hyperlink types, such as links inducing the article history, user pages, images or discussions.

Note, with respect to a graph-based representation of the *Wikipedia* collection (see Figures 3.5 - 3.7[22]), we only utilize the article and category contributions with their authored hyperlinks as described above. Let $G_{wiki} = (V, E, \sigma)$ be the graph representation of the *Wikipedia* collection, where V is the set of all article nodes and $E \subseteq V^2$ the corresponding set of edges (induced hyperlinks), and σ represents the set of edge types. Observing the graph structure of such a complex network more closely, we can argue that the characteristics of the *Wikipedia* article graph induces a *Small World* (SW) property [41, 183, 375] and [212, 221, 222]. In this context, following Watts and Strogatz [351],

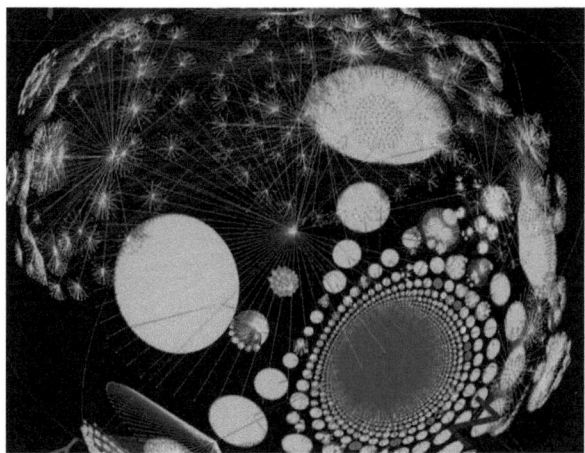

Figure 3.5: Forced minimum spanning tree representation of the German *Wikipedia* collection. Orange edges denote article hyperlinks, green edges denote category hyperlinks, red edges denote the links to the main category.

any randomly chosen pair of nodes in G_{wiki} should have, on the one hand – on average – a considerably short *geodesic distance* (in terms of the shortest path between two vertices in the graph), while having, on the other hand, a considerably higher level of *cluster formation*.

---

[22]The figures depict a forced minimum spanning tree representation of the German Wikipedia article and category graph, as calculated by the *Walrus* graph visualization tool (http://www.caida.org/tools/visualization/walrus/).

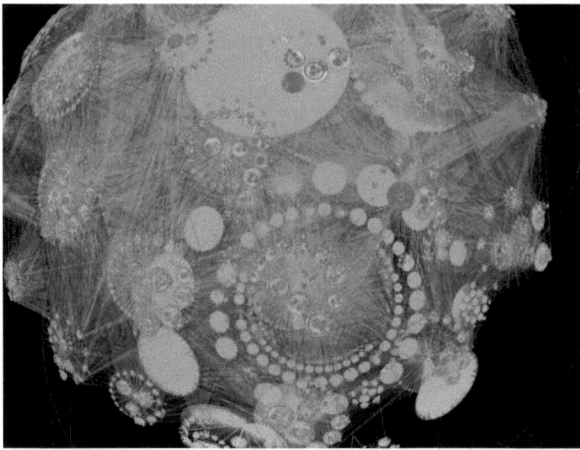

Figure 3.6: Graph representation of the German *Wikipedia* collection with all comprised edges, article-to-article, category-to-category and redirects. White edges are those not needed for the spanning tree representation.

Figure 3.7: Graph representation of the German *Wikipedia* collection, setting the root-category *Hauptkategorie* at the center of the concept universe.

With respect to the social network of Wikipedia (G_{wiki}), both SW properties can be identified [183, 191] (see Table 3.2). The average *geodesic distance* between two random articles of the German *Wikipedia* collection is 3.55. In other words, *Bielefeld* is only three clicks away from *Paradise*[23] but also from *Hell*[24].

Wiki	Lang	Nodes	Edges	C_d	L_d	CC_d	C_u	L_u	CC_u
German	de	1,467,762	31,858,920	0.06	4.36	0.76	**0.10**	**3.55**	0.95
French	fr	1,069,829	23,531,353	0.08	5.02	0.69	**0.13**	**3.53**	0.96
Dutch	nl	624,631	10,502,145	0.1	4.91	0.65	**0.14**	**3.63**	0.87

Table 3.2: Network topology of *Wikis* by language, nodes and edges. L denotes the average geodesic distance, C the cluster formation and CC denotes the cluster coefficient of the directed (d) and indirected (u) graph representation. (cf. [186, 191])

While the SW property obviously supports an high information flow [57], it also induces the complexity with respect to computational aspects. For example (see Table 3.2), the graph representation of the German *Wikipedia* induces $1,467,762$ nodes and $31,858,920$ edges (including user pages, images and so on) [186]. In contrast, the English pendant is more than three times larger than the German one (average geodesic distance $L_u = 3.28$ [375, pp. 7]). Thus, observing only edges that are directly pointing to or starting from an article as in the example of *Bielefeld*, which will lead to a total of 609 incoming links (see Figure 3.8) and 1602 outgoing links – inducing quite a dense graph representation. Nevertheless, similar to the algorithms applied to the web (e.g. most notable the *PageRank*-Algorithm [229]), an analysis of incoming links contributes toward the assessment of significance of contributed articles. In the line of Gabrilovich [90, pp. 55], we therefore make use of the internal and external hyperlink structure of $c_i \in V$ as an extended property of

---

[23] The shortest path comprising the English *Wikipedia* graph: Bielefeld → Design → Utopia → Paradise.

[24] The shortest path comprising the English *Wikipedia* graph: Bielefeld → Berlin → Lutheranism → Hell.

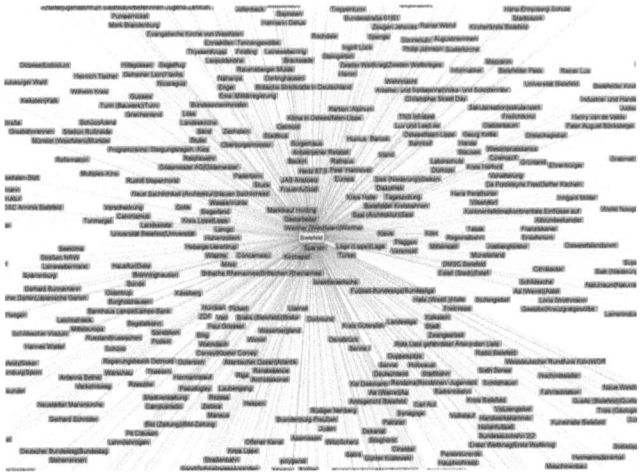

Figure 3.8: Extract of the German *Wikipedia* article graph using hyperlinks as edges starting from the article *Bielefeld* with a distance of one.

the used significance score $Score(c_i)$ of the CES by:

$$Score(c_i) = Score(c_i) \cdot \log(\log(num(Page2PageIncoming(c_i)))) \quad (3.1)$$

That is, highly interlinked, say referred, articles (e.g. 34,697 hyperlinks point to *Berlin*) reflect an higher content-based significance than articles with a lower number of *Page2PageIncoming* edges (e.g. 7 edges point to *Guttenbach*). In this sense, used concepts are not only represented through textual attributes, but are additionally rated by their relevance to the context by means of the hyperlink structure.

3.4.2 Constructing Social Semantic Vectors

In building a CES out of the document collection of *Wikipedia*, we are heading towards the construction of a *Social Semantic Vector Space*[25] of a *social network*. More precisely, we are proposing to construct a two-folded vector space

---

[25] Our term usage relates to a social semantics induced matrix representation, where the vector components of the constructed matrices are vectors.

representation, using both article and category concepts[26], which are interlinked to each other – instantiating the desired CES. Following this, we define the title information of *Wikipedia* articles as the set of concepts C_{art}, and the category nodes as the set of concepts C_{cat}. Concept attributes, defined as T_{art}, are thereby reflected through the words that occur in the individual articles. At the center of the *Wiki*-based CES, a *feature set reduction* is applied. In this context, we are reducing both, the number of concepts and attributes to a minimum representation, comprising only the most significant term features – pointing to their associated concepts. This is done for two reasons: first, the dataset is rather big in terms of its comprised token index[27]. For computational reasons, a reduction has to be applied in order to ensure a reasonable classification flow. Second, we are focusing only on the most informative word attributes, in order to circumvent feature noise in the classification process. Therefore, attributes rated as minor informative are removed from the vector space. Additionally, in the line of Gabrilovich and Markovitch [92], we are building an inverted vector space representation. That is, instead of sorting the concepts by attributes, we reverse the approach and construct an attribute-concept space. This accelerates the computational process, since we are able to access the term index in a direct manner during classification. Following the specification as described above, the construction of the *social network-induced semantic space* representation as a CES is conducted by the following steps:

1. **Document Preprocessing:** The *Wikipedia* XML dump[28] is downloaded. We used the the German *Wikipedia* snapshot as of January 19, 2009. After parsing the XML-dump (5, 2 Gb) comprising 756,444 articles, we conducted the preprocessing, inducing a tokenization, stop-word removal, lemmatization and PoS-Tagging of all article texts (as described in Chapter 2). In the second phase, a structure analysis was performed. Hence, text types such as article, category, discussion, user

---

[26]Note, we see article namespaces as concepts, which are typified by the article content (attributes). Category entries of the category taxonomy are typified by the associated article namespaces (attributes).

[27]The English Wikipedia version contains more than 300 million words. In contrast, the famous Britannica comprises 44 million words.

[28]A complete copy of all Wikimedia wikis in the form of wikitext source and metadata embedded in XML can be download at: http://download.wikimedia.org/

or disambiguation pages were identified, redirect pages resolved. Finally, the network topology on the basis of the induced hyperlinks was annotated.

2. **Feature Weighting:** In the line of traditional text categorization, word occurrences in texts are counted as feature units, used for the feature weighting task. As the function for validating these textual features, we make use of the *tfidf* weighting (see Section 2.2). *tf* reflects thereby the normalized term frequency, the *idf* refers to the inverse concept (article or category respectively) frequency. In addition, each concept weight is multiplied by the hyperlink-based significance weighting ($Score(c_i)$), quantifying the degree of concept and context (see previous Section).

3. **Concept and Attribute Reduction:** On the basis of the extracted and weighted attribute and concept features, but also by their hyperlink-based topology information, certain concepts and term features are removed from the initial KB. We ignored those articles, for example having fewer than five *Page2PageIncoming* or *Page2PageOutgoing* hyperlinks. Articles with less than 100 non stop-words or less than 10 "true"[29] features were also removed. In the final step, a vector-length reduction is performed. Thus, attributes whose feature weight falls below a threshold are excluded. As a result, the final vector representation comprised 248, 106 articles and 620, 502 lemmata. With respect to the category taxonomy, we have removed those categories with the highest *Page2Category* proportion (e. g. pages such as "List of ...", "Born in ..." or "Death in ..."). These categories were rated as overestimated in terms of the significance to the context. The category vector representation consisted of 55, 707 category entries utilizing the 248, 106 articles.

Thus, we build two connected *Social Semantic Vectors* matrices, utilizing article and category concepts out of the KB, inducing a rigorous reduced vector space representation. The idea behind our two-fold implementation is to enable the computation of concept similarities even if they do not have any direct (article-based) features in common [194, pp. 11]. This follows inter alia the

---

[29]True features are represented by their PoS-Tag. That is, we comprise only noun, adjective and verbs. All other features are ignored.

idea of the *weak contextual hypothesis* as described by Miller and Charles [213, pp. 8], which states that the *difference of meaning correlates with difference of its contextual distribution* [108, pp. 156].

Generally, similarity measures, utilizing the traditional BOW approach, are based mostly on the fraction of term features overlap. Since we are able to query additional category concepts, connected to other (topical-related) article concepts, which themselves again comprise a set of (article) term features, we are able to enhance the existing term feature representation within a certain scale. In this regard, we are not heading towards an *explicit* mentioned and shared feature information, but instead, using *implicit* relatedness obtained by common category reference. More formally, we construct a matrix using the article concepts as the row component and the terms that occur in the individual article text as the column. All term feature are weighted by using the $tfidf$ [272] scheme.

In the next step, we invert this matrix to a *term-article* matrix defined as V_{art}. Feature reduction is performed by sorting all weighted article concepts in descending order (of each row) and removing those entries whose $tfidf$ scores are below a certain threshold (below 10% in comparison to the highest article entry of the row). Subsequently, we observed the hyperlink-topology for each article concept as a reduction parameter. That is, we utilized only those article concepts having more than $>= 5$ of $Page2PageIncoming$ or $Page2PageOutgoing$ hyperlinks (see previous section). All other concepts are left out of the index.

Therefore, the final V_{art} representation consists of a minimum number of term features (represented as row entries in a matrix), with a minimum of associated article concepts (represented as column entries in a matrix), on the basis of our feature weighting function and the observed hyperlink structure. For computational reasons, we sort all features of V_{art} by their weights in descending order. Consequently, given an input word as a query request, we are able to retrieve a number of article concepts, starting from the highest to the lowest similarity[30].

As the second part of the *Social Semantic Vector* implementation, we connect article and category concepts of KB. In this sense, we construct an

---

[30]Similarity in the sense of $tfidf$ score.

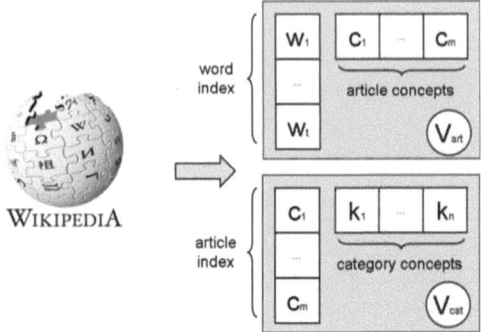

Figure 3.9: Overview of the construction of the *Social Semantic Vector* representation by means of the social network *Wikipedia* comprising article contributions and category taxonomy.

article-category matrix, defined as V_{cat}, where the rows represent article concepts and the column represent category nodes. Used article entries are those from V_{art}. That is, for each article a number of categories are assigned. In the line of the article-based matrix representation, the *tfidf* scheme is used for feature weighting. Again, we sort V_{cat} in descending order by assigned category weights (*tfidf* scheme). Therefore, given an article node as a query parameter, we are able to retrieve a number of associated category concepts that are also ordered by their feature weight.

Once both matrices (see Figure 3.9), V_{art} and V_{cat}, are constructed, we are in the position to retrieve, given any input word that occurs in the term index, a number of associated article concepts $V_{art}(i, 1:m)$, where i represents the index of the query term. Consequential, we are able to also request a number of category concepts $V_{cat}(l, 1:n)$, where l represents the index of the article. Moreover, this enables us to map a given text fragment onto a number of related article concepts on the basis of the matrix representation.

Let us consider some example texts, which were applied to the proposed CES by means of the *Social Semantic Vector* implementation. Article concepts refer thereby to the best[31] five index entries within V_{art}. Analogously, category concepts are derived from the best five index entries of V_{cat}.

---

[31]Best in the sense of the highest association score.

- **InputText**: *"Die Gesellschaft wird ihre Minderheitsbeteiligung an der Hermann Milke KG GmbH & Co gegen neue Vorzugsaktien in die Anneliese Zementwerke AG einbringen. Für die Ausgabe der neuen Vorzugsaktien wird ein Bewertungsgutachten notwendig, das eine in der Anneliese-Beteiligung steckende Stille Reserve aufdecken soll. [...]*[32]"

- **Representation**[33]: Gesellschaft, Minderheitsbeteiligung, KG, GmbH, Co, Vorzugsaktie, Anneliese, Zementwerk, AG, Ausgabe, Beteiligung, Stille, Reserve

- **Generated feature concepts**:

    – *Article Concepts*: Bauwelt / Agravis Raiffeisen / Baustoffkunde / Raiffeisen / Baustoffhandel[34]

    – *Category Concepts*: Wirtschaft / Unternehmen / Wirtschaftszweig / Handel und Dienstleistung / Handel[35]

- **InputText**: *"Die französische Großbank hat 1996 deutlich besser verdient. Es entstand ein zurechenbarer Reingewinn von 4,544 Milliarden Francs nach 3,817 Milliarden Francs im Vorjahr oder 52,1 (46,3) Franc je Aktie. Die Anteilseigner sollen daran mit einer Netto-Dividende von 17,5 (16,0) Franc je Aktie teilhaben.[...]*[36]"

- **Representation**[37]: Großbank, Reingewinn, Milliarde, Franc, Vorjahr, Aktie, Anteilseigner, Netto, Dividende

- **Generated feature concepts**:

    – *Article Concepts*: Kapitalerhöhung / Vorzugsaktie Aktie / Aktionär / Aktiensplit / Börsenkurs[38]

---

[32]Text excerpt: brackets introduced by the author.
[33]Lemmata-based noun representation used for the classification.
[34]English translation: construction materials world / Agravis Raiffeisen a company trading construction materials / construction material science / Raiffeisen the trading company / trade in construction materials
[35]English translation: economy / company / branch of economic activity / provision of services / business
[36]Text excerpt: brackets introduced by the author.
[37]Lemmata-based noun representation used for the classification.
[38]recapitalisation / preference stock / equity holder / stock split / stock exchange price

- *Category Concepts*: Finanzmarkt / Finanzierung / Ökonomischer Markt / Aktienmarkt / Wirtschaft[39]

- **InputText**: "*Ein Stargate, das kann man sich vorstellen wie eine jener Drehtüren, die im Slapstick Verbrecher oder Komödianten unvermittelt in den benachbarten Raum katapultiert haben. Mit dem Unterschied, daß der geheime Klappmechanismus sich nicht einfach nur zum Nebenzimmer öffnet, sondern zu einem Millionen Lichtjahre entfernten Planeten.[...]*[40]"

- **Representation**[41]: Stargate, Slapstick, Verbrecher, Komödiant, Raum, Unterschied, Nebenzimmer, Million, Lichtjahr, Planet

- **Generated feature concepts**:

  - *Article Concepts*: Stargate (Film) / Roland Emmerich / Karl Walter Lindenlaub / 10.000 B. C. / Zeitreise[42]

  - *Category Concepts*: Film / Darstellende Kunst / Filmtitel / Werk der Darstellenden Kunst / Medien[43]

- **InputText**: "*Wenn man in Sachsen ein Bett sucht. Wo finde ich abends um zwanzig Uhr noch ein Hotelbett für unter 100 Mark? Der Geschäftspartner bevorzugt chinesische Küche, wo kann ich mit ihm stilvoll essen? Welche Bar hat noch nachts um zwei offen?[...]*[44]"

- **Representation**[45]: Sachsen, Bett, Uhr, Hotelbett, Mark, Geschäftspartner, Küche, Bar

---

[39]financial market / financing / financial exchange / stock market / economy
[40]Text excerpt: brackets introduced by the author.
[41]Lemmata-based noun representation used for the classification.
[42]English translation: Stargate (the movie) / Roland Emmerich (German movie director) / Karl Walter Lindenlaub (director of photography) / 10.000 B. C. (american movie) / journey through time
[43]English translation: cinema / performing arts / film title / work of performing arts / media
[44]Text excerpt: brackets introduced by the author.
[45]Lemmata-based noun representation used for the classification.

- **Generated feature concepts**:

    - *Article Concepts*: Lastminute / Reisevertrag / Reise Individualreise / Tourismus in der DDR / Cluburlaub[46]
    - *Category Concepts*: Wirtschaftszweig / Dienstleistungssektor / Freizeitindustrie / Tourismus / Verkehrswirtschaft [47]

- **InputText**: "*Große Schlacht um den Euro. Waterloo, Verdun, Stalingrad - und jetzt Brüssel: Um den Euro zu retten und die Spekulanten zu zähmen, haben die Staats- und Regierungschefs der EU binnen Stunden Beschlüsse gefasst, die in vielen Jahren nicht vorstellbar gewesen waren. Es ist eine Revolution[...]*[48]"

- **Representation**[49]: Schlacht, Verdun, Stalingrad, Brüssel Euro, Spekulant, Staat, Regierungschef, EU, Stunde, Beschluß, Jahr, Revolution

- **Generated feature concepts**:

    - *Article Concepts*: Schlacht bei Wavre / Lohnausgleich / Devisenmarkt / Grenzschlachten / Lambert II.[50]
    - *Category Concepts*: Thema nach Staat / Geschichte nach Staat / Europa / Militärwesen / Europäische Geschichte[51]

As shown above, it seems that our *Wikipedia*-based feature generator (Social Semantic Vector (SSV)-based CES) is able to reveal the latent topic[52] of texts by means of topic-related category concepts on a satisfying level. As for instance: "Wenn man in Sachsen ein Bett sucht" ↦ Tourismus; "Stargate" ↦

---

[46]English translation: last-minute travel / tourist travel contract / personal tours / tourism in the German Democratic Republic (DDR)

[47]English translation: branch of the economy / services sector / leisure industry / tourism / transport economics

[48]Text excerpt: brackets introduced by the author.

[49]Lemmata-based noun representation used for the classification.

[50]English translation: Battle of Wavre / wage adjustment / exchange market / frontier battle / Lambert II. - German count of Brussels who died 1054 in a battle in Tournai.

[51]English translation: topic by country / history by country / europe / armed forces / european history

[52]Latent topics in the sense of the identification of topics in texts, were the actual assigned topic label do not necessarily need to occur in the observed document.

Film; "Großbank" ↦ Wirtschaft; However, "Große Schlacht um den Euro" ↦ Militärwesen. In this context, the features *Schlacht, Verdun* and *Stalingrad* have mislead the feature generator to the category military rather than currency in Europe. Nonetheless, with respect to our idea of a topic-based extension of a document representation model used for text categorization, we are now able to approach this task from two different points of view: As shown in Figure 3.10, we could apply $(V_{art})(V_{cat})_{i \leq j \leq p}$ as the *concept cloud*, which is added to the existing document representation. Thus, we map a given input document onto the representation of the social ontology using the SSV implementation, and utilize the constructed category or article concepts to enhance the existing document representation.

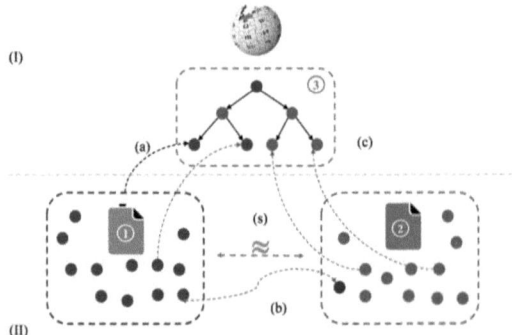

Figure 3.10: Enhancement-based document similarity model: Similarity (s) of document (1) and (2) by means of a feature enhancement of a shared concept cloud representation (3). (a) and (c) represent the links associated to enhanced (shared) concepts among individual texts and concepts derived from a social ontology. (b) denotes the initial overlap of textual features between (1) and (2) prior enhancement. (I) represents reference level (social ontology); (II) represents the document level.

On the other hand, as shown in Figure 3.11, we could also abstract from the entire input document representation after the concept construction. Instead of enhancing the existing document representation, we are using the comprised category information to determine the document similarity. Within the social ontology of the *Wikipedia* collection, each category node has a set of assigned article contributions. Therefore, the similarity of two documents d_i and d_j may be determined by:

$$\delta(d_i, d_j) = \delta(V_{art_{d_i}}, V_{art_{d_j}}); \qquad (3.2)$$

or

$$\delta(d_i, d_j) = \delta(V_{cat_{d_i}}, V_{cat_{d_j}}); \qquad (3.3)$$

In this context, the similarity of d_i and d_j is determined by the entire content features of the respective constructed *Wikipedia* document contributions $(V_{art_{d_i}}, V_{art_{d_j}})$. Even further, we could also use all articles that are associated to the constructed category concepts of $V_{cat_{d_i}}$ and $V_{cat_{d_j}}$ respectively, and calculate the similarity by means of the entire document content. Utilizing all articles that are comprised by the individual category nodes. In both cases, the compared input documents, d_i and d_j, are represented as attribute vectors using *all Wikipedia* article content. Attribute vectors are then compared using the cosine metric (see Section 2.2.3). The similarity of two documents is thereby determined by its similarity of comprised article-category information.

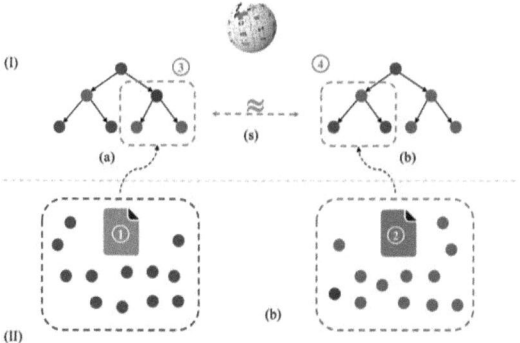

Figure 3.11: Ontology-based document similarity model: Similarity (s) of documents (1) and (2) by means of mapped concept cloud representations (3) and (4). (a) and (b) denotes the mapping of the respective text onto associated concepts from a social ontology. (s) denotes the average similarity between each mapped concepts. (I) represents the reference level (social ontology); (II) represents the document level.

3.4.3 Concluding Remarks

Our strategy in building a two-folded social network-driven semantic space, utilizing V_{art} and V_{cat}, focuses on the extraction of topic-related concepts derived from a large knowledge repository built by a multitude of volunteers of an online community. We therefore treat the task of concept extraction out of a KB, as a task of mapping a document onto the conceptual structure of a social ontology [51, 195, 209]. Different to the proposal of Gabrilovich and Markovitch [91], using *Wikipedia*-based article title information to construct a feature enhancement, we are focusing on the task of mapping a given text fragment or document onto the social ontology, instantiated by the *Wikipedia* category taxonomy. Our proposed algorithm serves as a method in finding the "right"[53] entry points into the taxonomy. Once the input text is connected to the category structure, we can apply different (text- *and* graph-related) algorithms from the domain of information retrieval to predict the overall topics of distinctive documents, or to enhance the existing document representation by means of category concepts. With respect to the tasks of topic identification and document similarity, we will present a detailed analysis of the proposed approach in the next chapter.

---

[53]"right" in the sense of the most significant and topical related categories in the *Wikipedia* dataset on the basis of a two-fold vector representation.

Chapter 4

Evaluation of Social Network-induced Content Models

In this chapter we present the evaluation of our model of a *Social Semantics in Information Retrieval*. In Section 4.1, we describe the analysis of the proposed *Social Semantic Vector* (SSV) representation with regards to term-term associations. That is, we formulate a method for assessing the semantic relatedness by exploring the distributional properties of the social network. As we argue that the incorporation of external knowledge (instantiated by topic-related concepts) derived from social networks and social ontologies will lead to an improvement of text classification, we will continue with the analysis by means of two subsequent evaluation scenarios:

- The first experiment focuses on the construction and evaluation of *Open Topic Models* by using a topic generalization technique. Hence, we aim to analyze the performance of a topic-related text analysis within a topic identification experimental setup, utilizing the proposed *Social Semantic Vector* implementation (Section 4.2.4) as a resource. More precisely, we will evaluate the accuracy of extracting topic labels by means of concepts derived from an open topic universe.

- The second experiment sets the focus on the semantic extension of existing document representations formats. That is, we systematically evaluate the performance of topic-orientated feature enhancement for the task of text categorization by means of *Closed Topic Models*. This approach will be analyzed by two different experiments. First, we utilize a large corpus of newspaper articles and compare the achieved results with reference implementations – utilizing the classical apparatus of text categorization (e. g. SVM). Second, we apply the method of feature construction to a corpus of meta data as provided by the *Open Archives Initiative* to derive document snippets as minimized document representations. This approach follows the idea of reducing both the time and space complexity of the document processing by using a minimum amount of textual information for the classification task. Thus, we circumvent the problem of data sparseness by providing reliable topic-related classifications.

4.1 Social Semantic Relatedness

In this section, we present a first analysis of the proposed SSV representation. That is, we want to analyze the SSV by means of quantifying semantic relatedness of texts from a social semantics perspective. In particular, we wish to answer the question of the influence of collaboratively constructed resources (instantiated by the SSV implementation) on the determination of term-term associations. While humans can intuitively assess the relatedness of two word forms or text fragments, determining it by automatic means is still a challenge. Consider the following example: How related are "Bill Gates" and "Yahoo"?[1] In general, the reasoning of semantic relatedness (SR) performed by humans plays a significant role in the lexical retrieval of human cognition. SR is one of the fundamental concepts in the study of the conceptual memory of humans. It has been shown [7, 55, 285] that semantically related terms do influence the (semantic) processing of one another. For example, a *mouse* is faster recognized, if it is primed by *cat*[2]. This follows the theory of *spreading activation* [55] or the related *ACT theory* of Anderson [7], which argues that long-term memory contains interlinked units of information. These connections produce associations between those units, controlling the information retrieval by a hu-

---

[1] On the basis of our proposed Semantic Relatedness method the answer would be 0.64
[2] While there are different areas within the phenomenon priming [84], e. g. repetition priming: mouse → mouse, the semantic priming mouse → cat, or the associative priming: mouse → elephant, we are focusing on the basic concept of SR from a computational perspective only.

man. Most importantly, these ties are based on personal experience and are not necessarily logical. Following this, humans are more likely to retrieve information from memory if it relates to information they already have processed (priming). With respect to the domain of NLP, the computation of semantic relatedness is an important task for a variety of applications such as spelling error detection, word sense disambiguation or information extraction. In the context of computational linguistics, we first have to distinguish between two closely related phenomena. Following Budanitsky and Hirst [36, pp. 1], we define the following:

Definition 4.1.1. *Semantic Similarity:*
If two terms are from a linguistic point of view similar and, share some aspects of meaning, e. g. connected through semantic relations such as hypernymy or synonymy (e. g. home - residence*), they are defined as semantically similar.*

Definition 4.1.2. *Semantic Relatedness:*
Two terms can be semantically strongly related without having a semantic similarity or meaning in common, but showing a strong associative relationship (e. g. car - street*), or are related by different linguistic categories (e. g.* grass - green*). This relationship is defined as semantic relatedness.*

This section aims to provide an algorithm to determine the SR of a given word pair by automatic means utilizing social network data. We utilize the proposed *Social Semantic Vectors* implementation, using the distributional properties of the comprised social concepts, as a resource for the computation of SR. We will first present an overview of current state-of-the-art approaches to SR. Second, we will provide the algorithm for the computation and measuring of SR, which good performance will be evaluated by means of an extensive experimental setup [345]. Hence, we will analyze sixteen different algorithms, inducing two languages, and four different resources, by means of a reference data set, which was obtained from two different human judgement experiments.

4.1.1 Related Work

A large variety of algorithms in computing SR has been proposed in the past decade. However, due to different evaluation setups, in terms of comprised resources or reference data sets, a clear picture of their ability to compute SR, which correlates to humans, remains unanswered. With respect to evaluation, most commonly, human judgement experiments are conducted. In this context, a number of volunteers rate, within a fixed scale, their interpretation of SR for an observed list of term pair candidates. The performance of the proposed SR algorithms are then evaluated by directly comparing the automatic computed scores with those obtained from the human judgement experiment. As the scoring function, the *Pearson correlation coefficient* is used.

With respect to English-based human judgement experiments, Rubenstein and Goodenough [269] compiled one of the first reference data sets comprising 65 word-pairs. The second most cited human-judged set of word pairs was compiled by Miller and Charles [213], inducing 30 word-pairs. In 2006, Boyd-Graber et al. [31] presented a collection of 120,000 concept pairs, rated by 20 volunteers, focusing on the *evocation*[3] of concepts. In 2001, Finkelstein et al. [85] presented the *WordSimilarity* collection, comprising 353 term pair entries. With respect to German reference data sets, there are two different proposals:

- First, a translation of the word-pair list of Rubenstein and Goodenough [269], proposed by Gurevych [104]

- Second and most recently, a data set compiled by Cramer and Finthammer [60]. This collection comprises two lists of word pairs. A set of 100 noun word pairs, manually collected from diverse semantic classes (e. g. autumn and winter). The other one induces 500 term pairs as part of collocations or associations (e. g. clown and marquee).

With respect to algorithms for an automatic modelling of associations between words or text fragments, various methods have been proposed in the past. Based on their used resources, we can identify three different groups. Distributional methods can be defined in approaches establishing relatedness on direct co-occurrence in text (1st order). For example, utilizing frequency information of co-occurrences [314, 355], using bi-grams [135], deducing an information-based sequence distance [157], by the induction of search engine indices as the *Google* page-counts [52, 53], or on comparing the similarity of contexts in which two terms occur, defined as 2nd order approaches. With

---
[3]The term evocation is defined as a shared meaning of concepts.

respect to the semantic processing, the *Latent Semantic Analysis* (LSA) [74] has obtained particular attention. As described in Section 2.2.4 the LSA is based on a term×context matrix A, displaying the occurrences of each word in each text context. Most recently, Widdows and Ferraro [356] proposed a *Java*-based implementation called *Semantic Vectors*, which promises to perform as successfully as techniques like LSA. However, it does not rely on complex procedures such as SVD. The second group, where numerous measure of SR ([117, 150, 159, 260, 364]) have been proposed, induce a lexical-semantic net like Princeton *WordNet* [83], *EURO-WordNet* [332] or its German counterpart *GermaNet* [154]. An overview of a broad variety of lexical-semantic net induced measures can be found in Cramer [59] and Waltinger et al. [345]. As a commonality, most of these SR measures are using only the hyponym relations in WordNet, and can therefore be regarded as measures of similarity [36, pp. 2]. As for example, the *Leacock-Chodorow* measure [150], computes the length of the shortest path between two synonym sets and scales it by the depth of the complete hyponym-tree.

$$\text{rel}_{\text{LC}}(s_1, s_2) = -\log \frac{2 \cdot \text{sp}(s_1, s_2)}{2 \cdot d_{Tree}} \qquad (4.1)$$

Let s_1 and s_2 be two synonyms and $\text{sp}(s_1, s_2)$ the length of shortest path between s_1 and s_2 in the hyponym-tree. d_{Tree} represents the overall depth of the hyponym-tree D_{Tree}. In contrast, the lexical-semantic net measure of Resnik [260], induces also the *hyponym-tree* and in addition a frequency list, utilizes the *information content* in order to compute the similarity between two synonym sets.

$$\text{p}(s) := \frac{\sum_{w \in W(s)} \text{freq}(w)}{TotalFreq} \qquad (4.2)$$

$$\text{IC}(s) := -\log \text{p}(s) \qquad (4.3)$$

$$\text{rel}_{\text{Res}}(s_1, s_2) = \text{IC}(\text{lcs}(s_1, s_2)) \qquad (4.4)$$

where $\text{freq}(w)$ defines the frequency of a word within a corpus. $W(s)$ is the set of the synonym set s and all its direct/indirect hyponym synonym sets. *TotalFreq* defines the sum of the frequencies of all words in the lexical semantic-net. $\text{IC}(s)$ is defined as the information content of the synonym set s.

However, by definition, all of the utilized lexical-semantic net measures are only able to access connections between words and synsets. Therefore, only systematic semantic relations, such as hyponymy or meronymy, can be directly accessed and calculated. Unsystematic connections, such as associations, are, due to the strongly specified resource, hardly determinable[4]. As a third group, we can identify measures establishing social networks such as the online encyclopedia *Wikipedia* as a resource for the computation of SR. These methods focus mainly on either the hyperlink structure [215], the vector space model (VSM) and/or on category taxonomy for graph related measures [246, 371]. Gabrilovich and Markovitch [92] proposed a method called *Explicit Semantic Analysis*, which represents term similarity by a high-dimensional space of article concepts derived from *Wikipedia*. SR of a pair of terms is computed by comparing the article concept vector A with B using the cosine metric.

4.1.2 The Measure of Wiki Semantic Relatedness

In this section, we propose the *Wiki Semantic Relatedness Measure*. In general, our approach determines the SR by the use of concept-based frequency information only, using the two-folded *Social Semantic Vectors* implementation. The basic idea behind our approach is that words with a related or associated meaning tend to occur together in a defined topic context [213][5]. We are following thereby a search-engine based word similarity distance presented by Cilibrasi and Vitanyi [53] proposing the so called *Google similarity distance*(GD)[6]. In a nutshell, the GD measure is derived by the number of returned search engine hits for a given pair of keywords weighted by the hits

---

[4] At the current version (April 2010) of *GermaNet* [154] there are 66,928 hyperonymy/hyponymy relations and 1,362 conceptual relations typified as association (http://www.sfs.uni-tuebingen.de/GermaNet/). With regards to *WordNet* [83], Gangemi et al. [94] developed a hybrid bottom-up top-down approach to autmatically extract associations in terms of a set of conceptual relations.

[5] weak contextual hypothesis: the contextual similarity of words - their tendency to occur in similar contexts - contributes to their meaning. That is, the more often two words can be substituted into the same contexts the more similar in meaning they are judged to be

[6] The semantic distance can be regarded as the inverse of both semantic relatedness and semantic similarity [37].

of the single keywords respectively. The GD is defined as:

$$GD(x,y) = \frac{G(x,y) - \min(G(x), G(y))}{\max(G(x), G(y))} \quad (4.5)$$

where the *Google* code of length $G(x)$ represents the shortest expected prefix-code word length of the associated Google event x. The expectation is taken over the *Google* distribution g. The g-distribution refers to the web pages indexed by *Google*. Therefore, this distribution changes over time, but holds in the sense of an *instantaneous snapshot*, as *an approximation of g* [53, pp. 6]. Hence, using the search index of *Google*, an almost unsurpassed quantity of information is accessible. Nevertheless, with respect to the resources used for the calculation we claim that a smaller although more controlled corpus is more important than a quantity as available by the *Google* search index [138]. We therefore follow the proposal of Cilibrasi and Vitanyi [53], however using the concept vectors representation as a resource to obtain needed frequency information. More formally, we define the *Concept Vector Distance CVD* as:

$$CVD(x,y) = \frac{\max\{\log(f(x)), \log(f(y))\} - \log(f(x,y))}{\log M - \min\{\log(f(x)), \log(f(y))\}} \quad (4.6)$$

where $f(x)$ is the number of concepts retrieved by word x (e.g. $f(x) = 10$, if ten *Wikipedia* categories are associated to the term x). $f(y)$ is the number of concepts associated to word y and $f(x,y)$ is the number of unique concepts returned by x, y together (e.g. $f(x,y) = 2$, if only two categories are associated with both terms x and y). M is the total size of our concept vector index. As described in Section 3.4.2, we have built a two-folded vector representation of the *Wikipedia* dataset. First, V_{art}, representing article concepts and term attributes as an inverted index. Second, V_{cat} gathering article and category concepts. Our approach combines both concept vectors to a weighted concept vector-driven distance. We refer to the article concept distance as $CVD_{art}(x,y)$ and $CVD_{cat}(x,y)$ as the distance derived from the category concept vector. Consequently, we define the *Wiki Semantic Distance (WSD)* as:

$$WSD(x,y) = \delta_i \cdot CVD_{art}(x,y) + \delta_j \cdot CVD_{cat}(x,y); \quad (4.7)$$

where δ is a weighting parameter. In order to determine the *Wiki Semantic Relatedness (WSR)* score of a pair of keywords we invert the resulting distance:

$$WSR(x,y) = 1 - WSD(x,y) \quad (4.8)$$

where $WSR(x,y) = 0$ equals no relatedness of the keyword candidates, and $WSR(x,y) = 1$ deduces a high semantic relatedness on the basis of the concept vectors. It is the combination of article and category related concepts which enables us to measure a relatedness score of term pair candidates that do not explicitly occur together within one article. Therefore, the extension of the frequency based concept contexts allow us to derive implicit relatedness scores. To use an example, consider the keywords *Bill Gates* and *Yahoo*. We can infer a semantic relatedness for both candidates, however they do not occur together within one article of the article vector representation[7]. Anyhow, both terms share related category information, which is comprised by CVD_{cat}. In the line of distributional properties, we combine direct co-occurrences information, using V_{art}, indirect (context-based) occurrences by the consideration of V_{cat}. That is, identifying the *latent* relationships from a category perspective. As Table 4.1 will depict in the next section, our approach allows us gain valuable relatedness scores within different domains.

Word 1	Word 2	WSR (Word1, Word2)
Google	Sergei Brin	.784
Microsoft	Sergei Brin	.645
Microsoft	Bill Gates	.875
Yahoo	Bill Gates	.525
Federal Bureau of Investigation	FBI	.970
Central Intelligence Agency	FBI	.618
CDU (German party)	Angela Merkel	.756
SPD (German party)	Angela Merkel	.633
Angela chancellor	Merkel	.952
winter	snow	.798
summer	snow	.515

Table 4.1: Example WSR scores for different domains

---

[7]There are actually three German *Wikipedia* articles online, where both keywords occur together. However, this holds not for the reduced vector representation as used in this thesis.

4.1.3 Experimental Evaluation

The purpose of our experiment is two-fold: first, to analyze the performance in comparison to a broad variety of current state-of-the-art algorithms for computing SR. That is, how does the WSR algorithms correlate to human-judged reference sets. Second, to observe the algorithms from a theoretical point of view. In this regard, we analyze the run-time and coverage property of the SR measures respectively.

Reference Dataset

Since our aim is to provide a comprehensive comparison to state-of-the-art approaches, we utilize three different data sets comprising two languages and compare the performance of the WSR method with sixteen other measures. For the German language, we utilize the set created by Gurevych [104]. It is a translation of Rubenstein and Goodenough [269], inducing 65 word pairs. Second, we conduct experiments on the two-folded reference line of Cramer and Finthammer [60], comprising a total of 600 word pairs. Test set (A) contains 100 word pairs (inducing semantic classes), and collection B contains 500 randomized word pairs with not more than 20 % of collocations and associations[8]. Note, the German net-based reference results were calculated on the German resource *GermaNet* v. 5.0^9. We use the *Pearson* correlation coefficient for the German dataset. With regards to the English language, we used the *WordSimilarity-353* dataset [85][10].

Results

In summarizing, the proposed semantic relatedness WSR measure performed very well. Tables 4.2, 4.3 and 4.4 show the results for all three German resources comparing lexical network (e. g. Leachock & Chodorow, Hirst & St-Onge, Resnik), distributional (LSA, Google) and *Wikipedia*-based measures.

---
[8]See Cramer and Finthammer [60] for detailed information about the experiment and the constructed data sets.

[9]All net-based measures have been kindly provided by Irene Cramer using *GermaNet Pathfinder v. 0.83* [87].

[10]The reference results for the English language were reported using the *Spearman* correlation coefficient. Although, we argue that the *Pearson* correlation coefficient should be applied.

Test set	Leacock & Chodorow	Wu & Palmer	Resnik	Jiang & Conrath	Lin
r Set A	0.48	0.36	0.44	0.46	0.48
r Set B	0.17	0.21	0.24	0.25	0.27
Coverage	86.9%	86.9%	86.9%	86.9%	86.9%
t/pair (ms)	<10	<10	<10	<10	<10

Test set	Hirst & St-Onge	Tree path	Graph path
r Set A	0.47	0.41	0.42
r Set B	0.32	0.11	0.31
Coverage	86.9%	86.9%	86.9%
t/pair (ms)	1110	<10	3649

Table 4.2: Pearson correlations results of the net-based measures by term coverage and processing time using the *Cramer* test set (German).

Table 4.5 shows the results for the German $GUR-65$ dataset. Reference results were obtained by Cramer [59] and Gurevych [104]; results of the LSA were kindly provided by Tonio Wandmacher [348]. A detailed description of the applied reference methods can be found in Waltinger et al. [345]. Table 4.6 shows the results of the English experiments. The results of the *Explicit Semantic Analysis* (ESA) were computed by applying the method of Gabrilovich and Markovitch [92] on the German and English *Wikipedia* document collection.

Primarily, we can identify that the measures comprising lexical networks as a resource for the determination of SR show rather low correlation coefficients (r= 0.11 - 0.48). The distributional measures (LSA, Google) perform better. However, WSR outperforms all other relatedness scores for the German language. With regards to the English dataset. The original ESA implementation reports a *Spearmann* correlation of 0.75 in contrast to WSR of 0.72. Our re-implementation of this method $ESA2$ shows a correlation of 0.70. This might be due to the selected snapshot of the *Wikipedia* dump or could relate to differences in the pre-processing of this resource. The results of the *Semantic*

Test set	PMI *Google*	*Google* Quotient	NSD *Google*	LSA (newspaper)
r Set *A*	0.37	0.27	0.37	0.64
r Set *B*	0.34	0.31	0.36	0.63
Coverage	100%	100%	100%	87.0%
t/pair (ms)	<10	<10	<10	<10

Table 4.3: Pearson correlations, coverage and processing time per pair of the distributional measures tested using the *Cramer* test set (German).

Test set	WSR	CVD_{cat}	ESA (Wiki)	Semantic Vectors	Wiki Graph Path	LSA (Wiki)
r Set *A*	**0.77**	0.57	0.51	0.52	0.49	0.65
r Set *B*	**0.64**	0.36	0.28	0.44	0.37	0.57
Coverage	100%	79.8%	99.1%	75.9%	92.0%	83.8%
t/pair (ms)	850	<10	1299	240	2301	<10

Table 4.4: Pearson correlations of the *Wikipedia*-based measures by coverage and processing time using the *Cramer* test set (German).

Vector package are based on the implementation of Widdows and Ferraro [356] using the *Wikipedia* dataset, gaining only mediocre results. In a nutshell, the *WSR* performs best on all three German datasets gaining a Person correlation of up to .77.

4.1.4 Concluding Remarks

In general, we can argue that based on the differences between the applied approaches, the choice of the resource has a strong influence on the calculation of SR. That is, determining the SR using small but expert-structured resources such as a lexical-semantic net perform inferior to completely unstructured (plain text) or semi-structured (WSR) resources as by using the *Wikipedia* collection. With reference to coverage, the web-based measures

Test set	Google	Lesk1 (DWDS)	Lesk2 (radial)	Lesk3 (hypernym)
r Set $GUR-65$	0.59	0.53	0.55	0.60
Test set	Resnik	WND (Wiki)	ESA1	WSR
r Set $GUR-65$	0.72	0.71	0.56	**0.75**

Table 4.5: Pearson correlations to human estimates utilizing the *GUR-65* dataset (German).

Test set	WordNet	Roget's Thesaurus	Wiki Relate	LSA
r Set $WordSim-353$	0.35	0.55	0.48	0.56
Test	ESA-ODP	ESA.	ESA2	WSR
r Set $WordSim-353$	0.65	0,70	0.75	**0.72**

Table 4.6: Spearman correlations to human estimates tested on the *Word-Similarity 353* dataset (English).

(but also the *WSR*) clearly outperform all other approaches (German). However, the lowest coverage scores are still over 75%, lexical-wordnet and LSA achieve almost 87% respectively. In conclusion, we can argue that the choice of the resource for determining SR by automatic means plays an important role. However, it obviously also depends on the implementation chosen. Nevertheless, entirely web-based methods were inferior to those that comprise a more controlled corpus. Therefore, we can observe that quality is more important than quantity [138]. Overall the results show that the proposed WSR algorithm on the basis of the *Social Semantics Vectors* implementation performs on an higher level than any other state-of-the-art approach in the case of the German language.

4.2 Social Network-induced Topic Identification

This section considers the problem of topic identification on *Open Topic Models* (OTM). That is, we are not heading towards a clustering of a document collection but labelling individual documents by the *best fitting* topic labels obtained from a social ontology. As described in Chapter 1, OTM are topic-related models in which content categories are not defined in advance but change over time – contributed by the open community. From a topic identification point of view, we are heading towards assigning a set of categories with characteristic terms or phrases to a document. These terms – called topic labels – characterize the textual content with reference to the remaining categories. Assigned topic labels may not be those that occur in the actual document. This section describes the characteristics of OTM and reviews recent algorithms. Furthermore, we propose a novel algorithm as well as experimental evaluations of a socially-induced topic identification (TI).

4.2.1 Related Work

Most approaches to TI relate to the domain of keyword extraction [5, 316] or text summarization [105]. That is, identified topics refer mostly to a set of documents, instead of detecting topics within single documents, or in a more sophisticated way, within specific text divisions. Therefore, the majority of proposed algorithms to TI are heading towards a clustering [156, 350] of a document collection within a traditional text categorization scenario [302, 366]. Thus, we can distinguish between two categorization types [5] [207, pp. 64]: Approaches to a flat categorization aim at identifying meaningful keywords with respect to a single document or an entire document collection. These methods primarily combine term occurrences from the beginning of the document with term frequencies using co-occurrence information [179, 362] of the entire corpus. This follows more or less a conditional probability model for observed term features of a clustered document collection. Following Popescul and Ungar [247, pp. 4] and Meyer zu Eißen [206, pp. 64], a topic-based term scoring function can be modeled by

$$f_C(t) = P(t|C) \cdot \frac{P(t|C)}{P(t)} \qquad (4.9)$$

where $f_C(t)$[11] acts as a scoring function for term t to be the topic label in a cluster denoted by C. $P(t|C)$ is the conditional probability of t from a document in cluster C. $P(t)$ denotes the probability of t from the entire document collection. Note that t can represent single tokens as well as frequent phrases. This approach is based on a rather simplistic heuristic. Even the highest scored topic labels ($f_C(t)$) are those obtained from the document cluster. As a second approach to TI, several algorithms [315, 300, 301] have been proposed to an automatic labelling of hierarchical clusters. Most of those methods use a two-fold algorithm. First, a hierarchical document clustering is conducted to obtain a tree-like cluster hierarchy. In this regard, each node of the tree represents a cluster with associated documents. Second, the tree representation is recursively parsed and for each term occurrence a significance test (e. g. χ^2 - distribution) is applied to obtain the information, whether or not the observed term has an equal occurrence in all of the children nodes. The method proposed by Meyer zu Eißen and Stein [207] combines thereby the clustering procedure with a suffix tree analysis called *Suffix Tree Clustering* (STC). Suffix tree paths are used for clustering *and* serve additionally as the assigned topic labels. Meyer zu Eißen and Stein [207, pp. 66] defines the ranking-based cluster label as:

$$k(w,i) = C \qquad (4.10)$$

where $k(w,i)$ is the cluster in which feature w occurs most frequently on the basis of a cluster ranking based on $tf_C(w)$. w denotes thereby the suffix trees. Hence, even though this approach reduces time complexity, the actual topic labels are extracted from the document clusters. Most recently, approaches in the progression or change of topics for a collection of documents have been proposed by Allan [5] and Heyer et al. [115]. These methods aim at identifying relevant terms in texts with respect to a predefined period of time [305, 306]. The relevance of terms in multiple documents are measured again based on the *tfidf* weighting or co-occurrence values (using a so called volatility measure [115, pp.3]), in comparison to the observed text segments. As a conclusion, most of the current approaches to TI utilize term features that occur in the

---

[11]Popescul and Ungar [247] refers to the first factor in f_C as an indicator that more frequent terms are favored, while the second factor regards the so called predictivenes (likewise the mutual information)

observed document collection. Single tokens are thereby interlinked (e. g. suffix trees, phrases) to representative topic labels on the basis of statistical properties of n-grams. One of the disadvantages in using these approaches to TI is that oftentimes the concatenate token streams end up with quite a confusing mix-up of individual terms as topic labels[12].

4.2.2 A Method for Open Topic Identification

In Chapter 3 we have introduced a general framework of social semantics. More specifically, we described the dynamic aspects of social ontologies, and how to construct a socially-induced feature generator, the *Social Semantic Vector* (SSV) representation, out of the dataset of *Wikipedia*. In this section, we will evaluate the SSV by means of proposing a method for an *Open Topic Identification*. In contrast to traditional approaches, our method for TI is based on human created topic labels. In this context, we utilize over 55,000 different categories as topic labels and combine both keyword extraction[13] as a type of text representation and categorization by means of topic labeling. Therefore, the domain of our approach heads towards a task of mapping text onto conceptual structures [51, 195] utilizing social ontologies by means of the SSV representation. In short, the proposed method to the domain of TI utilizes the category taxonomy of *Wikipedia* as a resource. Moreover, we utilize the tree-like structure of the social ontology in order to generate topic related concepts within a certain scale of generalization. We define this procedure as *concept generalization* (*CG*). Concepts reflect, in this sense, category labels from the category taxonomy, where assigned article contributions represent the attributes. The main principle in conducting *CG* is that we map a given input text to the most descriptive category as described in the previous section and *proverbially* take an uphill walk along the category taxonomy. As we can see in Figure 4.1, the category taxonomy structure can considered as a graph representation rather than a classical taxonomy tree representation.

---

[12]As for example search engine *Carrot* (http://search.carrot2.org) shows the following topic labels for the input query: "swine flu": "Swine Flue Vaccine UTube" and "Seeing this Message because your Web Browser". The cluster engine Clusty (http://clusty.com) shows "Worry That You" or simple "School", "Employees" and "Los Angeles" as a result set.

[13]We use only classification features covered by the SSV representation model.

More precisely, Mehler [191] has shown this in his comprehensive analysis with respect to the graph structure of social ontologies (focusing on the connectivity, multiplicity of sources, cyclicity, imbalance, bipartivity and cohesion of social ontology graphs):

> *SOG [Social Ontology Graphs] are not tree-like however they tend to be more tree-like than they are like unrestricted graphs. [...] whatever the differences of the branches used to represent the different fields of knowledge in a SOG, they tend to be balanced in terms of their depth. [...] any two randomly chosen daughter categories of the main category of a SOG [...] coincide in terms of their depth more or less irrespective of the order of the SOG.*[14] Mehler [191, pp. 24,33].

Mehler [191, pp. 33] refers to this phenomenon as a *sort of characteristic level of maximal specification or depth of field within this SOG*.

Figure 4.1: Graph representation of all category paths of the German Wikipedia social ontology, between the article concept *Bielefeld* and the root category *Hauptkategorie*. Edges comprise only category-to-category hyperlinks.

Since the aim of our approach is to perform a generalization with respect to category information, a conversion of the graph structure had to be applied. That is, we have extracted the category taxonomy of the *Wikipedia*

---
[14]Brackets introduced by the author.

collection in a top-down-manner. Starting from the most general category (*Category:Contents*), we subsequently connected all subordinated categories to their superordinated nodes. Hence, the taxonomy is forced in the representation of a directed tree defined as $D = (V, E)$ with one artificial root. The nodes $d \in V$ correspond to category concepts, edges are marked by their semantic relation – a hypernym relation. The procedure of "walking up" the taxonomy therefore implies to follow the hypernym edges. This means that we move upwards along the tree structure of the taxonomy, where for each edge we pass a more general category label is obtained. We define the number of edges L we pass within tree D as the extend of generalization CG.

In Section 3.4, we already described the method in mapping a given text fragment onto the conceptual structures of a social ontology ($W \mapsto KB$). Subsequently, we iterate over article namespaces (V_{art}) and request all associated category concepts of the article-category matrix (V_{cat}). In a next step, we use these category nodes as the next seed nodes for moving upwards the tree structure, and so on. It must be noted that we assign category weights to these entries by using the $tfidf$ score of the initial article that we started from. In order to circumvent an undesirable overestimation of specific categories and to avoid going in a circle, we 'dye' already visited entries.

A note on the variable L. The parameter L allows us to adjust the level of moving upwards within the tree structure and therefore acts as a sensitivity value of concept generalization. After having computed CG, we sort all requested category entries in descending order by their feature weights, having the most generalized concepts at the beginning and the most specific at the end of the vector. Therefore, the task of topic generalization is defined as making generalizations from specific concepts to a much broader context, as for example from *basketball* to the more general concept *sport*, or from *delegate* to *politics*. Let us consider some example texts, which were applied to the proposed topic generalization technique:

- **InputText**: "*Nowitzki's performance this year has vaulted him past the late Petrovic as the NBA's best-ever European import. But the Bavarian Bomber is fast becoming one of the NBA's best players, period. Maybe even a little like Mike. Last week, Dirk Nowitzki led the running, gunning Dallas Mavericks into the second round of the playoffs. He put up, as the sports guys say, "Big-time numbers." Those would be: 100 points and 47 rebounds in a mere three games. [...]*"

- **Output**:

    - *Related Article*: Dirk Nowitzki / Dallas Mavericks / Avery Johnson / Jerry Stackhouse / Antawn Jamison
    - *Specialized Topics*: basketball player / basketball / athlete / olympic athlete / basketball league
    - *Generalized Topics*: sport / United States / basketball / Germany / sport by country

- **InputText**: "*Das Grösste Kursplus seit 1985 wurde an den acht hiesigen Börsen im vergangenen Jahr erzielt. Beispielsweise zog der Deutsche Aktienindex um 47 Prozent an (vgl. SZ Nr. 302). Trotz Rezession und Hiobsbotschaften von der Unternehmensfront hatten sich zunächst britische und amerikanische Fondsverwalter bei hiesigen Standardwerten engagiert, woraufhin in der zweiten Hälfte des vergangenen Jahres der SZ-Index um 31 Prozent hochgeschnellt war. Hiesige Anleger - Investmentfonds oder Spezialfonds von Versicherungen - hatten lange Festgeld einer Wertpapieranlage vorgezogen [...]*"

- **Output**:

    - *Related Article*: Anlageklasse / Bundesanleihe / Nebenwert / Bullen- und Bärenmarkt / Börsensegment[15]
    - *Generalized Topics*: Finanzierung / Finanzmarkt / Ökonomischer Markt / Wirtschaft / Rechnungswesen[16]

---

[15]English translation: asset category / federal bond / second-tier stock / bull market
[16]English translation: financing / financial market / economical market / economy / accountancy

- **InputText**: *"Berwerbungsfrist läuft ab: Bis zum 15. Januar müssen die Bewerbungen für die zulassungsbeschränkten Studienplätze bei der Zentralstelle für die Vergabe von Studienplätzen (ZVS) in Dortmund eingetroffen sein. Die notwendigen Unterlagen sind bei den örtlichen Arbeitsämtern, Universitäten, Fachhochschulen ... Weniger Habilitationen: 1992 wurden an den Hochschulen in Deutschland rund 1300 Habilitationsverfahren abgeschlossen, 13 Prozent weniger als im Vorjahr. [...]"*

- **Output**:
    - *Related Article*: Provadis School of IMT / Approbationsordnung / Private Hochschule / Hochschulabschluss / Hochschule Merseburg[17]
    - *Generalized Topics*: Bildung / Deutschland / Bildung nach Staat / Akademische Bildung / Wissenschaft[18]

As the above examples show, specialized topics expresses very closely related categories attached to the initial article set such as *olympic athlete* or *basketball player*. Unlike, generalized topics, representing a much broader context of the detected topic such as *sport* or *basketball*, since these nodes are closer attached to the root node of the taxonomy. Moreover, with respect to the task of text categorization, we argue that topic related documents ideally should also share a subset of the generated, generalized topic concepts and consequently improve the performance of text categorization systems.

4.2.3 Experimental Evaluation

With respect to the evaluation of TI, individual documents or document clusters, which have been manually labelled by a topic are hardly available. Most of the approaches to TI therefore propose an evaluation on the base of certain topic-related quality criteria, in terms of properties of term features with respect to a document cluster [247, 207, 354], such as expressiveness, summarizing (e.g. topic labels appear only in a few documents of a category),

---
[17]English translation: Provadis School of International Management and Technology / Medical Licensure Act / private university / university degree / university of Merseburg

[18]English translation: education / Germany / education by country / university education / sciences

uniqueness (e. g. terms of distinct labels overlap) or discrimination. Hence, those approaches measure the quality of terms occurring in the observed document collection from an application point of view.

Reference Dataset

Since the novel method for TI proposed in this thesis uses the entries of a category taxonomy as topic labels, but not terms that occur in the observed document or division, we conducted our experiments in a different setup. More specifically, we compiled two different data sets each of 1,000 articles of the *Meyer-Lexikon* collection[19] (data set A) and 1,000 articles of the German *Wikipedia* (data set B). Since both resources are encyclopedia-based and categorized by a taxonomy (annotated by human), we further divided the corpus into ten categories (e. g. fashion, politics, sports) each consiting of 100 articles. In this context, we used the selected categories as the topics, which have to be identified by our method of TI. Subsequently, for each document, we computed the five and ten best generalized categories and analyzed whether one of the predicted topic labels match to the *initial*[20] category of the taxonomy. Note that we removed all category and HTML-markup information from the raw documents. With respect to the evaluation metric, we report the accuracy performance. Additionally, in the case of mismatches, we have analyzed how *close*[21] we were finally connected to the taxonomy tree with respect to the target category. Doing this, we included a category context window of five levels. See Table 4.7 for an overview of comprised sub-categories on the general topic level. Consider the following example: an article is finally categorized as a subordinate of our target category (level 1), if one of our five best topic labels matches one of the subordinate categories. For example, associated topic categories for the article of "Helmut Kohl" are within the first level "Federal Chancellor" and within the second level "Chancellor" and "politician (Germany)". On the third level there are "politician" and "politics (Germany)", on the fourth level "politics (Europe)" and on the fifth level the topic category

---

[19] http://lexikon.meyers.de/
[20] We considered only one category for each article even if *Wikipedia* articles are multiply categorized.
[21] Close in the sense of the tree-path of between the predicted and the target category within the taxonomy.

"politics" is associated. In this case, the fifth level is from a topic-related point of view actually not wrong, though we are at the first two levels closer to the topic - Helmut Kohl the former German Chancellor.

	info	spor	poli	medi	liter	cult	econ	mili	educ	cloth	relig
0	1	1	1	1	1	1	1	1	1	1	1
1	12	44	34	31	12	41	21	27	20	10	63
2	76	671	415	284	275	549	248	234	248	43	588
3	293	3339	1923	807	609	2760	1181	989	939	70	1781
4	631	8026	4403	1207	1075	6483	2995	1922	1951	81	2870
5	889	8618	8351	1483	1388	9930	4228	2440	2156	83	4083

Table 4.7: The number of considered subcategories of generalized topics by taxonomy level and category class.

	info	spor	poli	medi	liter	cult	econ	peda	reli	psycho
A0	.638	.745	.750	.710	.660	.495	.710	.710	.760	.462
A1	.670	.798	.940	.770	.750	.546	.710	.810	.850	.527
A2	.766	.957	1	.860	.830	.825	.940	.920	.960	.714
A3	.798	.979	1	.860	.970	.979	.980	.940	.960	.725
A4	.872	.979	1	.890	1	.989	1	.950	.970	.725
A5	.894	.979	1	.910	1	1	1	.950	.970	.824

Table 4.8: Accuracy results of the topic identification experiments by means of OTM using the *Meyers Lexicon* corpus and ten topic labels.

Results

The results of the experiments are shown in Tables 4.8 – 4.11 with respect to the taxonomy level[22]. As we can observe, our proposed method performs very well with an average accuracy[23] of .627 (level 0), .706 (level 1), .895 (level

---
[22]The used categories are: *info*rmatics, *spor*ts, *poli*tics, *medi*cine, *liter*ature, *cult*ure, *econ*omics, *mili*tary, *edu*cation, *cloth*ing, *reli*gion, *psycho*logy and *peda*gogy.

[23]Accuracy values of the best nine categories on ten comprised topics. Considering all ten categories accuracy values of 0.589 (level 0), 0.660 (level 1), 0.834 (level 2) and 0.871 (level 3) can be identified.

	info	spor	poli	medi	liter	cult	econ	peda	reli	psycho
A0	.553	.691	.680	.650	.640	.319	.580	.518	.710	.396
A1	.564	.702	.880	.720	.710	.392	.580	.639	.810	.439
A2	.691	.883	.980	.790	.800	.753	.880	.807	.920	.648
A3	.723	.936	.980	.800	.950	.969	.950	.928	.940	.659
A4	.777	.936	.980	.840	.990	.969	.980	.976	.950	.659
A5	.798	.936	.990	.880	.990	.979	.990	.976	.950	.747

Table 4.9: Accuracy results of the topic identification experiments by means of OTM using the *Meyers Lexicon* corpus and five topic labels.

	info	spor	poli	medi	liter	cult	econ	mili	educ	cloth
B0	.677	.630	.740	.660	.780	.520	.460	.620	.560	.240
B1	.768	.690	.880	.700	.850	.650	.490	.620	.710	.240
B2	.849	.870	.960	.810	.900	.970	.920	.890	.890	.280
B3	.879	.880	.970	.820	.960	.990	.990	.910	.950	.360
B4	.889	.900	.980	.830	1	1	.990	.930	.970	.360
B5	.929	.900	.990	.850	1	1	.990	.930	.980	.360

Table 4.10: Accuracy results of the topic identification experiments by means of OTM using the *Wikipedia* corpus and ten topic labels.

2) and .928 (level 3) on the topic identification experiment on the *Wikipedia* data set. Since our approach utilized a *Wikipedia* dump the results on data set B are not surprising. However, identifying the five/ten best topic labels out of a set of over 55,000 is still very good. Therefore, results on dataset A (1000 articles from Meyer-Lexikon) with an accuracy of .664 (level 0), .737 (level 1), .877 (level 2) and .919 (level 3) support the good performance on the topic identification task for OTM. Additionally, analyzing the results of the TI in more detail, we can observe that there are many examples that are truly "mapped" to the actual initial article within the *Wikipedia* collection, hence the generalization process "over-generalized" or "under-generalized" the computed category trails. Therefore most of the incorrectly-classified documents were actually labelled correctly – though not exactly the one we defined and therefore marked as *false*. For instance, the article *CD-burner* is tracked to

	info	spor	poli	medi	liter	cult	econ	mili	educ	cloth
B0	.606	.590	.690	.520	.740	.350	.410	.520	.500	.140
B1	.717	.650	.810	.550	.790	.510	.420	.530	.640	.150
B2	.788	.730	.940	.650	.830	.900	.870	.820	.820	.170
B3	.808	.740	.950	.660	.910	.970	.930	.830	.930	.230
B4	.828	.750	.980	.680	.990	.980	.940	.870	.940	.230
B5	.889	.750	.990	.790	1	.980	.970	.870	.940	.230

Table 4.11: Accuracy results of the topic identification experiments by means of OTM using the *Wikipedia* corpus and five topic labels.

the *Wikipedia* article concept *CD-burner* but generalized to *technical instrument*, *storage medium*, *hardware* but not directly to *informatics*. Moreover, since we randomly downloaded articles identified using the specific category information, we did not perform a corpus cleaning. That is, we did not remove inappropriate articles as for instance disambiguation pages or miss-classified articles within the document collection.

4.2.4 Concluding Remarks

The proposed algorithm of topic identification utilizes a social ontology to label documents by means of OTM. Different to previous algorithms, our approach is not headed towards the application of keyword extraction, document summarization or clustering, but considers the task of topic labelling as a task of document mapping within a social network. Therefore, the proposed method overcomes some of the disadvantages of conventional TI methods. First, computed topic labels are human readable, since the comprised taxonomy is manually created. Second, topic labels may not implicitly be terms that occur in the observed document, but are rather established from the (social) lexical semantic analysis. Third, the proposed approach enables us to identify topics even in the scenario, when only a small amount of textual data is present (such as identifying the topic in sentence, paragraphs or divisions of documents). The achieved performance with an average accuracy from .664 to .919, can be identified as a valuable contribution to the community of TI.

4.3 On Social Semantics-induced Closed Topic Categorization

In this section we approach the problem of text categorization by means of *Closed Topic Models* (CTM) from a social semantics perspective. As described in the first chapter, different to *Open Topic Models* (OTM) [196, 341], where topic labels represent content categories that change over time and are contributed by an open community, the category set of CTM is defined in advanced. In this regard, we deal with a fixed number of categories for the categorization process. Therefore, traditional machine learning techniques and document classification techniques can be applied. We utilize *Support Vector Machines* (SVM)[24] as the learning algorithm for text categorization (See Chapter 2). Prior studies [63, 130, 288, 366] have already proven that this machine learning technique contributes to the performance of text categorization even when dealing with a large set of features [70, 139, 308]). With respect to a social semantics-induced categorization of CTM, we follow the notion that document categorization is not only about the words occurring in texts, but also about common topic concepts texts represent.

We propose a novel feature enhancement technique for a text categorization, utilizing the concepts derived from the topic identification method as described in the previous section. That is, we use predicted generalized topic labels derived from a social ontology to enrich the existing document representation. We argue that the acquisition of semantic topic labels for a concept-based feature enhancement contributes significantly to the performance of text categorization systems – overcoming the famous bottleneck of information sparsity (see Chapter 2).

4.3.1 Related Work

In the past, various attempts have been made to expand or enhance the local context of texts with additional term features. Most recently, query expansion techniques have been proposed to augment search queries with additional term features [325, 324]. While the majority of approaches focus on co-occurrence

---

[24]The SVM^{light} 6.0 implementation provided by Joachims [126].

information of texts to expand a query, terminological resources such as *Word-Net* [83], dictionaries [365] or thesauri [330] are occasionally used as a source of *external* knowledge. Regarding approaches of text categorization that use feature enhancement techniques of different resources of knowledge, few approaches have been proposed in the past [82, 175]. Andreas and Hotho [8] proposed a method of using background knowledge from an ontology by means of the lexical-semantic net *WordNet* [83] to improve text classification. They explored the hypernym hierarchy to perform a generalization by completely replacing the BOW features by using a *bag-of-synsets* representation instead.

As one of the first in the field of social network-driven methods, Gabrilovich and Markovitch [91] induced directory concepts of the *Open Directory Project* (ODP) to enhance the existing document representation. With respect to methods comprising the online encyclopedia *Wikipeda*, Gabrilovich and Markovitch [89] and Zalan Bodo [370] conducted experiments combining article information with SVMs. Wang and Domeniconi [349] proposed a semantic kernel technique for text classification also based on the *Wikipedia* data set. In the field of bio-medicine Lu et al. [165] proposed a *Latent Dirichlet Allocation* model (LDA), evaluated on the *TREC* corpus [331] for an enhanced representation of biomedical knowledge.

As a commonality, all approaches have utilized the *article title* of Wikipedia to enhance the existing data representation. The performance of these feature enhancement techniques yield an improvement of up to 30.4% using the *Reuters RCV1* corpus and 18% for *OHSUMED* dataset [90, pp. 98]. Contrary to the described approaches, in this thesis we propose a *knowledge feature breath* on the basis of generalized *category concepts* extracted from a social ontology. Therefore, we label the individual texts of a document collection with a fixed number of topic-related category labels instead of article namespaces. Utilized category information, considered as the key topic information, are subsequently used for the topic generalization (e. g. from topic *tennis* to a more general label *sports*) as described in the last section and added to the initial representation format. Hence, we argue that topic related documents share semantically related generalized topic concepts.

4.3.2 Generalized Topic Concepts for Text Categorization

The method for a topic-oriented feature enhancement consists of two main parts. First, the input text is converted into the traditional BOW representation. In a second step, we conduct the topic generalization on the basis of the topic identification (TI) algorithm as described in the previous section. As a result, we have gained a set of associated topic labels defined as S_{topic}[25], but in addition a set of associated article labels[26] defined as $S_{article}$. We define the entire set of generated concept as $S_{sem} := S_{topic} \cup S_{article}$. Next, the bag of words merges with the set of generated features. Note that we use the 10 best-matching category *and* article concepts respectively, predicted by the TI method. The constructed concepts are subsequently used for the classification task either as feature enhancement or replacement candidates. Feature weights are computed by applying $tfidf$ weighting function. Feature reduction is performed by replacing initial features of the data vector with lower feature weight by higher weighted features of the corresponding S_{sem}.

4.3.3 Document-based Experimental Evaluation

The purpose of our categorization-oriented evaluation is twofold. First, we want to analyze how the approach will perform compared to the well-known LSA implementation. Second, we want to analyze the difference between a traditional SVM and a topic-enhanced SVM implementation. Within all experiments, we vary the initial amount of features. That is, for the classical SVM implementation we use all nominal, verbal and adjectival features (we refer to this method as *C-SVM*). In a second step, we reduced the initial feature set to nominal features only, delimited by a threshold (defined as *R-SVM*). In a next step, we enhanced the reduced representation (*R-SVM*) with all topical features of S_{sem}. After that, we followed a feature replacement strategy for building a fourth representation model (*M-SVM*). We replaced the number of initial features by the number of topic features. As a fifth document representation for a SVM classification, we used only the features gained from the

---
[25] Topic labels in the sense of category labels of the category taxonomy.
[26] Article labels in the sense of article namespaces.

topic generalization (S_{sem}) (*GO-SVM*). Finally, we used only the features of S_{sem} and additionally reduced it with a certain threshold (*MGO-SVM*). For each category, an SVM classifier was trained using *linear kernel*. The results were analyzed by means of a *leave-one-out cross-validation*. As a comparison to non-SVM approaches we computed various supervised and unsupervised baselines. First, a random clustering of all documents was performed. This served as the lower base line evaluation. Second, we computed an LSA [74]. The SVD is computed keeping the k best *eigenvalues*. In our experiments we defined k as *300*. The resulting matrix, served as an input for different clustering techniques including k-means, hierarchical and average linking. Note that we report only the best LSA-based clustering performance. The major aim of our experiments was to determine the effect of topic generalization within a SVM-based text classification environment. More precisely, to analyze which level a feature enhancement by means of semantically related topic concepts improves the classical SVM categorization.

Document Set

With respect to the evaluation benchmark of the topic-enhanced text categorization approach, we used a large corpus of newspaper articles. While there are benchmark collections for the English language available (*Reuters, OHSUMED* ...), there are no public benchmark collections for the German language (in terms of a golden standard for text categorization). Therefore, in this study we decided to use a 10 years newspaper corpus of *Süddeutsche Zeitung* (SZ) that has been compiled and preprocessed in a preliminary step by the *TextMiner* system [182]. The initial corpus comprised 135,546 texts within 96 categories (newspaper rubrics). Due to its unbalanced category-text proportions, an adjusted subset was extracted, consisting of 29,086 text, 30 categories and 232,270 unique textual features (see Table 4.12).

Results

Analyzing the results of the experiments (see Table 4.13), we can observe that all SVM, and therefore supervised methods, clearly outperform the unsupervised clustering results (LSA). With an average F-measure of 0.631, the best LSA clustering method obviously performs better than the baseline ap-

Number of classes	30
Number of unique features	232,270
Number of texts	29,086

Table 4.12: SZ-based newspaper article corpus statistics by comprised categories and texts.

Classifier	F-Measure
Generalized-SVM	0.915
Reduced-SVM	0.914
Min-SVM	0.913
Classical-SVM	0.836
Generalized-Only-SVM	0.884[1]
Minimal-Generalized-Only-SVM	0.855[2]
LSA	0.631
Random	0.15

Table 4.13: F1-Measure results of the different German-based SVM classification using the document-based benchmark collection.

proaches (F-measure of 0.15), but also confirms that within a classical text categorization scenario SVMs are most appropriate.

Comparing the different SVM implementations (Table 4.15), we can identify that feature enhancement (G-SVM with an average F-measure of 0.915) boosts with a difference of up to 0.700 (at category *gesp*) the C-SVM implementation using all noun, verb and adjective features (F-Measure 0.778). Yet, in comparison to a much reduced SVM implementation (R-SVM: 0.914) – using only nouns and limited to 5,000 features overall - only minor enhancement can be identified. However, a closer look at the data reveals that we can state, within categories that perform lower than an F-Measure of 0.900 in the reduced version, that the G-SVM improves the results. Nevertheless, since the average results of the R-SVM implementation are from the outset very high, not much improvement could be expected. Yet, what is more interesting is the aspect of using only the concepts derived from the topic generalization

ID	Name	Texts	Features	Generalized Features	Reduction
1	baro	465	71593	9300	-87.00%
2	camp	345	54451	6900	-87.33%
3	diew	276	36704	5520	-84.96%
4	fahr	313	53568	6260	-88.31%
5	film	2457	395226	49140	-87.57%
6	fird	2213	157340	44260	-71.87%
7	firm	1339	163189	26780	-83.59%
8	gesp	1234	276813	24680	-91.08%
9	inha	1933	86140	38660	-55.11%
10	kost	533	113094	10660	-90.57%
11	leut	911	85492	18220	-78.69%
12	loka	1953	169381	39060	-76.94%
13	mein	2240	221982	44800	-79.82%
14	mitt	677	53123	13540	-74.51%
15	nchg	1105	147305	22100	-84.99%
16	nrwk	349	29295	6980	-76.17%
17	nrwp	297	40154	5940	-85.21%
18	nrww	342	29062	6840	-76.46%
19	reit	286	28738	5720	-80.09%
20	schf	542	28470	10840	-61.92%
21	spek	375	23981	7500	-68.73%
22	spfi	318	69424	6360	-90.84%
23	stdt	700	58072	14000	-75.89%
24	szen	2314	269962	46820	-82.66%
25	szti	336	15562	6720	-56.82%
26	thkr	1613	330619	32260	-90.24%
27	tvkr	2355	222970	47100	-78.87%
28	woch2	375	63385	7500	-88.17%
29	zwif	409	51309	8180	-84.06%
30	zwiz	481	62836	9620	-84.69%

Table 4.14: Number of none unique features before and after topic generalization by reduction.

ID	Name	C-SVM	R-SVM	G-SVM	Imp-1	Imp-2
1	baro	0.995	0.998	0.998	+0.000	+0.003
2	camp	0.913	0.953	0.956	+0.003	+0.043
3	diew	0.925	0.994	0.995	+0.001	+0.070
4	fahr	0.924	0.978	0.989	+0.011	+0.065
5	film	0.865	0.955	0.954	-0.001	+0.089
6	fird	0.902	0.971	0.973	+0.002	+0.071
7	firm	0.969	0.995	0.995	+0.000	+0.026
8	gesp	0.393	0.751	0.817	+0.066	+0.424
9	inha	0.974	0.988	0.987	-0.001	+0.013
10	kost	0.926	0.964	0.966	+0.002	+0.040
11	leut	0.903	0.994	0.996	+0.002	+0.093
12	loka	0.728	0.772	0.781	+0.009	+0.053
13	mein	0.923	0.961	0.951	-0.010	+0.028
14	mitt	0.171	0.485	0.495	+0.010	+0.324
15	nchg	0.799	0.761	0.769	+0.008	-0.020
16	nrwk	0.871	0.957	0.936	-0.021	+0.065
17	nrwp	0.952	0.846	0.838	-0.008	-0.114
18	nrww	0.932	0.983	0.983	+0.000	+0.051
19	reit	0.933	0.946	0.953	+0.007	+0.020
20	schf	0.682	0.795	0.785	-0.010	+0.103
21	spek	0.712	0.975	0.950	-0.025	+0.238
22	spfi	0.908	0.984	0.983	-0.001	+0.075
23	stdt	0.767	0.850	0.853	+0.003	+0.086
24	szen	0.827	0.869	0.878	+0.009	+0.051
25	szti	0.947	0.979	0.973	-0.006	+0.026
26	thkr	0.817	0.939	0.945	+0.006	+0.128
27	tvkr	0.846	0.949	0.951	+0.002	+0.105
28	woch2	1.00	1.00	1.00	+0.000	+0.000
29	zwif	0.666	0.862	0.829	+0.033	+0.163
30	zwiz	0.918	0.968	0.969	+0.001	+0.051

Table 4.15: Results of SVM-Classification comparing Reduced-SVM and Generalized-SVM (Imp. 1) and Classical-SVM and Generalized-SVM (Imp. 2) by category.

for the classification, and therefore discarding all BOW features of texts. Using only twenty concepts per text, we still reach a promising F-measure of 0.884 (Generalized-Only-SVM[27]). The Minimal-Generalized-Only-SVM[28] implementation, which utilized only 1000 features for all 29,086 texts, show a very promising F1-Measure of 0.855. However, both SVMs had to be aborted due to their run-time complexity (we aborted the learning algorithm after two months of calculation). When comparing the number of used features (see Table 4.14) using the GO-SVM and the R-SVM, we see that we were able to reduce the actual reduced features again with an average percentage of 80.10%. Therefore, the results of using only the topic generalization concepts for text categorization may seem to be very up-and-coming, however the complexity in predicting the SVM hyperplane increases to a non-satisfactory amount.

4.3.4 OAI-based Experimental Evaluation

As a second evaluation scenario, we apply the feature enhancement technique to a corpus of document meta data. Hence, we utilize a minimized document representation by means of meta data as provided by the *Open Archives Initiative* (OAI). We thereby follow the idea of reducing the time and space complexity of the document processing by using only a minimum amount of textual information for the classification task. Thus, the topic-based document representation extension shall circumvent the problem of data sparseness. In the line of web result snippets, as provided by search engines, meta data reflect in the context of digital libraries a query list of document descriptors (metadata: data about data). One of the most popular meta data protocols in the area of digital library services is the Protocol for Metadata Harvesting (OAI-PMH) of the *Open Archives Intitative*. OAI-PMH represents thereby a standardized and uniform exchange description model, following the recommendations of the *German Initiative for Network Information* (DINI) for the OAI-PMH (see Table 4.16). With respect to approaches to the categorization

---

[27]The Generalized-Only-SVM results are based upon eleven categories, the algorithm was aborted after two months of calculation.

[28]The Minimal-Generalized-Only-SVM was reported on the basis of five computed categories, since in the line of the GO-SVM, the algorithm of SVM^{light} was still calculating after two months.

```
 1  ... <metadata> <oai_dc:dc
 2  xmlns:oai_dc="http://www.openarchives.org/OAI/2.0/oai_dc/" ... >
 3      <dc:title>Search engine technology and digital libraries :
 4      libraries need to discover the academic internet</dc:title>
 5      <dc:creator>Summann, Friedrich</dc:creator>
 6      <dc:creator>Lossau, Norbert</dc:creator>
 7      <dc:subject>information retrieval</dc:subject>
 8      <dc:subject>digital library</dc:subject>
 9      <dc:description>This article describes...</dc:description>
10      <dc:publisher>Universität Bielefeld ; Universitätsbibliothek</dc:publisher>
11      <dc:type>Article</dc:type>
12      <dc:language>en</dc:language>
13      ...
14  </metadata>...
```

Table 4.16: Outline of the OAI meta data of Lossau [163]. Dots indicated omitted content. ([196, pp. 6])

by means of using meta data as a reference document representation, only few methods have been proposed in the literature. They primarily focus either on text clustering, with regards to the subject area of the actual documents [106], or the extension of search queries using reference ontologies [106, 267]. That is, new keywords are assigned to the actual – already categorized – meta data entry. In our experiments, we focus on the construction of a topic classification model by using the *Dewey Decimal Classification* (DDC) [226] as the target scheme. The DDC can be considered as one of the most common classification schemes within the domain of scientific library services. In short, the taxonomy of the German translation of the DDC is hierarchically structured by using three levels. It starts with ten main classes (see Table 4.17), where each of the respective classes is twice subdivided into ten areas (100 hundred classes at level two). The third level of the DDC comprises a number of $1,000$ categories. In our experiments we comprised only the first level of the DDC taxonomy, that is we used ten predefined categories for the OAI classification task.

ClassName	Number of OAI-PMH
DDC 000: Computer science, information	5,117
DDC 100: Philosophy & psychology	2,181
DDC 200: Religion	570
DDC 300: Social sciences	7,553
DDC 400: Language	531
DDC 500: Science	9,598
DDC 600: Technology	6,813
DDC 700: Arts & recreation	4,281
DDC 800: Literature	446
DDC 900: History & geography	1,183
Overall	38,273

Table 4.17: German meta data corpus by DDC classes and number of comprised OAI-PMH protocols.

OAI-Corpus

With the absence of an existing reference corpus for OAI-PMH, we decided to compile a OAI-benchmark collection independently. We accessed the taxonomy of the DDC by means of the *Bielefeld Academic Search Engine* (BASE) [242], which provided the API for querying DDC-annotated OAI meta data protocols of (primarily) scientific documents. With respect to the constructed document representation, we reduced the set of OAI-specific meta data fields to title, subject, and description only. Note that we explored the document data without the need to parse the entire document, but only by accessing document snippets in the form of the OAI data fields. In the line of the SZ-based document classification experiments (see previous section), we also performed the usual pre-processing of the reduced OAI protocols by means of language identification, tokenization, sentence boundary detection, PoS-tagging and lemmatization with a subsequent conducted stop word removal (filtering non-lexical tokens and function words). The final OAI-PMH-based corpus (see Table 4.17) consisted of 10 DDC classes utilizing 38,273 meta data snippets. Note that we selected only those records for corpus construction whose Dublin Core description fields contain more than 100 bytes of text to avoid problems of data sparseness (5,868 English and 7,473 German records). Each entry served subsequently as an input for constructing the topic enhanced document representation model (see previous section). Thus, we appended additionally the ten best topics and article concepts to the existing document representation. Consequently, we utilized both representation models (with and without feature enhancement) as an input for a SVM-based classification using the *leave-one-out cross-evaluation* by means of SVM^{light} [126]. As a reference line for the evaluation, we are comprising the results of Mehler and Waltinger [196][29], which utilized a total corpus size of 1,000 OAI-records (as a balanced corpus of 100 documents per DDC category) by also using an SVM-based classifier.

DDC	Precision	Recall	F-Measure
000	0.911	0.720	0.804
100	0.691	0.380	0.490
200	0.682	0.580	0.627
300	0.564	0.310	0.400
400	0.825	0.470	0.599
500	0.694	0.430	0.531
600	0.509	0.290	0.369
700	0.778	0.700	0.737
800	0.605	0.460	0.523
900	0.625	0.300	0.405
Overall	0.689	0.464	0.549

Table 4.18: Baseline results of traditional SVM classification on the basis of German OAI-Data using a reduced benchmark collection comprising 1000 OAI meta data records.

Results

By analyzing the results of both OAI-classification experiments, we observed that using meta data only for a DDC-based categorization by means of 1,000

---

[29]This contribution has been authored by Alexander Mehler and the author of this thesis comparing five different classifiers on OAI-based meta data records.

DDC	Pre.	Rec.	F-Measure	DDC	Pre.	Rec.	F-Measure
000	0.948	0.878	0.912	000	0.952	0.934	0.943
100	0.906	0.815	0.858	100	0.923	0.876	0.899
200	0.903	0.719	0.801	200	0.913	0.791	0.848
300	0.852	0.691	0.763	300	0.929	0.907	0.918
400	0.828	0.621	0.709	400	0.822	0.627	0.711
500	0.868	0.819	0.843	500	0.928	0.937	0.932
600	0.857	0.764	0.808	600	0.909	0.875	0.892
700	0.812	0.630	0.710	700	0.959	0.928	0.943
800	0.805	0.620	0.701	800	0.803	0.666	0.728
900	0.878	0.745	0.806	900	0.879	0.753	0.811
Overall	0.730	0.866	0.791	Overall	0.829	0.902	0.863

Table 4.19: Results of traditional SVM classification on the basis of 7,473 meta data snippets.

Table 4.20: Results of feature enhanced document representation using SVM on the basis of German OAI-Data.

OAI records for training and evaluation a machine learning classifier, only mediocre results can be achieved (see Table 4.18). However, extending the size of the comprised feature set by means of a large corpus of 7,473 meta data snippets, we can raise the resultant F-Measure from 0.549 to a nearly acceptable level of 0.791 (see Table 4.19). Note that we used only a minimized document representation by means of meta data as provided by the OAI. This means that the actual documents behind these records are like, for example, journal contributions and research theses comprising more than 100 pages. The results of the topic enhanced document model (see Table 4.20), with a resultant F-Measure of 0.863, can therefore be considered as a valuable contribution to the domain of digital libraries. We can argue that topic enhanced SVMs provide an adequate DDC-related method of classify documents based on their OAI metadata. More than 86% of the used records were classified within the right DDC category.

In addition, we can state that a topic enhanced representation model, *combining title, summary, keywords* of a document and semantically related *topic concepts* provide sufficient information for a successful DDC-oriented classification.

4.4 Concluding Remarks

Unsupervised and supervised methods play an important role in the field of text processing and categorization. While in the past, the LSA - *as a solution to Plato's problem* [149] - has drawn major attention in the NLP community, with respect to experiments within the field of text categorization, this approach can be seen as inferior to SVMs. It is not only the computational complexity of the LSA/SVD procedure, but also the overall classification performance. When comparing the proposed topic-enhanced SVM implementation to the best LSA-clustering technique (see Section 4.3.3), we can identify a significant improvement of 45%. By analyzing the results of the traditional SVM with those using the topic-enhanced SVM, we can identify an improvement of 9.45% within the document-based experimental setup. With respect to the classification of OAI-PMH records (see Section 4.3.4), we were able to improve the classification accuracy by 9.10%, and therefore almost to the same extent as within the newspaper-based setup. Our experiments clearly indicate that the topic enhanced document model has a significantly positive influence on the performance of text processing applications. Moreover, we can state that a collaborative constructed knowledge enhanced TC improves the effectiveness and accuracy. In addition, it circumvents the data sparseness problem of traditional BOW approaches even under the condition of operating with a minimum amount of textual information.

Chapter 5

Application Scenarios of Social Semantics

In this chapter, we apply our model of social semantics to three different application scenarios. That is, we use external knowledge, as constructed by an online community, to improve retrieval components within the domain of IR. In the first section, we propose a novel method for the task of *Named Entity Recognition*. In this regard, we focus not only on identifying a proper name within a text, but also on disambiguating the respective entity (named entity instance). Thereby, *concept clouds* (Section 3.3) are used to construct an enhanced context representation around the identified entity. In the second application scenario, we propose a novel method for the task of *Sentiment Analysis*. In the line of CTMs, the proposed method induces *concept clouds* to construct a sentiment-enhanced document representation, which is used within a sentiment polarity identification experimental setup. The third section proposes a method to *Hypertext Type Classification*. Therefore, instead of using textual *or* structural features for a classification, we utilize the macro-structure created by the users to predict the overall web genre category. This follows a two-level approach for the exploration of web genre structures, where the individual segments (spanned by a website) are considered as generic units on the sub-genre level.

5.1 Named Entity Instance Recognition

This section proposes a novel algorithm to predict the proper instance of a recognized named entity (NE) in texts by using information from a social network in order to expand the local context around the entity itself. In the domain of IR, information extraction plays a crucial role. Moreover, the subtask in identifying named entities in text or web documents is becoming more and more important in different areas such as person-orientated websearch, link analysis and KB construction (think of the RDF-idea of Berners-Lee et al. [20]). By now, named entity recognition (NER), as the task of PoS-Tagging individual terms and classifying them into a predefined category set such as *"Person"* or *"Company"*, has already been done successfully [1, 66, 134]. However, the disambiguation of a given named entity is still a challenge. Identifying the proper instance of a name within the context the name that actually occurs has been hardly tackled. Bunescu and Pasca [38] applied SVM-kernel methods to disambiguate *Wikipedia* article concepts. They used a set of queries from the *Wikipedia* collection to predict the proper article name within the same dataset. Hence, no external dataset is used to evaluate their approach. Nguyen and Cao [223] proposed a hybrid statistical and rule-based approach to interlink named entities to the *Wikipedia* collection. Their two-fold approach primarily uses a constructed pattern and heuristics to narrow down the number of possible named entity instances and further uses the classical VSM to rank the remaining entries. Most recently, Han and Zhao [107] used a semantic relatedness measure in order to pick the right candidate out of the *Wikipedia* collection. Their proposed approach, measured in this context, the semantic relatedness between the input query and the respective named entity instances.

Different to the methods above, our approach focuses on an *extension* of the external local context *around* to disambiguate a named entity. Our goal is to enhance the existing context of the term, with additional term descriptors (context cloud) in order to improve the classification accuracy. Consider the following example as an input for the named entity instance recognition system:

> "David Haye of Britain said he was hoping for a mega-showdown with the oldest *Klitschko* brother."

When focusing on the proper name *Klitschko* to disambiguate, we enhance the local context by the following topic descriptors: *boxing, ukraine, world champion*, and are therefore able to link the entity *Klitschko* to the domain of *boxing* and as a consequence, since there are two *Wikipedia* articles about the boxing-brothers *Klitschko*, to link the named entity to the older brother – *Vitali Klitschko*. Consider now, just knowing the name *Müller*[1], the probability of predicting the right entity reduces drastically, when not having the local context around it. This clearly shows that a semantic disambiguation of named entities is not a trivial task.

5.1.1 The Algorithm to Named Entity Instance Recognition

At the center of the proposed algorithm of the Named Entity Instance Recognition (NEIR) is the assumption that any named entity *always* appears within a specific textual context – the lexical neighborhood – instantiating the initial addressed entity instance. Take for example the proper name *Michael Jordan*. This name may only get positively disambiguated, if a further (lexical) context is provided by term descriptors such as *machine learning* or *artificial intelligence*. Based on the enhanced background information we are able to link this named entity (NE) to *Michael I. Jordan*[2], a professor at UC Berkeley, rather than to the famous basketball athlete *Michael Jeffrey Jordan*[3]. With respect to the comprised textual context, we can assume that any context is delimited by the units of the logical document structure (LDS) [249], inducing sentences, paragraphs or divisions. Therefore, a context window within the LDS has to be incorporated. Since an NE, for example in paragraph one is more likely to be connected to terms occurring in the subsequent sentences than in the last paragraph of a document, this context window has to be chosen carefully. We argue that all terms that occur within this defined lexical-based window are instantiating the examined entity by conveying the actual context information.

---

[1] There are 336 different article about the name Müller in the German Wikipedia collection.
[2] http://en.wikipedia.org/wiki/Michael_I._Jordan
[3] http://en.wikipedia.org/wiki/Michael_Jordan

NE-based KB

As an important precondition of NEIR systems is the existence of a NE-induced KB, comprising different NE instances to query. Thus, any system can only be as successful as it has at least one instance of the NE already in the knowledge base. In the line of the methodology proposed in the previous chapter, we introduce the document collection of the social network *Wikipedia* in order to construct a NE-based KB. More precisely, we use both the article and the hyperlink structure of the collection, in order to construct the needed KB to query. Extracting all articles that are associated to the *Wikipedia-Category:People* let us establish a number of 183, 554 articles of different people instances.

Different to the CES (see Chapter 2), using the term features of the document collection, we extract only the hyperlinks that occur within the respective article, all other textual content is dropped. Subsequently, we convert the resultant NE and hyperlink features into a graph representation. More formally, we define the NE-related graph as $G_{\text{NE}} = (V, E, \omega)$, where V is the set of vertices and $E \subseteq V^2$ the set of edges. Note, $V = N \cup H$ consists of two subsets. We define N as the set of article names of the used Wikipedia articles, and H as the set of hyperlinks, which start from the entries N. That is, $(v, w) \in E$ iff there is an article $w \in N$, such that $v \in H$ is the name of the hyperlink within the respective article.

Therefore, G_{NE} represents a bipartite digraph – not having multiple edges and not having a reverse edge from the article title to the article content. With respect to the edge weighting function ω, we differentiate between three different structure constraints of the comprised *Wikipedia* articles. As for example, the personal data of an NE can be prevalently found in the first paragraph of the article[4][340]. Such vertices are specially treated by ω. More precisely, let C_1, C_2 and C_3 be classes of H, where

- $C_1 \in H$ is the set of all vertices, for which there is at least one article in which they occur in the first paragraph as a substring of the title.

---

[4]The first paragraph of the Wikipedia article comprises mostly detailed information about a person such as full name, birthday and place and profession. The search engine Yahoo refers to this information as to the Yahoo-Abstract corpus.

- $C_2 \in H$ is the set of all vertices, for which which there is at least one article in which they occur in the first paragraph, but *not* as a substring of the title.

- $C_3 \in H$ represents the set of all remaining vertices as $C_3 = H \setminus (C_1 \cup C_2)$.

The actual edge weight $e \in E$ is calculated using the conditional probability function $P(v|w)$, where $v \in N$ is the NE represented as an article for which $w \in H$ occurs as the anchor of the edge. Thereby $P(v|w)$ denotes the probability on the basis of the occurrences of term w within the article v defined as $f(w,v)$, and the frequency within the entire corpus ($f(w)$):

$$P(v|w) = \frac{f(w,v)}{f(w)} \qquad (5.1)$$

By combining structural information and hyperlink topology features of the social network, we finally define the weighting function ω for any $(w,v) \in E$ as:

$$\omega((w,v)) = \begin{cases} 1 \cdot \text{idf}(w) \cdot P(v|w) : w \in C_3 \\ 2 \cdot \text{idf}(w) \cdot P(v|w) : w \in C_2 \\ 3 \cdot \text{idf}(w) \cdot P(v|w) : w \in C_1 \end{cases} \in [0,3] \qquad (5.2)$$

Therefore, G_{NE} represents a weighted bipartite digraph, where anchor names within the Wikipedia collections refers to the comprised set of NE entries.

Co-occurrence-based Term Clouding

According to the methodology of the social semantic-induced closed content models (see Chapter 2), we also used additional topic-related term candidates to enrich the existing document content – the delimited context window. However, in this case we use statistically significant co-occurrences information to build the desired context cloud around the to classify NE. More precisely, we apply the technique of sentence-based statistical co-occurrence [114]. In general, the repeated occurrences of two words within a defined context is defined as a statistical co-occurrence. Most prominent, a significance measure, similar to the log-likelihood [25] is used to calculate the significant co-occurrences. The calculations in constructing the co-occurrence-based KB were computed by using the software package *TinyCC* provided by Biemann et al. [22] on the basis

Searched Name	Instances	Activity Ranking
H. S. (athlete)	H. S. (athlete)	2.4
	H. S.(skier)	0.09
M. K. (writer)	M. K. (writer)	0.024
	M. K.(politics)	0.0005
	M. K.(soccer)	0.00004

Table 5.1: Activity Ranking of Hubert Schwarz (H. S.) and Michael Krüger (M. K.) (cf. Waltinger and Mehler [340, pp. 3])

of a lemmatized reference corpus (688,728 lemmata) extracted from the German newspaper *Die Zeit*. On the basis of the calculated sentence-based significant co-occurrences, we build a second graph defined as $G_\sigma = (V', E', \sigma)$, where V' represents the set of lemmata out of the reference corpus, and $E' \subseteq V'^2$ the corresponding set of edges (as terms $v' \in V'$ that occur significantly within the defined context window). Note that we kept only those edges (v, w) in E', which significant score defined as σ are above a defined threshold τ. The actual method, in enhancing the local context (terms occur in the article context window – v in x) of a to classified NE, is performed by building a context cloud, which also is defined as a graph (V'', E'', σ') such that $V'' \subseteq V'$ is the set of all lemmata of G_σ occur in x *and* E'' and σ' are the restrictions of E' and σ' to V'', respectively. These properties enable us to acquire for a given query term t_1 a set of significant nodes – ranked in descending order by ω – representing the enhanced co-occurrence cloud, used as an input for the NEI prediction algorithm.

NEI Activity Ranking

Given the NE-induced KB defined as G_{NE}, the NE to disambiguate within the text A_2 and the context enhancement graph G_σ, we use a spreading activation technique (see Algorithm 2) to predict the proper instance defined as $NE_{instance}$.

Step 1. For each label $v \in A_1$ - these are those v_i who are not pointing to another vertex in E (the constructed entity instances of the *Wikipedia* collection) - of G_{NE} to its own activity class defined as C_i. During the initialization, all activity classes W_i are defined as zero.

Step 2. A context cloud w is constructed using G_σ as a resource for the enhancement of each input token t within the defined context window. For each constructed context descriptor, defined as w_i, we add the edge value ω to those $v \in A_1$ classes, where an edge between V and V' exists. We define z as the number of enhanced descriptor comprised within the instance prediction.

Step 3. Building the sum of the edge weight of ω_{NE} and σ', the co-occurrence graph, we obtain the new activation value W_i of a class C_i Hence, for every comprised term within the context window, z, the corresponding $v \in A_1$ will 'grow' in their activation value. Finally, after sorting the ranking of $v \in A_1$ by their activation value in descending order, we choose that entity instance $NE_{instance}$ whose $v \in A_1$ value was maximized during the calculation (see Table 5.1).

$$C_i = W_i(E_i \cap E'_i) \tag{5.3}$$

$$W_i = W_{i-1} + \omega_{NE} + \sigma' \tag{5.4}$$

$$NE_{instance} = \arg\max_{0<w<z+1}\{C_i\} \tag{5.5}$$

5.1.2 Experimental Evaluation

The purpose of the experiments is set to evaluate a NE disambiguation on the basis of different foreknown knowledge. Consequently, we varied the given NE information by using either the first name only, the surname or both entity information in combination.

Algorithm 2 Named Entity Instance Recognition.

1: set all activation values of all $v \in A_1$ to 0
2: **for** each token t of the input text **do**
3:     build context cloud w of t
4:     **for** each item in w **do**
5:         **if** w is element of A_2 **then**
6:             **for** augment for all $v \in A_1$ for which $(w,v) \in E$ **do**
7:                 $v = v + activation\_value.$
8:             **end for**
9:         **end if**
10:     **end for**
11: **end for**
12: Select that $v \in A_1$ which has the highest activation value.

Reference Corpus

Two volunteers, who randomly collected articles out of the German online newspaper *Zeit Online*, compiled the evaluation corpus. For each article they were asked to copy one paragraph (the defined context window), where a certain person was mentioned. After that, the volunteers were prompted to remove all occurrences of the person's name in the paragraph. This is done, because there should be no detailed information (the complete name) of the observed person available. In addition, we instructed the volunteers not to analyze the extracted paragraph in more detail. This is done, to prevent that the most appropriate term descriptors occur within the texts. They should more or less be blindfolded copying the paragraph into the corpus file. As a resultant, they constructed a number of 195 unique NE of persons, each represented by a context window of one paragraph. In order to obtain the golden standard, the volunteers individually interlinked the actual NE instances to the instances of the constructed KB of the *Wikipedia* collection. In addition, we performed a parameter study of the activity value W_i. That is, we set $\omega_{\text{NE\_w}} + \omega_{\text{sig\_w}} = 1$ (*e1*) ,$\omega_{\text{NE\_w}}$ and $\omega_{\text{sig\_w}}$ without their *idf* (*e2*) and with *idf* value (*idf*).

Foreknown Knowledge	Accuracy
Fullname (idf)	0.98
Surname (idf)	0.72
Forename (idf)	0.55
Fullname (e2)	0.96
Surname (e2)	0.70
Forename (e2)	0.45
Fullname (e1)	0.93
Surname (e1)	0.68
Forename (e1)	0.57

Table 5.2: Evaluation results of a named entity instance recognition by varying the foreknown knowledge. $e1$, $e2$ and idf refers to different edge weighting settings for ω.

Results

By analyzing the results (see Table 5.2), we can observe that, given a full name and one paragraph as a context window, a promising accuracy value of 0.98 can be obtained. In contrast, using only the surname, with its context for the disambiguation, an acceptable accuracy of 0.72 can be achieved. The number of possibilities increases significantly when using only the first name such as 'Helmut', however, we were still able to reach an accuracy of 0.55.

5.1.3 Concluding Remarks

In conclusion, we can state that the proposed algorithm to NEI recognition performs very well when having at least one constituent of a person's name given. The analysis of the local context of one paragraph, in combination with an enhancement of co-occurrence-based term descriptors within a spreading activation technique, enabled us to perform a disambiguation of NE. At large, the document collection improved the task of traditional NE recognition by exposing the semantic interrelation between detected NEs and their hold instances. This clearly shows that social networks and social ontologies such as the *Wikipedia* dataset are of high interest to the area of entity recognition and disambiguation. This related not only for the development and evaluation of new methods (e. g. the creation of test collections and algorithms), but in the context of NER and for the creation of high-quality gazetteers. As NE dictionaries and gazetteers are an essential part for the performance of NER systems, the construction and the ongoing maintenance are time consuming tasks. The *Wikipedia* collection is, precisely because of its rich data structure (e. g. named entities are categorized) and its openness character (e. g. new named entities are added constantly), of vital importance toward the development of large-scale NLP applications.

5.2 Social Semantics-induced Sentiment Analysis

In this section we apply the methodology of our social semantics definition to the area of *Sentiment Analysis*. While a majority of approaches in IR focus on the thematic- or topic-based classification of texts (as we described in the previous chapters), applying content-based models [130] or structure-orientated [202] methods, the task of sentiment analysis refers to the non-topical opinion mining (OM) [233]. The area of opinion mining thereby focuses on the detection and extraction of opinions, feeling and emotions in text with reference to a specific subject. As a subcategory of OM, the categorization of sentiment polarities have drawn attention in the IR community. That is, being able to distinguish between positive, neutral or negative expressions or statements of extracted textual or spoken elements [10, 71, 120, 234, 360]. More sophisticated methods additionally analyze the level of polarity – referred to as the intensity level – using a rating inference model [234] (as for example a stars-rating within the scale of one and five), or focusing on primary and secondary emotion conditions [16]. With respect to the computational aspects of a polarity classification, most of the proposed methods focus on the determination of polarity-related term features in order to deduce the overall polarity orientation of the entire document. However, in the majority of cases both, positive and negative expression do occur within the very same document. Therefore the prediction and classification of the overall polarity is still challenging.

Consider the following example of an *Amazon* product review [339]:

Product-Review[5]: <u>Wonderful</u> when it works... I owned this TV for a month. At first I thought it was <u>terrific</u>. <u>Beautiful</u> <u>clear</u> picture and <u>good</u> sound for such a <u>small</u> TV. Like others,however, I found that it did not always retain the programmed stations and then had to be reprogrammed every time you turned it off. I called the manufacturer and they <u>admitted</u> this is a <u>problem</u> with the TV.

While focusing on polarity-based term features (e. g. wonderful, terrific, beautiful...), we might infer that this review should be classified with a positive polarity label. However, this contribution is actually classified as a negative review, which is not exposed until the last sentence ("...this is a *problem* ..."). Therefore traditional text categorization approaches, such as the BOW representation, need to be seized to the domain of sentiment analysis, in order to fulfill positively the task polarity classification. At the core of the recent approaches to polarity identification, the determination of polarity-based linguistic features (e. g. terms or phrases) within different document levels (e. g. sentences or overall document) need to be established. That is, to draw conclusions of the overall document polarity on the basis of identified subjectivity terms (such as words or phrases rated as positive, negative or neutral polarity) that occur in the observed document. More formally, Liu [161, pp. 5] define an opinion-oriented document model as follows:

Let d be a polarity-related document, and $O = \{o_1, o_2, \ldots, o_j\}$ be a set of opinion objects from $H = \{h_1, h_2, \ldots, h_p\}$, as a set of opinion holders. Further, let each opinion object o_j be represented by a set of polarity-related sentiment features $F = \{f_1, f_2, \ldots, f_j\}$. In addition, let each feature $f_j \in F$ be represented in d by a set of term or phrases $W = \{w_{i1}, w_{i2}, \ldots, w_{im}\}$, which are indicated by a set of feature indicators $I_i = \{i_{i1}, i_{i2}, \ldots, i_{ip}\}$. Therefore, an opinion object o_j is expressed through a opinion polarity s_j (e. g. positive) with respect to the embraced set of features f_j of o_j and the opinion holder h_i. Note that the feature indicator i_j thereby reflects the strength of the opinion (e. g. rating scale). This leads to the definition that a contrary opinion within

---
[5]This text is a product review extracted form the Amazon website at: http://www.amazon.com/

a document correlates to a low opinion similarity of two opinion objects defined as $S(o_j, o_k)$, while a opinion consistency within a document is indicated by a high similarity value. With respect to machine learning-based classifiers, the similarity function $S(o_j, o_k)$ refers to the similarity between the supervised trained SVM-based opinion models (o_j) and the evaluation set of document opinions (o_k).

Following this definition, a mapping $W \mapsto F$ of the term features of the input document to the comprised polarity features, with corresponding indicators needs to be established. In this regard, most of the proposed unsupervised or (semi-)supervised sentiment-related approaches make use of external resources. These constructed lists contain a set of textual features with assigned polarity orientation (e. g. boolean or within a rating scale). We refer to these resources as *subjectivity dictionaries* used for document-based polarity classification. In recent times, various annotated data sets have been proposed in the research community, however only a small number of them have been made freely available to the public, most of them for the English language. Currently, to the best of our knowledge, there are hardly subjectivity resources freely available for the German language[6]. Therefore, regarding the domain of sentiment analysis, the contributions of this thesis are two-fold. First, we propose an English-based polarity identification method using associated term features out of a social network, to enhance the existing polarity-oriented document representation. We thereby are heading towards a polarity reinforcement strategy in order to improve the overall classification accuracy. Second, we present a new resource – *German Subjectivity Clues* – for a German-based sentiment analysis, covering a set of German polarity term features, annotated with their polarity-related orientation.

5.2.1 Related Work

In this section, we present related work on sentiment analysis. In recent years, a variety of different algorithms have been applied to the task of polarity identification. Tan and Zhang [312] presented an empirical study of sentiment categorization on the basis of different feature selection (e. g. document frequency,

---

[6]Remus et al. [259] presented just recently a German-language resource for sentiment analysis.

chi square, subjectivity terms) and different learning methods (e.g k-nearest neighbor, Naive Bayes, SVM) on a Chinese data set. The results indicated that the combination of sentimental feature selection and machine learning-based SVM performs best compared to other tested sentiment classifiers. Chaovalit and Zhou [49] published a comparative study on supervised and unsupervised classification methods in a polarity identification scenario of movie reviews. Their results also confirmed that machine learning on the basis of SVM are more accurate than any other unsupervised classification approaches. Hence, a significant amount of training and building associated models is needed.

Prabowo and Thelwall [250] proposed a combined approach for sentiment analysis using rule-based, supervised and machine learning methods. An overview of current sentiment approaches is given, comparing their model, data source, evaluation methods and results. However, since most of the current attempts based their experiments on different setups, using mostly self-prepared corpora or subjectivity resources, a uniform comparison of the proposed algorithms is barely possible. The results of the combined approach shows that no single classifier outperforms the other, and the hybrid classifier *can* result in better effectiveness. With respect to different methods applied to the sentiment polarity analysis, we can identify two different branches. On the one hand we have rule-based approaches, for instance, counting positive and negative terms [319] on the basis of subjectivity dictionaries or combining it with so-called discourse-based contextual valence shifters [136]. On the other hand we have machine-learning approaches [318] on different document levels, such as the entire documents [234], phrases [3, 307, 360], sentences [231] or on the level of words [169], using extracted and enhanced linguistic features from internal (e.g. PoS- or text phrase information) and/or external resources (e.g. syntactic and semantic relationships extracted from lexical resources such as *WordNet* [83]) [49, 219].

Most notably, sentence-based models have been quite intensively studied in the past, combining machine learning and unsupervised approaches by using inter-sentence information [147, 369], sentence-based linguistic feature enhancement [359] or most famously by following a sentence-based minimum cut strategy [231, 232]. In general, sentence-based polarity identification contributes to a higher accuracy performance, but induces also a higher computational complexity. Nevertheless, depending on the used methods the reported increase of accuracy of document and sentence classifier range between $2-10\%$ [231, 359], mostly compared to the baseline (e. g. *Naive Bayes*) implementations. However, in the majority of cases, only slightly better results were achieved [147, 359].

At the core of almost all approaches, a set of subjectivity terms is needed, either to train a classifier or to extract polarity-related terms following a bootstrapping strategy [369]. With respect to the used sentiment or subjectivity resources, only a few of them are publicly available, mostly inducing the English language. Hatzivassiloglou and McKeown [109] used a small set of manually annotated $(1, 336$ adjectives) in order to extract polarity-related adjectives using a bootstrapping strategy, inducing *adjective conjunction* $(13, 426)$ that hold the same semantic orientation.

Various resources used the linguistic resource *WordNet* [83] as the basis of construction for sentiment resources, inducing graph-related distance measures [169], classifying *word-to-synset* relations [304] (*WordNet-Affect* comprises $2, 874$ synsets and $4, 787$ words) or combining semantic relations with co-occurrence information extracted from corpus using the *Ising Spin Model* [48, pp. 119] (*SentiSpin* induces $88, 015$ words) [309]. Also, on the basis of *WordNet*, Esuli and Sebastiani [81] proposed a method for the analysis of glosses and associated synset (*SentiWordNet* comprises $144, 308$ terms). Wiebe et al. [358], Wilson et al. [360], Wiebe and Riloff [357] presented the most fine-grained polarity resource. In total, $8, 221$ term features were not only rated by their polarity (positive, negative, both, neutral) but also by their reliability (e. g. strongly subjective, weakly subjective).

5.2.2 The Social Network-induced Polarity Enhancement

Following the CES methodology, we applied a feature enhancement method, in order to improve the accuracy of polarity categorization. Thereby, we enhanced the existing polarity-orientated document representation with additional concept features defined as a *polarity-based feature cloud* and derived from a social network. As described in the previous chapter, a concept enhancement system (CES) consists of a knowledge base as the main resource in constructing semantically related feature concepts for a given input fragment to enhance.

With respect to the task of polarity identification, this resource needs to fulfil two premises. First, at most the data set should be constructed from data provided by a social network in order to factor the open character of the concept 'universe', such as terms and texts, which will get constantly extended, updated and improved by a multitude of online users. Therefore, no 'expensive' expert knowledge is needed in keeping the data set up-to-date. Second, computational methods must be able to extract *sentiment-related* term definitions, in order to derive polarity-related features for the enhancement task.

A resource, that fulfils both needs, is the data set of the social network-driven online project Urban Dictionary (UD)[7]. This online dictionary, which was launched in 1999, currently consists of $3,933,862$ different definitions and term description, contributed by an online community. The basic principle of this social network is, that users are able to introduce a new coined or existing term definition. The online community is then able to reshape the current definition and rate the existing descriptions based upon of its relevance to the target term or phrase, by using a 'thumb up vs. thumb down' strategy. One of the major advantages of this procedure, is the desired online dynamic of the community itself. This resource is constantly growing in its corpus size, and each contribution gets constantly extended by multiple contributed descriptions (see Table 5.3).

In addition, the online project offers a list of the most frequently-associated concepts on the basis of their assigned descriptors (see Table 5.4). Most of the associated concepts are based upon semantic relations such as synonymy and meronymy (e.g. tight $\mapsto$ cool). With respect to the procedure of feature enhancement, we aim to request for a given textual context – such as an input document within a certain context window – a set of polarity-related descriptors defined as the *polarity term clouds* of the KB, the converted UD data set. In the line of the *Social Semantic Vector* implementation (see Chapter 3), the construction of $UD \mapsto KB$ is based upon an inverted term index representation of UD. This is done in two steps. First, we utilize an existing list of words and phrases with polarity values assigned. In this case, the data set of Takamura et al. [309], which assembled a list of $80,000$ words including their semantic polarity orientation, defined as T. Note that each new constructed

---

[7]http://www.urbandictionary.com

Seed Word	Concept Description
Tight	Stylish, cool, having everything together; Scrooge
	cool or hip
	Original use: the mood or spirit between members of a music group who are having a particularly excellent performance.
	Modern use: describes something particularly enjoyable or awesome.

Table 5.3: Seed word and concept description as presented by the urban dictionary project.

Seed Word	Associated Concepts
awesome	sound cool, amazing, sweet, great, rad, sick, fantastic, wicked ...
marvelous	wonderful, superb, excellent, stunning, splendid, magnificent...
shiznit	shizzle, tight, sweet, foshizzle, awsome, badass, aiight ...
crappy	shitty, lame, stupid, horrible, sucky, useless, cruddy, cheesy

Table 5.4: Seed words enriched by urban dictionary based associated concepts.

lexical feature of KB needs to have a sentiment orientation, therefore the induction of polarity orientation is mandatory. Second, we use each entry of T as a seed word w_i in requesting new associated concepts of the KB. That is, for each seed word we retrieved the term definitions – represented as a set of urban concepts – of UD. More formally, let $s_i \in S$ be a vector of a polarity seed word $w_i \in W$, its polarity value $k_i \in K$ and its associated urban concepts $ud_j = \{u_{jt}, ..., u_{jM}\}$ where M defines the total number of considered concepts. In order to obtain the semantic orientation, each ud_{jt} inherits the polarity value k_i of w_i. Consequentially, there exist certain ud_{jt}, which has both polarities assigned (positive and negative). Therefore, a term-specific polarity disambiguation on the basis of the maximum likelihood probabilities $\hat{P}_{fix}$ needs to be computed, which are derived from the relative frequency defined as

$$\hat{P}_{pos}(ud_{jt}) = \frac{p(ud_{jt}|C_{pos})}{p(ud_j)} \qquad (5.6)$$

$$\hat{P}_{neg}(ud_{jt}) = \frac{p(ud_{jt}|C_{neg})}{p(ud_j)} \qquad (5.7)$$

where $p(ud_{jt}|C_{pos})$ and $p(ud_{jt}|C_{neg})$ are the number of occurrences of the term ud_{jt} as a positive or negative polarity feature with respect to the overall occurrences $p(ud_j)$, and

$$\hat{P}_{fix}(ud_{jt}) = \max\{|\hat{P}_{pos}(ud_{jt})|, |\hat{P}_{neg}(ud_{jt})|\} \qquad (5.8)$$

where, $\hat{P}_{fix}(ud_{jt})$ classifies the concept ud_{jt} as either positive or negative.

As we have mapped the social network UD to the KB of the CES, we proceed with the actual concept enhancement and polarity classification. The polarity-enhanced classification is computed in three steps: First, a *feature candidate selection* is performed. Single- and multi-word expression within a context window of five are mapped onto the inverted index of the KB. Second, the actual *feature enhancement* is computed by adding a fixed set of polarity-related concepts to the existing document representation. The last step is the actual *polarity classification* of the new enhanced concept representation. In this thesis, we used supervised SVM-based machine-learning classifier for the categorization of sentiment polarities.

5.2.3 The German Polarities Clues

As stated above, there are various sentiment-related resources and data sets proposed in the research community, however most of them induce the English language. Currently to the best of our knowledge, there are hardly annotated dictionaries (terms with associated semantic orientation) freely available for the German language [259]. Therefore, this section proposes a new lexical resource for sentiment analysis of the German language - the *GermanPolarityClues*. In contrast to other approaches [75] that propose to translate the input text into the English language, and to use English-based resources such as *SentiWordNet* for the polarity classification, we have built a new German

Resource:	Subjectivity Clues	Senti Spin	Senti WordNet	Polarity Enhancement
No. of Features:	6,663	88,015	144,308	137,088
Positive-AMean:	76.83	236.94	241.36	239.25
Positive-StdDevi:	30.81	84.29	85.61	84.98
Negative-AMean:	69.72	218.46	223.11	221.25
Negative-StdDevi:	26.22	74.08	75.37	74.68
Text-AMean:	707.64	707.64	707.64	707.64
Text-StdDevi:	296.94	296.94	296.94	296.94

Table 5.5: The standard deviation (StdDevi) and arithmetic mean (AMean) of subjectivity features by English resource, text corpus (Text) and polarity category (Positive, Negative).

subjectivity dictionary by translating the dictionary entries of different English resources. Hence, we have translated the two most comprehensive dictionaries of the English language: the *Subjectivity Clues* [357, 358, 360] comprising 9,827 term features (further called *German Subjectivity Clues*) and the *SentiSpin* [309] dictionary comprising 105,561 polarity features (further called *German SentiSpin*), into the German language by automatic means. For each translated term, we have used the sentiment orientation score (e.g. positive or negative) of the English seed word, as the polarity score for the German pendant. In addition, we constructed a more sophisticated dictionary, defined as *GermanPolarityClues*, by further manually assessing each term feature of the *German Subjectivity Clues* dataset with respect to their semantic orientation (see Table 5.8). We comprehensively appended not only 290 different German negation-phrases, such as *not bad* or *not good*, but also the most frequent positive and negative synonyms of the most popular polarity features. The corpus size of the *GermanPolarityClues* could thereby be extended to 10,141 different polarity features (See Table 5.7).

Resource:	German SentiSpin	German Subjectivity	German Polarity Clues
No. of Features:	105,561	9,827	10,141
Positive-AMean:	53.63	27.70	26.66
Positive-StdDevi:	6.90	4.59	5.01
Negative-AMean:	50.18	25.68	24.14
Negative-StdDevi:	10.40	5.88	5.41
Text-AMean:	109.75	109.75	109.75
Text-StdDevi:	24.52	24.52	24.52

Table 5.6: The standard deviation (StdDevi) and arithmetic mean (AMean) of subjectivity features by German resource, text corpus (Text) and polarity category (Positive, Negative).

5.2.4 Experimental Evaluation

The evaluation of the proposed sentiment analysis methods is threefold. First, we evaluate the existing English-based polarity resources by means of the combination of a polarity-based feature selection and machine learning-based classifier in a comparative manner. With the existence of significant variations within the comprised polarity feature set $(6,663 - 144,308)$, a question that arose was: At what amount do the number of used features influence the classification accuracy? Therefore, we systematically evaluated the three most widely used English-based sentiment resources (*Subjectivity Clues* [358], *SentiSpin* [309], *SentiWordNet* [81]) within a polarity-based feature selection and subsequent classification. That is, we analyzed all English resources within the same experimental setup. Second, we analyzed the effect of polarity-based feature enhancement using the proposed knowledge base for the feature construction process. Third, we analyzed the new constructed *GermanPolarityClues* (GPC) resource within the same experimental setup as the English resources. More precisely, we used the two automatic-translated polarity sets and the English-based results as the baseline for the evaluation of GPC approach. This approach was needed, since there are no reference results for a German-based polarity classification. For the actual classification task, we

Overall Features:	10,141
No. Positive Features:	3,220
No. Negative Features:	5,848
No. Neutral Features:	1,073
No. Negation Features:	290
No. Noun Features:	4,408
No. Verb Features:	2,728
No. Adj/Adv Features:	2,604

Table 5.7: *GermanPolarityClues* feature statistics by polarity and grammatical categories.

Id	Feature	PoS	+	-	o
5953	elementar	ADJD	0	0	1
7076	hoffnungslos	ADJD	0	1	0
7077	hofieren	VVINF	1	0	0

Table 5.8: Overview of the *GermanPolarityClues* data schema by polarity feature, grammatical category (PoS using the *STTS*-Tagset [9]), positive (+), negative (−) and neutral (o) polarity orientation.

utilized a supervised machine learning classifier by means of SVM, using a *leave-one-out cross-validation*.

Corpora

In general, the evaluation is based upon two different reference corpora. With respect to the English language, we performed the polarity classification experiments on the most widely used reference data set – the movie review corpus – initially compiled by Pang et al. [234]. In short, this corpus consists of a positive and a negative polarity category, where for each category 1,000 movie review articles are assigned with an average number of 707.64 textual features. With the absence of an existing German-based reference dataset, we decided to manually create a reference corpus for the German language. According to the data set proposed by Pang et al. [234], we compiled the German reference corpus using product review documents from the *Amazon*-Website[8]. In general, product review documents within the web project Amazon correspond to human-rated reviews, where a rating scale between 1 (worst) to 5 (best) stars is used in order to place the meaning (corresponds to the polarity) of a certain subject (product). The final German reference corpus consists of 1,000 product reviews for each of the five rating levels, where each level comprises 5 different categories (e.g. books, furniture ...). For the actual classification experiments, we removed all category, star label and review authorship information. The average number of term features per review was 109.75.

Results

Sentiment-Method	Accuracy
Naive Bayes - unigrams [234]	78.7
Maximum Entropy - top 2633 unigrams [234]	81.0
SVM - unigrams+bigrams [234]	82.7
SVM -unigrams [234]	**82.9**
Polarity Enhancement - PDC (without feature enhancement)	81.9
Polarity Enhancement - PDC (with feature enhancement)	**83.1**
Subjectivity-Clues SVM Linear-Kernel	**84.1**
Subjectivity-Clues SVM RBF-Kernel	83.5
SentiWordNet SVM Linear-Kernel	**83.9**
SentiWordNet SVM RBF-Kernel	82.3
SentiSpin SVM Linear-Kernel	**83.8**
SentiSpin SVM RBF-Kernel	82.5

Table 5.9: Accuracy results comparing four subjectivity resources and four baseline approaches.

With respect to the English polarity experiment (see Table 5.10), we have used the published accuracy results of Pang et al. [234], using the *Naive Bayes* (NB), the *Maximum Entropy* (ME) and the *N-Gram*-based SVM implementa-

---
[8]http://www.amazon.de

Resource	Kernel	F1-Pos	F1-Neg	F1-Av
E-Subjectivity Clues	SVM-Linear	.832	.823	**.828**
	SVM-RBF	.828	.823	.826
E-SentiWordNet	SVM-Linear	.832	.828	**.830**
	SVM-RBF	.816	.812	.814
E-SentiSpin	SVM-Linear	.831	.827	**.829**
	SVM-RBF	.815	.811	.813
E-Polarity Enhancement	PDC	.828	.827	**.828**
	SVM-Linear	.841	.837	**.839**

Table 5.10: F1-Measure valuation results of a English (E) subjectivity feature selection by resource, SVM-Kernel method (Linear and RBF), positive (F1-Pos) and negative (F1-Neg) polarity category. F1-Av denotes the average performance of the positive and negative results.

tion as the corresponding baselines. As Table 5.9 shows, the smallest resource, *Subjectivity Clues*, performs best with $acc = 84.1$. However, *SentiWordNet* ($acc = 83.9$), SentiSpin ($acc = 83.8$) but also the *Polarity Enhancement* using the Polarity Difference Coefficient (PDC) [337] ($acc = 83.1$), perform almost within the same accuracy. It can be stated that all subjectivity feature selection resources clearly outperform not only the well known NB and ME classifier but also the N-Gram-based SVM implementation. Not surprisingly, with respect to the feature coverage of the used subjectivity resources (see Table 5.6), we can argue that the size of the dictionary clearly correlates to the coverage (arithmetic mean of polarity-features selected varies between $76.83 - 241.36$). Interestingly, the biggest dictionary with the highest coverage property does not outperform the resource with the lowest number of polarity-features. In contrast, we can state that operating in the present settings, on $6,663$ term features (in contrast to $144,308$ of *SentiWordNet*), seem to be a sufficient number for the task of document-based polarity identification. This claim is also supported by the evaluation F1-Measure results as shown in Table 5.10. All subjectivity resources nearly perform equally well (F1-Measure results range between $82.9 - 83.9$). The *leave − one − out cross − validation*, the polarity-enhanced

Resource	Kernel	F1-Pos	F1-Neg	F1-Av
G-Senti Star12 vs. Star45	SVM-L	.827	.828	.828
	SVM-RBF	.830	.830	**.830**
G-Senti Star1 vs. Star5	SVM-L	.857	.861	**.859**
	SVM-RBF	.855	.858	.857
G-Sub Star12 vs. Star45	SVM-L	.810	.813	**.811**
	SVM-RBF	.804	.803	.803
G-Sub Star1 vs. Star5	SVM-L	.841	.842	**.841**
	SVM-RBF	.834	.834	.834

Table 5.11: F1-Measure valuation results of a German (G) subjectivity feature selection by resource, SVM-Kernel method (Linear and RBF), positive (F1-Pos) and negative (F1-Neg) polarity category. F1-Av denotes the average performance of the positive and negative results.

implementation performs a bit better than the other resources. Combining the polarity-enhanced document representation with a SVM-based classifier let us gain a promising F1-Measure of 83.9, outperforming all other three English-based resources. However, the amount of improvement is rather low, which might be due to differences in the language between the KB and the evaluation corpus. Table 5.11 shows the results of the newly built German subjectivity resources, used for the document-based polarity identification. With respect to the correlation of subjectivity dictionary size and classification performance, similar results can be achieved. Using the *German SentiSpin* version, comprising 105,561 polarity features, lets us gain a promising F1-Measure of 85.9. The *German Subjectivity Clues* dictionary, comprising 9,827 polarity features, performs with an F1-Measure of 84.1 almost at the same level. In general, in terms of Kernel-Methods, we can argue that the Linear-Kernel outperform the RBF-Kernel SVM implementation, even though it is only to a minor extent. With reference to the coverage of subjectivity dictionaries for a polarity-based feature selection – *size does matter*. However, the classification accuracy results indicate – for both languages – that a smaller but controlled dictionary contributes to the accuracy performance (almost equally to big-sized data) of opinion mining systems.

5.2.5 Concluding Remarks

The proposed English-based sentiment enhancement method used for a polarity classification shows that polarity identification is related to a sentiment sensitive feature extraction and classification. In contrast to traditional text categorization approaches, where more or less all textual and structural features contain valuable classification features, within the domain of sentiment analysis, only a subset comprehends polarity-related information. Therefore, the usage of subjectivity dictionaries is mandatory, but are – handcrafted – expensive to build. We proposed a polarity-enhancement algorithm that utilizes a social network to construct and extend current dictionaries by automatic means. Even further, we proposed a new subjectivity dictionary – *GermanPolarityClues* – as the first freely available resource for the German language[9]. The proposed resources and methods were analyzed by means of different comparative studies, where good results could be achieved. We can argue that the sentiment-sensitive feature-enhancement also improves the polarity classification accuracy, even if its only to a minor extent. However, this method can be useful to the community with respect to a needed extension of existing resources with recent polarity-features by automatic means. The newly constructed German resources performed in a document-based classification setup, with an F1-Measure of 85.9, surprisingly high. Overall, we can state that combining a polarity-based feature selection with machine learning, SVMs using Linear-Kernel exhibit the best performance.

5.3 Web Genre Classification

While the former aspects relate to the domain of topic, polarity and text categorization of different open- and closed content models, this section presents an approach to the classification of hypertext types by means of a *Closed Genre Model* [196]. We will explore the task of web genre categorization by means of document *and* genre-related structural components [199, 200, 203], seizing the

---

[9]The constructed resource is freely available at: http://hudesktop.hucompute.org/

notion of web genre subtype features as proposed by Mehler and Gleim [192] and Waltinger et al. [347]. Instead of using textual or structural features derived from a social network, we utilize the macro-structure authored by users on the web. Therefore, in lieu of comprising textual content only, created by a social community, we focus on the structural components of hypertext as contributed by the actual users, say authors, themselves. In general, the usage of 'genre' is primarily used within the 'offline world' referring to literature (e. g. biography, poem, thriller, ...) or music (e. g. musical, opera, ...) [78, 86, 282]. However, there also exists the notion of genre or document types within the 'online world', which is in the line of the offline genre definition, defined by means of purpose and function [268]. In this regard, web-based genre types, subsequently called *web genre* or *hypertext types* [190, 203], are instantiated in web pages through their functionality and aim to fulfil. We can consider documents of a web-based communication as new types, which are *much more unpredictable and individualized than documents on paper* [281, p. 1]. Possible web genre candidates represent in this context hypertext types such as *blogs*[10], *advertisements, web-shops, search-engines portals, faq-websites*[11] but also *private* or *academic hompages*. With respect to IR systems, hypertext type classification is of great interest to the NLP community in application areas such as search engines [78] or information extraction [86], for example, finding relevant documents that are most suitable to a certain user query with regard to their respective types. That is, providing the scope from where to extract meta data (e. g. FAQ webpage of a product website, contact segment of a personal website, and so on). In the following section, we describe how hypertext types are instantiated on the web, and propose a method for an automatic identification of web genres in web pages using a hypertext subtype classification approach.

---

[10]The term Blog refers to an Weblog-Website, an online-driven personal diary, where a single or a multitude of users can contribute to.

[11]FAQ refers to Frequently-Asked-Questions, a website that contains a list of question and associated answers.

5.3.1 Related Work

In recent years, the exploration and classification of hypertext types has drawn attention in the research community[12]. Regarding computational models, primarily (supervised) machine learning techniques, such as SVM or NB, have been applied, to focus on different notions of structural (in terms of structure and layout-oriented markup) and textual (in terms of linguistic) classification features [283, pp.33]. More precisely, the majority of approaches to web genre identification form their basis by utilizing linguistic features toward the learning process [133, 137], such as using character n-grams, PoS-tag information or the traditional bag-of-words (BOW). Others build genre classification models focusing on the structural components [152, 153, 158, 281] of the hypertext markup [279, 280] following a bag-of-structure[13] strategy. Several approaches combined thematic *and* structural features from web pages for the task of web genre classification [78, 131, 160, 257]. However, all of the cited methods follow the notion that hypertext types are manifested by the extracted features on the level of the individual, let's say single, website as a whole. Hence, focusing on the entire single web document as an instance of a web genre, is used for building the classifier. Our notion of hypertext types differs to them by following Mehler et al. [200] and Mehler [190] and their described aspects of informational uncertainty with respect to the phenomenon of *polymorphism* within web documents. That is, *hypertext units are compound manifestations of web genres* and consequently, hypertext type *classification goes hand-in-hand with* the spanned *genre-related segments* [347]. This follows the notion of Mehler [190]:

> *You shall know the genre of a hypertext unit by its genre-related structuring, that is, by the genre-related types of its segments.*[14]

Meaning that if we are able to identify the structural and genre-related segments of a web document, we are also able to draw a conclusion about the

---

[12] See Santini et al. [282] for an comprehensive overview to the area of web genre learning

[13] The bag-of structure representation follows the idea of the BOW as an unordered collection of words though only structural features (e.g. headers, paragraphs) are considered.

[14] But not only by its lexical, textual or hypertextual features (i.e. by the classical bag-of-features approach).

overall hypertext type of the web document. Consequently, this follows a two-level approach to web genre classification as described in Mehler [190], Mehler et al. [203] and Waltinger et al. [347], where hypertext segments are used as building blocks for the actual instantiation of a specific web genre. These central aspects will be picked up and continued by expanding the notion of *polymorphism* and *monomorphism* of hypertext types. Firstly, we focus on hypertext segment types as a reference point of hypertext segmentation in order to, secondly, use the learned segmentation of a hypertext unit as a reference point to its categorization [200]. Look, for example, at conference websites that typically consist of website segments, such as a *call for papers*, a *conference venue description* or a *conference program*. These segments pose as the reference points for the categorization of the overall web genre category. Therefore, we identify web genres by their prototypical segments, which may be manifested by one or more web pages[15].

5.3.2 Hypertext Type Classification Algorithm

The proposed algorithm of hypertext type classification implements the two-level model of hypertext categorization, following the notion that distinctions of hypertext types correlate with differences in their spanned segment types. In this sense, instances of different hypertext types are seen to be separable by the types of segments manifested by these instances. In order to implement this approach we argue that every web document is a class of hypertextual units defined as a number of hypertext segments that characterizes the instance through its content, structure and layout function membership. Thus, structure and textual units vary in dependence on their type categorization. With the presence of mono- and polyfunctionality within the structure of web documents, the task of hypertext type categorization is challenging. Consider for example, the structure of a *personal academic website*. There might be

---

[15]The approach to web genre learning has been primarily developed within the *DFG-Research Group 437 "Text Technological Modelling of Information"* at Bielefeld University. More precisely, the A4 Indogram project *"Induction of Document-Grammars for the representation of logic hypertextual Document-Structures"*. The Indogram project was headed by Prof. Dr. Alexander Mehler. Team members were Dr. rer. nat. Matthias Dehmer, Dr. phil. Armin Wegner, Rüdiger Gleim, Olga Pustylnikov, Tobias Feith, Arne Seemann and Carolin Kram. (http://www.text-technology.de/)

identified segment types, such as *publications* or *research*, containing a list of references with the same author name or contact person. However, observing only a segment, such as *contact*, will obviously lead to difficulties in classification due to its type ambiguity (e.g. conference website, project website, personal website). That is, certain segments vary in terms of their location within the website structure but also within different web genre types. We therefore follow Mehler et al. [203] and their definitions on hypertext segment type structures:

Definition 5.3.1. *polymorphic* (Mehler et al. [203])
From the perspective of a website, which consists of a number of webpages, instantiating a certain web genre, its structure is defined as polymorphic, *if the webpage contains at least two segments of different types.*

Definition 5.3.2. *monomorphic* (Mehler et al. [203])
In contrast to the inclusion of multiple segments of different types, a webpage is defined as monomorphic, *if it only consists of a fixed number of the same segment type.*

While the presence of *monomorphic* websites allows a strict separation of segment types with respect to the other web pages, the inclusion of *polymorphic* websites (the predominant case) will lead to difficulties in their needed differentiation of hypertext types. Thus, we need to be able, in first order, to separate a *polymorphic* website into its spanned segment types, in order to apply in second place the classical apparatus of document classification. The algorithm of web genre classification works therefore in two steps:

- First, we apply a method for an automatic extraction of segments within instances of different hypertext types, defined as hypertext type segmentation.
- Second, we utilize all extracted segments as our building blocks for the hypertext type classification, defined as hypertext segment type classification.

Hypertext Type Segmentation

In principle, the approach to hypertext type segmentation follows the notion of a segmentation by means of the visual depiction of web document as perceived by the user [256]. Since the structure of web documents is coded by means of a markup language (XHTML) while their layout is (partly) coded by means of (cascading) style sheets (CSS), both need to be taken into account. In general,

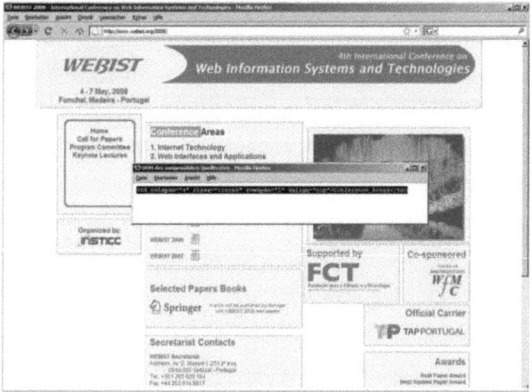

Figure 5.1: Hypertext Type – Conference Website: Type Segments marked by headlines

we utilize the logical document structure as a reference point, when focusing on the structural components of a web document, and observing primarily the associated style sheet language that specifies the actual visual presentation, when focusing on the layout of the document. As a premise of a web document segmentation, we argue that divisions, say segments, which are visually and prominently dividable, correlating with different sections on the content level – instantiating different hypertext segment types. Following this notion, we define a segment border as a conspicuous intersection of content divisions by textual elements, such as headings or text with an above-average font-size, image or clear visual space (no textual or graphical presentation). This task is challenging, since the visual depiction, as stated above, is encoded within web document by style- and structure elements, where both may imply layout-relevant information. As for example, textual headers can be authored by markup language using traditional html-tags (e.g. `<h1>title</h1>`, `<h2>`, `<h3>`,...), but also by using style sheet information (e.g. `.class { font-size: 20px;}` or `<span style='font-size:15px;'>`) Note that the latter layout information can be included within the web document or by external style sheets references. Therefore, the actual task of hypertext type segmentation is conducted in two phases. First, a *segment cutting* is applied, where all possible segment boundaries are detected. That is, a set of predefined separation features (e. g. div, h1, h2, a, font-size that exceeds a certain threshold, image, blank space, ...) are used for the exploration of possible indicators of hypertext type boundaries. In the second phase, we conduct a *segment re-connecting*, where each potential segment gets reviewed by its appropriateness as a true segment boundary. That is, parts of the extracted segments are often considered too small, in terms of textual content, to be an appropriate type segment boundary. We therefore amalgamate those candidates with their subsequent instances within the observed document. In the majority of cases, these candidates refer to single items of the navigation or headlines. Note, we defined a threshold for the minimum length of segments, where the number of characters without markup is used as a limitation criteria. As a result, each input web document is represented by its spanned hypertext type segments, which themselves are further used for the classification task.

Hypertext Segment Type Classification

In the line of the proposed two-level approach to web genre classification, we utilize identified hypertext segment types to be able to draw conclusions about the overall web genre instance. Therefore the actual classification is established by two phases. First, a segment type identification, and second an overall genre classification is performed. This is a sort of a two-level categorization as we categorize compound units by the classification of their segments. In the line of traditional data categorization, we have used SVM-based machine learning techniques by means of the SVM^{light} implementation of Joachims [126] for the actual classification task. While the SVM-based categorization of documents mainly focuses on the BOW representation, and therefore comprising mostly token information as classification features, the categorization of web documents differs. As described in the previous chapters, SVMs have proven to be an efficient and accurate technique within the domain of text [127, 130, 131, 288] but also genre [78, 281] classification. Therefore, the usage of SVMs seems to us to be the best choice for the two-level stage classification approach. With the presence of structural and textual information within the

---
Algorithm 3 Hypertext Type Segmentation.

Require: String H as the input website
String C as the stylesheet information
SF as the set of predefined segment features
SV as the set of output segments
min_l as the minimum threshold (string length)

Parse website H and stylesheet information C;
// *Segment Cutting*
p:=0; m:=0;
for each occurrence of $f \in SF$ in H at p **do**
    add substring $H[m,p]$ to SV;
    m:=p;
end for
// *Segment Re-Connection*
for each entry in SV as i **do**
    if $i_{length} < min_l$ **then**
        connect $SV[i]$ with $SV[i+1]$;
    end if
end for
return SV
---

classified web document corpus, a sensitive feature selection is applied, which can be divided into three classes of feature matrices:

- Tag-Matrix: Frequency of HTML-tags.
- Term-Matrix: Frequency of tokens.
- Structure-Matrix: Frequency of segment structure-related numerical features.

The class of HTML-tags (see Table 5.12) takes all occurrences of markup tags into account, considering primarily the tags that occur within the logical document structure of the segment except scripts or comments. With respect to the traditional token information, we utilized only stemmed tokens of certain part-of-speech categories, such as nouns, verbs, adjectives, adverbs, numerals, punctuation marks and named entities (e.g. email, proper names, location and country entities). The third class utilizes document structure relevant infor-

a	abbr	acronym	address
base	basefont	bdo	big
button	caption	center	cite
dd	del	dfn	dir
em	fieldset	font	form
h2	h3	h4	h5
html	i	iframe	img
kbd	label	legend	li
meta	noframes	noscript	object
p	param	pre	q
select	small	span	strike
sup	table	tbody	td
thead	title	tr	tt

Table 5.12: Html-Tags used as features for the construction of the tag-matrix

mation by means of numerical characteristics according to the calculation of the individual length of sections, paragraphs and sentences. Hereby, we argue that there are certain segment types that are supported by their structural representation. For example, the average sentence lengths within the contact section will differ strongly from those extracted from a project description or a publication list. The three-folded segment representation model (combining term, tag and structure matrix), is subsequently used as input for the machine learning classification.

5.3.3 Experimental Evaluation

With the absence of an existing benchmark corpus for a segment-based web genre classification, a new reference corpus that contains a set of web documents with annotated hypertext type segments had to be compiled[16]. We deployed two different machine learning-based classifier using not only the traditional *bag-of-features* but also a *bag-of-segments* document representation to compare the achievable classification performance. Moreover, we analyzed the

---
[16]Corpus compilation has been done by the team members of the A4 Indogram project.

proposed method of hypertext segmentation, enabling us to extract the set of hypertext subtypes used for the classification process. In the following section, we will describe the conducted experiments.

Corpus Collection

There have been a few attempts made in building reference corpora for web genre categorization [258], most of them for the English language [281, 279, 206]. With respect to the proposed method of a hypertext segment classification, a more sophisticated web genre corpus is needed, since type segments need to be annotated. However, with the absence of this kind of reference collection, we have compiled a new reference corpus ourselves. To achieve this, we focused on a set of three different hypertext types: *conference websites*, *personal academic websites* and *academic project websites*. While the majority of the previous attempts to web genre classification, focused on more or less distinguishable genre categories such as *listings* or *search pages*, the employed experiments deal with a set of very closely related categories, by means of their thematic background. The corpus was compiled by three volunteers who annotated 150 different web pages for the German language. Each of the resultant web pages have been manually segmented by means of their genre-related structures such as *contact* or *research*. That means that the volunteers identified the monomorphic segments within each (polymorphic and monomorphic) web page, and annotated them as reference examples used for the learning phase of the classifier. See Table 5.13 for an overview of the comprised hypertext type segments. Thereby the final compiled corpus consists of 3 web genre categories, 150 web pages and 1,250 spanned hypertext segments.

Classification

We conducted a *leave-one-out cross-validated* classification using a SVM-based machine learning classifier. Thus, all annotated segments with associated segment labels were used for building the feature set. With respect to a feature selection analysis, we have used the *GSS coefficient* [93], which neither improved nor degraded the classification accuracy. The experimental setup was two-fold. First, we extracted for each hypertext type, the feature matrix (as described in the previous section) and trained for each segment type one SVM (one against

Type	Conference	Personal	Project
Segments	about	contact	contact
	accommodation	personal	events
	call	publications	framework
	committees	research	links
	contact	teaching	news
	disclaimer		objectives
	organizer		project
	program		publications
	registration		staff
	sightseeing		
	sponsors		
Corpus-Size	50	50	50

Table 5.13: Hypertext type with assigned segment types by corpus size

Type	Structure	Tag	Token	Sites	Pages	Segments
Project.	29	91	11734	50	2,779	435
Conference.	29	91	56994	68	1,569	292
Personal.	29	91	10260	52	1,591	612

Table 5.14: Number of features by feature category and hypertext type.

the other). See Table 5.14 for a statistical analysis of the comprised feature set. Thereon, the overall web genre classification was performed. This is done by means of a developed weighted finite-state transducer[17]. Hereby, we argue that each web genre instance can be represented by its document grammar - its sequence of spanned hypertext segments, which can be typified through a weighted direct graph. The actual genre-related grammar is appointed through its calculated transition probabilities of accumulated segments. With this, am-

---

[17] The document grammar and the feature selection analysis is based on the calculations of Dr. phil. Armin Wegner, who was part of the *DFG-Research Group 437 "Text Technological Modelling of Information"* at Bielefeld University.

Model	Recall	Precision	F-Measure
Segmenter	.936	.625	.745
Baseline	.263	.446	.331

Table 5.15: Evaluation results for automatic segmentation experiment

biguities in the categorization of segment types can be dissolved and the most likely sequence pattern can be detected.

For the analysis of the overall web genre classification, we randomly selected 60 web sites (20 for each genre category) of the reference corpus with different structural status (*polymorphic* and *monomorphic*) This approach follows a *bag-of-structure* model including a hypertext type stage disambiguation (hypertext stage grammar), following the idea that different web genre types in many cases share similar segment instances. In a second experimental setup, we focused on a *bag-of-stages* model. Thereby, the hypertext stage-based segmentation is comprised in order to induce the feature set, following Eissen and Stein [78], Santini et al. [281, 282], Waltinger et al. [347], by using the entire web document for the classification. However, we set the focus on the accumulated segment types as the features used for the SVM classification. Therefore, we would seize the archetype of a *text structure-based* classification, by including the *stage-based structure* characteristics of web documents, rather than using the traditional text-based feature set.

Results

In addition to the overall classification performance on web genre categorization, we were interested in the performance of the automatic web document segmentation algorithm, which builds the foundation of the *bag-of-stages* representation model. Table 5.15 shows the results of the proposed segmenter algorithm. As a baseline scenario, we have implemented a method, that splits any given web document by means of the most prominent html-tags that occur in the LDS (e.g. div, h1, hr, ...). The achieved results indicate, with an F1-Measure of 0.745, that an automatic splitting of a web document into its spanned segments is successful in approximately three-quarter of all cases. With reference to the baseline scores (F1-Measure of 0.331), the achieved ac-

Classes	Recall	Precision	F-Measure
about	.578	.703	.634
accommodation	.680	.700	.690
call	.350	.389	.368
committees	.609	.609	.609
contact	.581	.720	.643
disclaimer	.706	.667	.686
organizer	.455	.417	.435
program	.692	.838	.758
registration	.729	.771	.749
sightseeing	.708	.739	.723
sponsors	.542	.650	.591
Average	.603	.655	.626
Baseline			.200

Table 5.16: Results of SVM classification and included segments for the web-genre: conference website

curacy can be interpreted as positive results since we were using a very strict experimental setup. We classified only those segments as *true positive* if the manually annotated and the automatically set segment borders overlap by means of the same character length. Therefore, the split has to be made on the exact same position in the document (not even one html-tag before or after).

The results of the first level web genre categorization are shown in Tables 5.16–5.18. Note that we classified each extracted segment by its hypertext stage category with labels, such as *contact* or *research*. As the a baseline scenario, we performed a random clustering, where each segment is randomly classified into one of segment categories. The results of the stage classification show that we are, again, able to outperform the baseline score, however, with an average F-Measure of 0.65 it is not as good as we hoped to achieve. Similar results (see Table 5.19) can be achieved using the second-level categorization approach, as we combine stage classification and the predicted document grammar, for the overall web genre identification setup. While we

Classes	Recall	Precision	F-Measure
contact	.947	.857	.899
links	.583	.636	.608
personal	.661	.709	.684
publications	.795	.720	.756
research	.485	.800	.604
teaching	.581	.643	.610
Average	.675	.728	.694
Baseline			.280

Table 5.17: Results of SVM classification and included segments for the web-genre: personal academic website

could clearly outperform the random baseline, the results are again, with an F-Measure of .625, far distant from more desirable values of above 0.90. In contrast to the *bag-of-structures* approach, when using the *bag-of-stages* model as an overall web genre classification (see Table 5.20), we were able to achieve both specification and we clearly outperform the baseline scores for web genre classification by reaching, with an average $F1$-Measure of 0.920, the upper field of classification accuracy.

5.3.4 Remarks

In conclusion, we see web genre identification primarily as a classification task. Different to previous approaches, we focus on the structural properties of web documents, seizing the paradigm of poly- and monomorphism. While in the past the identification of web genre categories on the web has been done by focusing on the classification of web documents as a whole, using a structural (in terms of markup-language) and/or a textual (in terms of linguistic) feature set, we concentrate on a two-level classification setup. By splitting and classifying a web documents stages – hypertext segments – we were able to identify the overall genre category. Although there are related experiments for the English language, reporting accuracy scores between 0.80 and 0.90 [78, 279] by using a bigger category set (seven classes), these results cannot be directly

Classes	Recall	Precision	F-Measure
contact	.823	.869	.849
events	.525	.636	.575
framework	.447	.568	.500
links	.471	.421	.444
news	.539	.560	.549
objectives	.603	.734	.662
project	.799	.789	.794
publications	.761	.761	.761
staff	.500	.807	.617
Average	.608	.683	.639
Baseline			.240

Table 5.18: Results of SVM classification and included segments for the web-genre: project website

compared. Their approaches primarily deal with a much broader and diverse thematic subject area, such as *FAQs* and *Search Engine Pages*. The differences in corpus collection are of vital importance. Nonetheless, we have proposed two different methods for the task of web genre identification by means of a two-level web document representation model. Our analysis reveals that by the exploration and categorization of restrained hypertext segments, we were able to classify over 90% of the used documents correctly when using the proposed *bag-of-stages* approach. Therefore, we can argue that the proposed solution for a web genre classification goes beyond the focus of the traditional approaches of hypertext categorization by the consideration of structural properties of web documents above the level of the logical document structure – but as authored by the user.

Classes	Recall	Precision	F-Measure
conference	.640	.640	.640
personal	.618	.627	.622
project	.620	.608	.614
Average	.626	.625	.625
Baseline			.428

Table 5.19: Results of hypertext type classification using stemmed token features using the hypertext stage grammar model

Classes	Recall	Precision	F-Measure
conference	.894	.919	.906
personal	.917	.941	.929
project	.930	.923	.927
Average	.914	.928	.920
Baseline			.428

Table 5.20: Results of hypertext type classification using bag-of-stages approach with stemmed token attributes and enhanced named entity recognition.

Chapter 6

Conclusion

In this thesis we analyzed the performance of *Social Semantics in Information Retrieval*. By means of collaboratively built knowledge derived from social networks, inducing both common-sense and domain-specific knowledge constructed by a multitude of users, we could improve existing tasks within different areas of information retrieval.

This work connected the concepts and the methods of social networks [189] and the semantic web [228] to support the analysis of a social semantic web [28] that combines human intelligence with machine learning and natural language processing. In this context, social networks (as instances of the social web) were not only capable of delivering social network data and document collections on a tremendous scale, but also induced a wealth of (collaborative constructed) knowledge, which could not have been achieved by traditional expert resources. In this regard, we can argue that the technologies of the semantic web supported the aggregation of information across variously knowledge repositories, and profited by the user-generated (crowd-source) information tuples and annotated metadata [208, 209, 298].

Following the idea that the internet is a *"Web of Data"* as stated by Berners-Lee et al. [20] or *"Data is the Next Intel Inside"* as shaped by O'Reilly [228] – and the notion that information on the web needs to be primarily converted into a machine readable format (think of RDF) – the question of an automatic conversion, annotation and processing was central to the debate of the benefits of the social semantic web.

We have therefore asked the question, which kind of technologies and methods were available, adequate and contributed to the processing of this rapidly rising flood of information. While Section 3.2 described the issues and problems due to the knowledge acquisition bottleneck when building content models, we proposed in the subsequent sections how to overcome the problem of data sparsity of the traditional bag-of-words approach (Section 3.2.2) by inducing a concept space of external knowledge (Section 3.3.2). Hence, in Section 3.4 we proposed the method in constructing the *Social Semantic Vectors* (SSV) representation, inducing the most distinctive document collection of social networks, instantiated by the electronic encyclopaedia *Wikipedia*, as a concept-based knowledge repository. Therefore, we used hierarchically organized (social) knowledge, comprising article and category information, as a resource for aggregating semantically-related topic concepts (Section 3.2.1).

In Section 4.1, we analyzed the quality of the SSV feature space by means of a comprehensive comparative study on semantic relatedness. That is, we utilized the constructed feature representation as a resource for aggregating frequency scores of associated concepts. Moreover, we presented a novel technique (Section 4.1.2) for assessing the semantic relatedness of word pairs, but also for text pairs by automatic means. In comparison to sixteen other approaches, utilizing two different languages, we could achieve notable improvements ($r = 0.64 - 0.75$) with respect to the correlation of three different human judgement experiments. In addition, in contrast to the *Latent Semantic Analysis* and other graph-based measures (e. g. applied to *GermaNet* and *WordNet*), we could reduce both the complexity and the cost of resource construction by using social ontologies.

In Section 4.2.4, we approached the problem of topic identification on *Open Topic Models*. In this context, we assigned for a given text fragment, the best fitting topic labels obtained from a social ontology. Content categories themselves were aggregated by the constantly growing social ontology itself. We presented a method of topic generalization (Section 4.2.2), which utilizes the hierarchical property of a social ontology in order to predict different topics within a certain generalization scale. We have evaluated the proposed method on the basis of two different corpora, each comprising $1,000$ articles and 10 categories. The achieved performance with an average accuracy ranging from

0.66 to 0.92 could be identified as a valuable contribution to the domain of topic identification.

Based on the findings of the TI model, we employed the SSV as a topic-based feature generator to enhance the existing document representation within a closed topic identification setup (Section 4.3). We systematically evaluated the performance of topic-orientated feature enhancement to the task of text categorization by means of *Closed Topic Models*. The results showed that feature enhancement contributes to the classification process, increasing both accuracy and coverage (Section 4.3.2). We analyzed the performance of the proposed topic-enhanced SVM implementation by using a large corpus of 29,086 documents comprising 30 categories. In comparison to the best LSA-clustering technique, we could identify a significant improvement of 45%, with respect to the traditional SVM implementation, we could achieve with an F1-Measure of 0.92 an improvement of 9.45%. With respect to the classification of OAI-PMH records, we were able to improve the classification accuracy by 9.10%. The experiments clearly indicated that a social network-induced topic enhancement influences significantly the positive performance of text processing applications, and circumvents the data sparseness problem of traditional BOW approaches even under the condition of operating with a minimum amount of textual information.

In Section 5, we applied the methodology of our social semantics definition to three different task within the field of information retrieval. We therefore used external knowledge, as constructed by an online community, to improve retrieval components within the domain of IR. In Section 5.1, we proposed a novel method for the task of *Named Entity Recognition* (NER). We focused not only on identifying a proper name within a text, but also performed a disambiguation of the respective entity. In the line of the methodology of this thesis, we constructed an enhanced context representation – concept cloud – around the entity itself, in order to improve the NER classification performance. With resultant accuracy values of 0.55 − 0.98, we could identify that our notion of social semantics contributes to the exposure of semantic interrelations between detected NEs and their hold instances.

Subsequently, in Section 5.2 we applied the feature generation methodology to the domain of *Sentiment Analysis*. By that, polarity-related features were constructed using a social network of term definitions as a subjectivity dictionary. Extracted polarity descriptors were used to build a sentiment-enhanced document representation. In addition, with respect to the German language, we constructed a new subjectivity dictionary, *German Polarity Clues* (Section 5.2.3), as the first freely available resource of a German sentiment analysis.

We analyzed our proposed methods and resources to sentiment analysis within a comprehensive experimental setup, using two languages, two reference corpora and seven different subjectivity resources. While the results of the English-based sentiment-enhanced document representation yields only minor improvements (F1-Measure of 0.84), the results of the German experiments showed with an F1-Measure between 0.83 − 0.86 its good applicability.

In Section 5.3 of this thesis, we proposed a method in classifying *Closed Genre Models* by resizing the notion of hypertext subtypes. We analyzed the impact of textual, structural and subtype features for the task of web genre classification in a comprehensive evaluation setup. Our analysis revealed that by the exploration and categorization of restrained hypertext segments, as annotated by users, we were able to classify over 90% of the used documents correctly, when using the proposed bag-of-segments approach.

Currently, content and information on the web is primarily prepared especially for the users using markup and other document formats, which are effectual to human cognition. However, in order to convert the web of data also in a machine (processing) understandable format, as of a decentralized knowledge repository, it is necessary to induce meta-information as syntax and context information at a semantic level [181], which is not explicitly present. By the processing and expression of the user-centered meaning of data, this research focused on adding the actual semantics in the semantic web, and to improve the standardized exchange between application and humans. Moreover, we focused on the aspects to express the semantics of structured and semi-structured information that support the communication between human and technology [28].

As information retrieval deals with accessing a comprehensive amount of data, the techniques derived from the web- and text mining contributed significantly to support the improvement of a human-machine interaction. In this thesis, we set the focus on the methods, techniques and application-oriented analysis within the field of information retrieval that enabled us to identify and extract semantic information of textual units, rather than to annotate metadata tuples using RDF or OWL markup. We therefore set the methodology and instruments to derive the needed semantic meta information out of text- and web documents at the center. Moreover, we set an emphasis on the exploration of the effect of collective constructed knowledge in combination with statistical methods of information processing derived from the text- and web mining domain in order to improve the accuracy performance within selected areas of information retrieval. We could clearly show that significant improvements can be achieved by incorporating collaborative knowledge as a stimulus for building concept-enhanced document models.

6.1 Outlook

We believe that the contributions of this thesis represents a valuable step towards the demand of an automatic-driven identification of semantic units and meta data in texts and web documents. However, the current study can only be seen as the beginning of what is potentially possible when incorporating information and ontology structures derived from social networks and online communities. With the exponential growth of the World Wide Web, social knowledge might also be useful to develop new algorithms and methods for other information retrieval tasks such as within the collaborative image tagging (e.g. identifying and annotating objects in images), the question answering area or for the construction of automated decision-support systems. In the present form, our methods can be applied towards the improvement of an existing document representation of (written) textual elements within classification tasks. However, in the future it would be of interest how to apply the methodology to spoken language, as we incorporate instances such as conversational agents or interactive robot systems [333].

Can collaborative knowledge improve the interaction of human and (social) software agents? For instance, detecting the emerging topic during a conversation, or providing background information - as a constructed feedback - to a specific mentioned object. It might be the incorporation of social knowledge that will help to shape a closer and more human centered communication

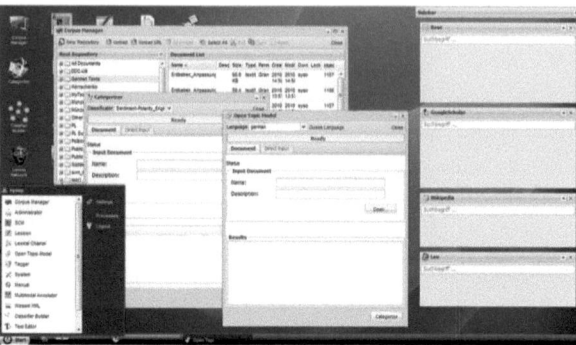

Figure 6.1: Screenshot of the eHumanities Desktop

within human-machine dialog systems [335]. Another direction for further research might be to apply the methodology to the phenomenon of semantic entailment [73]. That is, determining whether the meaning of a text fragment entails that of another (e. g. *For Chancellor Angela Merkel, selling the German public on the countries nearly $30 billion share of the bailout deal for Greece may prove even harder ...* ↦ *Chancellor Angela Merkel tries to persuade Germans on bailout.*) We believe that with the incorporation of collaboratively constructed resources, the ability to abstract and generalize over the semantic but also syntactic variability of natural language will be enabled. Social ontologies, as a unified knowledge representation, can thereby provide the hierarchical encoding of the relational and semantic properties to induce information from raw text and support a semantic inference which helps to improve natural language understanding applications. With respect to the applicability of the methods and results of this thesis, we could implement at present the majority of algorithms as proposed in this work in a developed[1] web-based desktop environment - the *eHumanities Desktop*[2] [97, 98, 205]. The main goal of this software system (see Figure 6.1) is to enable researchers in the humanities to work and process their resources online. It aims to combine

---

[1] The software systems of the *eHumanities Desktop* has been engineered by a number of software developer of the Working Group *Text Technology* at Bielefeld University and Goethe University Frankfurt am Main. The author of this thesis is a member of the software engineering team.

[2] http://hudesktop.hucompute.org/

methods and algorithms from the computer science domain with an intuitive user interface. The developed online application offers thereby not only to collaboratively work on shared resources, as constructing collaboratively corpora or annotating data, but also enables to apply the algorithms and text analysis methods, as proposed in this thesis, directly to the users need.

Bibliography

[1] Nist 2007 automatic content extraction evaluation official results. http://www.aclweb.org/anthology/D/D07/D07-1073 [accessed May 25, 2010], 2007.

[2] Karl Aberer, Philippe C. Mauroux, Aris M. Ouksel, Tiziana Catarci, Mohand S. Hacid, Arantza Illarramendi, Vipul Kashyap, Massimo Mecella, Eduardo Mena, Erich J. Neuhold, and Et. Emergent semantics principles and issues. In *Database Systems for Advances Applications (DASFAA 2004), Proceedings*, pages 25–38. Springer, March 2004.

[3] Apoorv Agarwal, Fadi Biadsy, and Kathleen McKeown. Contextual phrase-level polarity analysis using lexical affect scoring and syntactic n-grams. In *EACL2009*, Athens, Greece, 2009.

[4] Harith Alani, Martin Szomszor, Ciro Cattuto, Wouter Van den Broeck, Gianluca Correndo, and Alain Barrat. Live social semantics. In *International Semantic Web Conference*, pages 698–714, 2009.

[5] James Allan, editor. *Topic detection and tracking: event-based information organization*. Kluwer Academic Publishers, Norwell, MA, USA, 2002. ISBN 0-7923-7664-1.

[6] Keith Allan. *Natural Language Semantics*. Wiley-Blackwell, 2001. ISBN 978-0631192978.

[7] John R. Anderson. A spreading activation theory of memory. *Journal of Verbal Leaning and Verbal Behaviour*, 22:261–295, 1983.

[8] Stephan Bloehdorn Andreas and Andreas Hotho. Boosting for text classification with semantic features. In *In Proceedings of the MSW 2004*

Workshop at the 10th ACM SIGKDD Conference on Knowledge Discovery and Data Mining, pages 70–87, 2004.

[9] Christine Thielen Anne Schiller, Simone Teufel and Christine Stöckert. Vorläufige guidelines für das taggen deutscher textcorpora mit stts. Technical Report IMS-95, Universität Stuttgart, 1995.

[10] Michelle Annett and Grzegorz Kondrak. A comparison of sentiment analysis techniques: Polarizing movie blogs. In *Canadian Conference on AI*, pages 25–35, 2008.

[11] S. Auer, C. Bizer, J. Lehmann, G. Kobilarov, R. Cyganiak, and Z. Ives. Dbpedia: A nucleus for a web of open data. In *Proceedings of the 6th International Semantic Web Conference and 2nd Asian Semantic Web Conference (ISWC/ASWC2007)*, 2007. URL http://www.aclweb.org/anthology-new/W/W06/W06-3812.pdf.

[12] Ricardo Baeza-Yates and Berthier Ribeiro-Neto. *Modern Information Retrieval*. Addison Wesley, May 1999.

[13] Douglas L. Baker and Andrew K. Mccallum. Distributional clustering of words for text classification. In Bruce W. Croft, Alistair Moffat, Cornelis J. van Rijsbergen, Ross Wilkinson, and Justin Zobel, editors, *Proceedings of SIGIR-98, 21st ACM International Conference on Research and Development in Information Retrieval*, pages 96–103, Melbourne, AU, 1998. ACM Press, New York, US.

[14] Jan Bakus and Mohamed S. Kamel. Higher order feature selection for text classification. *Knowl. Inf. Syst.*, 9(4):468–491, 2006.

[15] D. T. Barnard, L. Burnard, S. J. DeRose, D. G. Durand, and C. M. Sperberg-McQueen. Lessons for the www from the tei. In *Proc. of the 4th Int. WWW Conf.*, Boston, Massachusetts, 1995.

[16] Christian Becker-Asano and Ipke Wachsmuth. Affective computing with primary and secondary emotions in a virtual human. *Autonomous Agents and Multi-Agent Systems*, 20(1):32–49, 2010. ISSN 1387-2532.

[17] Paul N. Bennett, Susan T. Dumais, and Eric Horvitz. Inductive transfer for text classification by using generalized reliability. In *Proceedings of the ICML-2003 Workshop on*, 2003.

[18] Ansgar Bernardi, Stefan Decker, Ludger van Elst, Gunnar Grimnes, Tudor Groza, Siegfried Handschuh Mehdi Jazayeri, Cedric Mesnage, Knud Moeller, Gerald Reif, and Michael Sintek. *The Social Semantic Desktop: A New Paradigm Towards Deploying the Semantic Web on the Desktop.* IGI Global, October 2008. ISBN 978-1-60566-112-4.

[19] T. Berners-Lee. *Weaving the Web.* Orion Business Books, 2000.

[20] Tim Berners-Lee, James Hendler, and Ora Lassila. The Semantic Web. *Scientific American*, 284(5):34–43, 2001.

[21] M. Berthold and D. Hand. Intelligent data analysis. *Springer-Verlag*, 1999.

[22] C. Biemann, U. Quasthoff, G. Heyer, and F. Holz. ASV Toolbox – A Modular Collection of Language Exploration Tools. In *Proceedings of the 6th Language Resources and Evaluation Conference (LREC) 2008*, 2008.

[23] Chris Biemann, Sa-Im Shin, and Key-Sun Choi. Semiautomatic extension of corenet using a bootstrapping mechanism on corpus-based co-occurrences. In *COLING '04: Proceedings of the 20th international conference on Computational Linguistics*, page 1227, Morristown, NJ, USA, 2004. Association for Computational Linguistics. doi: http://dx.doi.org/10.3115/1220355.1220533.

[24] Christian Biemann. Extraktion von semantischen relationen aus natürlichsprachlichem text mit hilfe von maschinellem lernen. *LDV Forum*, 18(1/2):12–25, 2003.

[25] Christian Biemann, Stefan Bordag, Gerhard Heyer, Uwe Quasthoff, and Christian Wolff. Language-independent methods for compiling monolingual lexical data. In *CICLing*, pages 217–228, 2004.

[26] David M. Blei, Andrew Y. Ng, and Michael I. Jordan. Latent dirichlet allocation. *Journal of machine Learning Research*, 3:993–1022, 2003.

[27] Avrim L. Blum and Pat Langley. Selection of relevant features and examples in machine learning. *Artif. Intell.*, 97(1-2):245–271, 1997.

[28] Andreas Blumauer and Tassilo Pellegrini, editors. *Social Semantic Web: Web 2.0 - Was nun?* X.media.press. Springer, 2009. ISBN 978-3-540-72215-1.

[29] Andreas Blumauer and Tassilo Pellegrini. Semantic web revisited - eine kurze einführung in das social semantic web. In *Social Semantic Web*, pages 3–22. 2009.

[30] Robert Blumberg and Shaku Atre. Automatic classification: Moving to the mainstream. *Information Management Magazine*, 2003.

[31] J. Boyd-Graber, C. Fellbaum, D. Osherson, and R. Schapire. Adding dense, weighted, connections to wordnet. In *Proceedings of the 3rd Global WordNet Meeting*, pages 29–35, 2006.

[32] Thorsten Brants. Tnt – a statistical part-of-speech tagger. In *Proceedings of the Sixth Conference on Applied Natural Language Processing*, pages 224–231, Seattle, Washington, USA, April 2000. Association for Computational Linguistics. doi: 10.3115/974147.974178. URL http://www.aclweb.org/anthology/A00-1031.

[33] Simone Braun, Claudiu Schora, and Valentin Zacharias. Semantics to the bookmarks: A review of social semantic bookmarking systems. In *International Conference on Semantic Systems (I-SEMANTICS 2009), Graz, Austria*, pages 445–454, 2009.

[34] Eric Brill. A simple rule-based part of speech tagger. In *Proceedings of the Third Conference on Applied Natural Language Processing*, pages 152–155, 1992.

[35] Eric Brill. Transformation-based error-driven learning and natural language processing: a case study in part-of-speech tagging. *Comput. Linguist.*, 21(4):543–565, 1995. ISSN 0891-2017.

[36] Alexander Budanitsky and Graeme Hirst. Semantic distance in wordnet: An experimental, application-oriented evaluation of five measures. In *Workshop on WordNet and Other Lexical Resources (NAACL2000)*, 2001.

[37] Alexander Budanitsky and Graeme Hirst. Evaluating wordnet-based measures of semantic relatedness. *Computational Linguistics*, 32 (1): 13–47, 2006.

[38] Razvan C. Bunescu and Marius Pasca. Using encyclopedic knowledge for named entity disambiguation. In *EACL*. The Association for Computer Linguistics, 2006.

[39] Cody Burleson. Introduction to the semantic web vision. http://www.semanticfocus.com/ [accessed May 25, 2010], 2007.

[40] Lou Burnard. New tricks from an old dog: An overview of TEI P5. In Lou Burnard, Milena Dobreva, Norbert Fuhr, and Anke Lüdeling, editors, *Digital Historical Corpora- Architecture, Annotation, and Retrieval*, number 06491 in Dagstuhl Seminar Proceedings. Internationales Begegnungs- und Forschungszentrum fuer Informatik (IBFI), Schloss Dagstuhl, Germany, 2007.

[41] Guido Caldarelli. *Scale-Free Networks: Complex Webs in Nature and Technology (Oxford Finance)*. Oxford University Press, USA, June 2007. ISBN 0199211515.

[42] Maria Fernanda Caropreso, Stan Matwin, and Fabrizio Sebastiani. A learner-independent evaluation of the usefulness of statistical phrases for automated text categorization. *Text databases and document management: theory and practice*, pages 78–102, 2001.

[43] Ciro Cattuto, Christoph Schmitz, Andrea Baldassarri, Vito Servedio, Vittorio Loreto, Andreas Hotho, Miranda Grahl, and Gerd Stumme. Network properties of folksonomies. *AI Commun.*, 20(4):245–262, 2007. ISSN 0921-7126.

[44] William B. Cavnar and John M. Trenkle. N-gram-based text categorization. In *In Proceedings of SDAIR-94, 3rd Annual Symposium on Document Analysis and Information Retrieval*, pages 161–175, 1994.

[45] Scott Cederberg and Dominic Widdows. Using lsa and noun coordination information to improve the precision and recall of automatic hyponymy extraction. In *Proceedings of the seventh conference on Natural language learning at HLT-NAACL 2003*, pages 111–118, Morristown, NJ, USA, 2003. Association for Computational Linguistics.

[46] Soumen Chakrabarti. *Mining the Web: Discovering Knowledge from Hypertext Data*. Morgan-Kauffman, 2002. ISBN ISBN 1-55860-754-4.

[47] Soumen Chakrabarti. *Mining the Web: Analysis of Hypertext and Semi Structured Data*. Morgan Kaufmann, August 2002.

[48] David Chandler. *Introduction to Modern Statistical Mechanics*. Oxford University Press, 1987.

[49] Pimwadee Chaovalit and Lina Zhou. Movie review mining: a comparison between supervised and unsupervised classification approaches. *Hawaii ICSS*, 4, 2005.

[50] Eugene Charniak, Curtis Hendrickson, Neil Jacobson, and Mike Perkowitz. Equations for part-of-speech tagging. In *Proceedings of the Eleventh National Conference on Artificial Intelligence*, pages 784–789, 1993.

[51] Namyoun Choi, Il-Yeol Song, and Hyoil Han. A survey on ontology mapping. *SIGMOD Rec.*, 35(3):34–41, 2006. ISSN 0163-5808.

[52] Rudi Cilibrasi and Paul Vitanyi. Automatic meaning discovery using google. In *Manuscript, CWI, 2004; http://arxiv.org/abs/cs.CL/0412098*, 2004.

[53] Rudi Cilibrasi and Paul M. B. Vitanyi. The google similarity distance. *IEEE Transactions on Knowledge and Data Engineering*, 19:370, 2007.

[54] Guillaume Cleuziou, Lionel Martin, Viviane Clavier, and Christel Vrain. Ddoc: Overlapping clustering of words for document classification. In *SPIRE*, pages 127–128, 2004.

[55] A.M. Collins and E.F. Loftus. A spreading activation theory of semantic processing. *Psychological Review*, 82:407–428, 1975.

[56] Michael Collins and Yoram Singer. Unsupervised models for named entity classification. In *Proceedings of the Joint SIGDAT Conference on Empirical Methods in Natural Language Processing and Very Large Corpora*, pages 100–110, 1999.

[57] Rui A. Costa and João Barros. Network information flow in small world networks. *CoRR*, abs/cs/0612099, 2006.

[58] Kristof Coussement and Dirk Van den Poel. Churn prediction in subscription services: An application of support vector machines while comparing two parameter-selection techniques. *EXPERT SYSTEMS WITH APPLICATIONS*, 34(1):313–327, 2008. ISSN 0957-4174.

[59] Irene Cramer. How Well Do Semantic Relatedness Measures Perform? A Meta-Study. In Johan Bos and Rodolfo Delmonte, editors, *Semantics in Text Processing. STEP 2008 Conference Proceedings*, volume 1 of *Research in Computational Semantics*, pages 59–70. College Publications, 2008. URL http://www.aclweb.org/anthology/W08-2206.

[60] Irene Cramer and Marc Finthammer. An evaluation procedure for word net based lexical chaining: Methods and issues. In *Proceedings of the 4th Global WordNet Meeting*, pages 120–147, 2008.

[61] Fabio Crestani and Mounia Lalmas. Logic and uncertainty in information retrieval. *Lectures on information retrieval*, pages 179–206, 2001.

[62] Fabio Crestani, Ian Ruthven, Mark Sanderson, and C. J. van Rijsbergen. The troubles with using a logical model of ir on a large collection of documents. In *TREC*, 1995.

[63] Nello Cristianini and John Shawe-Taylor. *An Introduction to Support Vector Machines and Other Kernel-based Learning Methods*. Cambridge University Press, March 2000. ISBN 0521780195.

[64] Nello Cristianini, John Shawe-Taylor, and Huma Lodhi. Latent semantic kernels. In *ICML*, pages 66–73, 2001.

[65] W. B. Croft and D. J. Harper. Using probabilistic models of document retrieval without relevance information. *Document retrieval systems*, pages 161–171, 1988.

[66] Silviu Cucerzan. Large-scale named entity disambiguation based on Wikipedia data. In *Proceedings of the 2007 Joint Conference on Empirical Methods in Natural Language Processing and Computational Natural Language Learning (EMNLP-CoNLL)*, pages 708–716, 2007. URL http://www.aclweb.org/anthology/D/D07/D07-1074.

[67] Philippe Cudré-Mauroux. Emergent semantics. In *Encyclopedia of Database Systems*, pages 982–985. 2009.

[68] Hamish Cunningham, Kalina Bontcheva, Valentin Tablan, and Diana Maynard. Gate - a general architecture for text engineering. http://gate.ac.uk/ [accessed May 25, 2010], 2007.

[69] Wenyuan Dai, Gui-Rong Xue, Qiang Yang, and Yong Yu. Transferring naive bayes classifiers for text classification. In *AAAI'07: Proceedings of the 22nd national conference on Artificial intelligence*, pages 540–545. AAAI Press, 2007. ISBN 978-1-57735-323-2.

[70] Anirban Dasgupta, Petros Drineas, Boulos Harb, Vanja Josifovski, and Michael W. Mahoney. Feature selection methods for text classification. In *KDD '07: Proceedings of the 13th ACM SIGKDD international conference on Knowledge discovery and data mining*, pages 230–239, New York, NY, USA, 2007. ACM. ISBN 978-1-59593-609-7.

[71] Kushal Dave, Steve Lawrence, and David M. Pennock. Mining the peanut gallery: opinion extraction and semantic classification of product reviews. In *Proc. of WWW '03*, pages 519–528. ACM Press, 2003.

[72] Dmitry Davidov, Evgeniy Gabrilovich, and Shaul Markovitch. Parameterized generation of labeled datasets for text categorization based on a hierarchical directory. In *SIGIR '04: Proceedings of the 27th annual international ACM SIGIR conference on Research and development in information retrieval*, pages 250–257, New York, NY, USA, 2004. ACM. ISBN 1-58113-881-4.

[73] Rodrigo De Salvo Braz, Roxana Girju, Vasin Punyakanok, Dan Roth, and Mark Sammons. An inference model for semantic entailment in natural language. In *AAAI'05: Proceedings of the 20th national conference on Artificial intelligence*, pages 1043–1049. AAAI Press, 2005. ISBN 1-57735-236-x.

[74] S. Deerwester, S. Dumais, T. Landauer, G. Furnas, and R. Harshman. Indexing by Latent Semantic Analysis. *Journal of the American Society of Information Science*, 41(6):391–407, 1990.

[75] Kerstin Denecke. Using sentiwordnet for multilingual sentiment analysis. In *ICDE Workshops*, pages 507–512. IEEE Computer Society, 2008.

[76] Inderjit Dhillon, Subramanyam Mallela, Rahul Kumar, Subramanyam Mallela, Isabelle Guyon, and Andre Elisseeff. A divisive information-theoretic feature clustering algorithm for text classification. *Journal of Machine Learning Research*, 3:2003, 2003.

[77] Kaibo Duan, S. Sathiya Keerthi, and Aun Neow Poo. Evaluation of simple performance measures for tuning svm hyperparameters. *Neurocomputing*, 51:41–59, 2003.

[78] Sven Meyer Zu Eissen and Benno Stein. Genre classification of web pages: User study and feasibility analysis. In *In: Biundo S., Fruhwirth T., Palm G. (eds.): Advances in Artificial Intelligence*, pages 256–269. Springer, 2004.

[79] Asif Ekbal and Sivaji Bandyopadhyay. A hidden markov model based named entity recognition system: Bengali and hindi as case studies. In *Pattern Recognition and Machine Intelligence, Second International*

Conference, PReMI 2007, Kolkata, India, December 18-22, 2007, Proceedings, pages 545–552, 2007.

[80] Asif Ekbal and Sivaji Bandyopadhyay. Part of speech tagging in bengali using support vector machine. In *ICIT '08: Proceedings of the 2008 International Conference on Information Technology*, pages 106–111, Washington, DC, USA, 2008. IEEE Computer Society. ISBN 978-0-7695-3513-5. doi: http://dx.doi.org/10.1109/ICIT.2008.12.

[81] Andrea Esuli and Fabrizio Sebastiani. Sentiwordnet: A publicly available lexical resource for opinion mining. In *In Proc. of the LREC-06*, pages 417–422, 2006.

[82] Tom Elliott Fawcett. *Feature discovery for problem solving systems*. PhD thesis, Amherst, MA, USA, 1993.

[83] Christiane Fellbaum, editor. *WordNet. An Electronic Lexical Database*. The MIT Press, 1998.

[84] Ludovic Ferrand and Boris New. Semantic and associative priming in the mental lexicon. pages 25–43, 2003.

[85] Lev Finkelstein, Evgeniy Gabrilovich, Yossi Matias, Ehud Rivlin, Zach Solan, Gadi Wolfman, and Eytan Ruppin. Placing search in context: the concept revisited. In *WWW*, pages 406–414, 2001.

[86] Aidan Finn and Nicholas Kushmerick. Learning to classify documents according to genre: Special topic section on computational analysis of style. *J. Am. Soc. Inf. Sci. Technol.*, 57(11):1506–1518, 2006. ISSN 1532-2882. doi: http://dx.doi.org/10.1002/asi.v57:11.

[87] Marc Finthammer and Irene Cramer. Exploring and navigating: Tools for germanet. In *Proceedings of the 6th Language Resources and Evaluation Conference*, 2008.

[88] Norbert Fuhr. Probabilistic models in information retrieval. *The Computer Journal*, 35:243–255, 1992.

[89] Gabrilovich and Markovitch. Overcoming the brittleness bottleneck using wikipedia: Enhancing text categorization with encyclopedic knowledge. *Proceedings of the Twenty-First National Conference on Artificial Intelligence, Boston, MA*, 2006.

[90] Evgeniy Gabrilovich. Feature generation for textual information retrieval using world knowledge. *SIGIR Forum*, 41(2):123–123, 2007. ISSN 0163-5840. doi: http://doi.acm.org/10.1145/1328964.1328988.

[91] Evgeniy Gabrilovich and Shaul Markovitch. Feature generation for text categorization using world knowledge. In *Proceedings of The Nineteenth International Joint Conference for Artificial Intelligence*, pages 1048–1053, Edinburgh, Scotland, 2005.

[92] Evgeniy Gabrilovich and Shaul Markovitch. Computing Semantic Relatedness using Wikipedia-based Explicit Semantic Analysis. *Proceedings of the 20th International Joint Conference on Artificial Intelligence*, pages 6–12, 2007.

[93] Luigi Galavotti, Fabrizio Sebastiani, and Maria Simi. Experiments on the use of feature selection and negative evidence in automated text categorization. In *ECDL '00: Proc. of the 4th European Conf. on Res. and Adv. Tech. for DL*, pages 59–68, London, UK, 2000. Springer-Verlag. ISBN 3-540-41023-6.

[94] Aldo Gangemi, Roberto Navigli, and Paola Velardi. The ontowordnet project: extension and axiomatization of conceptual relations in wordnet. In *WordNet, Meersman*, pages 3–7. Springer, 2003.

[95] Bin Gao, Tie-Yan Liu, Guang Feng, Tao Qin, Qian-Sheng Cheng, and Wei-Ying Ma. Hierarchical taxonomy preparation for text categorization using consistent bipartite spectral graph copartitioning. *IEEE Transactions on Knowledge and Data Engineering*, 17(9):1263–1273, 2005. ISSN 1041-4347.

[96] Dan Geiger, Moises Goldszmidt, G. Provan, P. Langley, and P. Smyth. Bayesian network classifiers. In *Machine Learning*, pages 131–163, 1997.

[97] Rüdiger Gleim, Alexander Mehler, Ulli Waltinger, and Olga Pustylnikov. ehumanities desktop — an extensible online system for corpus management and analysis. In *5th Corpus Linguistics Conference, University of Liverpool*. 2009.

[98] Rüdiger Gleim, Ulli Waltinger, Alexandra Ernst, Alexander Mehler, Tobias Feith, and Dietmar Esch. eHumanities Desktop - an online system for corpus management and analysis in support of computing in the humanities. In *Proceedings of the Demonstrations Session at EACL 2009*, pages 21–24, Athens, Greece, April 2009. Association for Computational Linguistics.

[99] Teresa Gonçalves and Paulo Quaresma. Enhancing a portuguese text classifier using part-of-speech tags. In *Intelligent Information Systems*, pages 189–198, 2005.

[100] Gregory Grefenstette and Pasi Tapanainen. What is a word, what is a sentence? problems of tokenization. Technical Report MLTT-004, Xerox Research Centre Europe, MLTT, 1994.

[101] Thomas R. Gruber. Toward principles for the design of ontologies used for knowledge sharing. *Int. J. Hum.-Comput. Stud.*, 43(5-6):907–928, 1995. ISSN 1071-5819. doi: http://dx.doi.org/10.1006/ijhc.1995.1081.

[102] R. Guha, Rob McCool, and Eric Miller. Semantic search. In *WWW '03: Proceedings of the 12th international conference on World Wide Web*, pages 700–709, New York, NY, USA, 2003. ACM.

[103] Rakesh Gupta and Lev Ratinov. Text categorization with knowledge transfer from heterogeneous data sources. In *AAAI'08: Proceedings of the 23rd national conference on Artificial intelligence*, pages 842–847. AAAI Press, 2008. ISBN 978-1-57735-368-3.

[104] Iryna Gurevych. Using the structure of a conceptual network in computing semantic relatedness. In *Proceedings of the IJCNLP 2005*, pages 767–778, 2005.

[105] Iryna Gurevych and Thade Nahnsen. Adapting lexical chaining to summarize conversational dialogues. In *Proc. of the Recent Advances in Natural Language Processing Conference (RANLP 2005)*, 2005.

[106] Kat Hagedorn, Suzanne Chapman, and David Newman. Enhancing search and browse using automated clustering of subject metadata. *D-Lib Magazine*, 13(7), 2007.

[107] Xianpei Han and Jun Zhao. Named entity disambiguation by leveraging wikipedia semantic knowledge. In *CIKM '09: Proceeding of the 18th ACM conference on Information and knowledge management*, pages 215–224, New York, NY, USA, 2009. ACM. ISBN 978-1-60558-512-3.

[108] Zellig S. Harris. Distributional structure. *Word*, 10:146–162, 1954.

[109] Vasileios Hatzivassiloglou and Kathleen R. McKeown. Predicting the semantic orientation of adjectives. In *Proc. of the eighth EACL*, pages 174–181. ACL, 1997.

[110] Patrick Hayes. Rdf semantics. http://www.w3.org/TR/2004/REC-rdf-mt-20040210/ [accessed May 25, 2010], 2004.

[111] Martin Hepp, Pieter De Leenheer, Aldo de Moor, and York Sure, editors. *Ontology Management, Semantic Web, Semantic Web Services, and Business Applications*, volume 7 of *Semantic Web And Beyond Computing for Human Experience*. Springer, 2008.

[112] Brekle Herbert. *Semantik: Eine Einfuehrung in die sprachwissenschaftliche Bedeutungslehre*. Fink, 1972. ISBN 3-7705-0635-9.

[113] Ivan Herman. W3c semantic web activity. http://www.w3.org/2001/sw/ [accessed May 25, 2010], 2001.

[114] Gerhard Heyer, Uwe Quasthoff, and Thomas Wittig. *Text Mining: Wissensrohstoff Text – Konzepte, Algorithmen, Ergebnisse*. W3L-Verlag, 2003.

[115] Gerhard Heyer, Florian Holz, and Sven Teresniak. Change of topics over time and tracking topics by their change of meaning. In *KDIR '09:*

Proc. of Int. Conf. on Knowledge Discovery and Information Retrieval, October 2009.

[116] T. Hill and P. Lewicki. Statistics methods and applications. *StatSoft*, 2006.

[117] Graeme Hirst and David St-Onge. Lexical chains as representation of context for the detection and correction malapropisms. In Christiane Fellbaum, editor, *WordNet: An Electronic Lexical Database*, pages 305–332. The MIT Press, 1998.

[118] Andreas Hotho, Andreas Nürnberger, and Gerhard Paaß. A brief survey of text mining. *LDV-Forum, Journal for Computational Linguistics and Language Technology*, 20(1):19–62, 2005.

[119] Andreas Hotho, Robert Jäschke, Christoph Schmitz, and Gerd Stumme. Bibsonomy: A social bookmark and publication sharing system. In *Proceedings of the Conceptual Structures Tool Interoperability Workshop at the 14th International Conference on Conceptual Structures*, pages 87–102. Aalborg University Press, 2006.

[120] Minqing Hu and Bing Liu. Mining and summarizing customer reviews. In *Proc. of the tenth ACM SIGKDD KDD '04*, pages 168–177, New York, NY, USA, 2004. ACM.

[121] David Hull. Improving text retrieval for the routing problem using latent semantic indexing. In *SIGIR '94: Proceedings of the 17th annual international ACM SIGIR conference on Research and development in information retrieval*, pages 282–291, New York, NY, USA, 1994. Springer-Verlag New York, Inc. ISBN 0-387-19889-X.

[122] Nancy Ide and C. M. Sperberg-McQueen. The TEI: History, goals, and future. *Computers and the Humanities*, 29(1):5–15, 1995.

[123] Georgiana Ifrim, Martin Theobald, and Gerhard Weikum. Learning word-to-concept mappings for automatic text classification. In Luc De Raedt and Stefan Wrobel, editors, *Proceedings of the 22nd International Conference on Machine Learning - Learning in Web Search (LWS 2005)*, pages 18–26, Bonn, Germany, 2005. ISBN 1-59593-180-5.

[124] Wolfgang Lezius Ims and Wolfgang Lezius. Morphy – german morphology, part-of-speech tagging and applications. In *Proceedings of the 9th EURALEX International Congress*, pages 619–623, 2000.

[125] Hideki Isozaki and Hideto Kazawa. Efficient support vector classifiers for named entity recognition. In *Proceedings of the 19th international conference on Computational linguistics*, pages 1–7, Morristown, NJ, USA, 2002. Association for Computational Linguistics. doi: http://dx.doi.org/10.3115/1072228.1072282.

[126] T. Joachims. SVM light, http://svmlight.joachims.org, 2002.

[127] Thorsten Joachims. Text categorization with suport vector machines: Learning with many relevant features. In *ECML '98: Proceedings of the 10th European Conference on Machine Learning*, pages 137–142, London, UK, 1998. Springer-Verlag. ISBN 3-540-64417-2.

[128] Thorsten Joachims. Transductive inference for text classification using support vector machines. pages 200–209. Morgan Kaufmann, 1999.

[129] Thorsten Joachims. Making large-scale SVM learning practical. In B. Schölkopf, C. Burges, and A. Smola, editors, *Advances in Kernel Methods - Support Vector Learning*, chapter 11, pages 169–184. MIT Press, Cambridge, MA, 1999.

[130] Thorsten Joachims. *Learning to Classify Text using Support Vector Machines*. Kluwer, 2002.

[131] Thorsten Joachims, Nello Cristianini, and John Shawe-Taylor. Composite kernels for hypertext categorisation. In *Proc. of the 11th Int. Conf. on Machine Learning*, pages 250–257. Morgan Kaufmann, 2001.

[132] Karen Spärck Jones. A statistical interpretation of term specificity and its application in retrieval. *Journal of Documentation*, 28:11–21, 1972.

[133] Jussi Karlgren and Douglass Cutting. Recognizing text genres with simple metrics using discriminant analysis. In *Proc. of the 15th Conf. on CL*, pages 1071–1075. ACL, 1994.

[134] Jun'ichi Kazama and Kentaro Torisawa. Exploiting Wikipedia as external knowledge for named entity recognition. In *Proceedings of the 2007 Joint Conference on Empirical Methods in Natural Language Processing and Computational Natural Language Learning (EMNLP-CoNLL)*, pages 698–707, 2007. URL http://www.aclweb.org/anthology/D/D07/D07-1073.

[135] Frank Keller and Maria Lapata. Using the web to obtain frequencies for unseen bigrams. *Computational Linguistics*, pages 459–484, 2003.

[136] Alistair Kennedy and Diana Inkpen. Sentiment classification of movie reviews using contextual valence shifters. *Computational Intelligence*, 22(2):110–125, 2006.

[137] Brett Kessler, Geoffrey Numberg, and Hinrich Schütze. Automatic detection of text genre. In *ACL-35: Proceedings of the 35th Annual Meeting of the Association for Computational Linguistics and Eighth Conference of the European Chapter of the Association for Computational Linguistics*, pages 32–38, Morristown, NJ, USA, 1997. Association for Computational Linguistics. doi: http://dx.doi.org/10.3115/979617.979622.

[138] A. Kilgarriff. Googleology is bad science. *Computational Linguistics*, 33(1):147–151, 2007.

[139] Hyunsoo Kim, Peg Howland, and Haesun Park. Dimension reduction in text classification with support vector machines. *J. Mach. Learn. Res.*, 6:37–53, 2005.

[140] Svetlana Kiritchenko. *Hierarchical text categorization and its application to bioinformatics*. PhD thesis, Ottawa, Ont., Canada, Canada, 2006.

[141] Tibor Kiss and Jan Strunk. Scaled log likelihood ratios for the detection of abbreviations in text corpora. In *Proceedings of the 19th international conference on Computational linguistics*, pages 1–5, Morristown, NJ, USA, 2002. Association for Computational Linguistics.

[142] Tibor Kiss and Jan Strunk. Viewing sentence boundary detection as collocation identification. In *Proceedings of KONVENS 2002*, pages 75–82, Saarbrücken, Germany, 2002.

[143] Tibor Kiss and Jan Strunk. Unsupervised multilingual sentence boundary detection. *Comput. Linguist.*, 32(4):485–525, 2006. ISSN 0891-2017.

[144] Graham Klyne and Jeremy Carroll. Resource description framework (rdf): Concepts and abstract syntax. http://www.w3.org/TR/rdf-concepts/ [accessed May 25, 2010], 2004.

[145] Ron Kohavi and Foster Provost. Glossary of terms. In *Machine Learning*, pages 271–274. Kluwer Academic Publishers, Boston, 1998.

[146] Daphne Koller and Mehran Sahami. Toward optimal feature selection. In *International Conference on Machine Learning*, pages 284–292, 1996.

[147] Satoshi Sekine Kugatsu Sadamitsu and Mikio Yamamoto. Sentiment analysis based on probabilistic models using inter-sentence information. In Nicoletta Calzolari, editor, *Proc. of LREC'08*, Marrakech, Morocco, may 2008. European Language Resources Association (ELRA).

[148] W. Lam and Am. Segre. A distributed learning algorithm for bayesian inference networks. *IEEE Trans. on Knowl. and Data Eng.*, 14(1):93–105, 2002. ISSN 1041-4347.

[149] T. Landauer and S. Dumais. A solution to Plato's problem: The Latent Semantic Analysis theory of the acquisition, induction, and representation of knowledge. *Psychological Review*, 104(1):211–240, 1997.

[150] Claudia Leacock and Martin Chodorow. Combining local context and wordnet similarity for word sense identification. In Christiane Fellbaum, editor, *WordNet: An Electronic Lexical Database*, pages 265–284. The MIT Press, 1998.

[151] Changki Lee and Gary Geunbae Lee. Information gain and divergence-based feature selection for machine learning-based text categorization. *Inf. Process. Manage.*, 42(1):155–165, 2006.

[152] Yong-Bae Lee and Sung Hyon Myaeng. Text genre classification with genre-revealing and subject-revealing features. In *SIGIR '02: Proc. of the 25th Int. ACM SIGIR*, pages 145–150, New York, NY, USA, 2002. ACM.

[153] Yong-Bae Lee and Sung Hyon Myaeng. Automatic identification of text genres and their roles in subject-based categorization. In *HICSS '04: Proc. of the 37th HICSS'04*, page 40100.2, Washington, DC, USA, 2004. IEEE Computer Society. ISBN 0-7695-2056-1.

[154] Lothar Lemnitzer and Claudia Kunze. Germanet - representation, visualization, application. In *Proceedings of the 4th Language Resources and Evaluation Conference*, pages 1485–1491, 2002.

[155] Stefan Lessmann, Ming-Chien Sung, and Johnnie E.V. Johnson. Identifying winners of competitive events: A svm-based classification model for horserace prediction. *European Journal of Operational Research*, 196 (2):569–577, July 2009.

[156] Hang Li and Kenji Yamanishi. Topic analysis using a finite mixture model. *Inf. Process. Manage.*, 39(4):521–541, 2003. ISSN 0306-4573.

[157] M. Li, J. H. Badger, X. Chen, S. Kwong, P. Kearney, and H. Zhang. An information-based sequence distance and its application to whole mitochondrial genome phylogeny. *Bioinformatics*, 17(2):149–154, 2001.

[158] C. Lim, K. Lee, and G. Kim. Automatic genre detection of web documents. Springer, 2005.

[159] Dekang Lin. An information-theoretic definition of similarity. In *Proceedings of the 15th International Conference on Machine Learning*, pages 296–304, 1998.

[160] Christoph Lindemann and Lars Littig. Coarse-grained classification of web sites by their structural properties. In *Proc. of the 8th ACM - WIDM'06*, pages 35–42, New York, NY, USA, 2006. ACM Press. ISBN 1-59593-525-8.

[161] Bing Liu. Sentiment analysis and subjectivity. *Handbook of Natural Language Processing*, 2:568, 2010. ISSN 978-1-4200-8592-1.

[162] Tie-Yan LIU, Yiming YANG, Hao WAN, Qian ZHOU, Bin GAO, Hua-Jun ZENG, Zheng CHEN, and Wei-Ying MA. An experimental study on large-scale web categorization. In *WWW '05: Special interest tracks and*

posters of the 14th international conference on World Wide Web, pages 1106–1107, New York, NY, USA, 2005. ACM. ISBN 1-59593-051-5.

[163] Norbert Lossau. Search engine technology and digital libraries: Libraries need to discover the academic internet. *D-Lib Magazine*, 10(6), 2004.

[164] Jianguo Lu, John Mylopoulos, Masateru Harao, and Masami Hagiya. Higher order generalization and its application in program verification. *Annals of Mathematics and Artificial Intelligence*, 28(1-4):107–126, 2000. ISSN 1012-2443.

[165] Xinghua Lu, Bin Zheng, Atulya Velivelli, and Chengxiang Zhai. Enhancing text categorization with semantic-enriched representation and training data augmentation. In *J Am Med Inform Assoc*, pages 66–72, 2006.

[166] Apache Lucene. Apache lucene - a full-featured text search engine library. http://lucene.apache.org/ [accessed April 18, 2010], 2010.

[167] H. P. Luhn. The automatic creation of literature abstracts. *IBM Journal of Research and Development*, 2(2), 1958.

[168] K. Lund and C. Burgess. Producing high-dimensional semantic spaces from lexical co-occurrence. *Behaviour Research Methods, Instruments and Computers*, 28(2):203–208, 1996.

[169] Jaap Kamps Maarten, Maarten Marx, Robert J. Mokken, and Maarten De Rijke. Using wordnet to measure semantic orientations of adjectives. In *National Institute for*, pages 1115–1118, 2004.

[170] Rila Mandala, Takenobu Tokunaga, and Hozumi Tanaka. Improving information retrieval system performance by combining different text-mining techniques. *Intell. Data Anal.*, 4(6):489–511, 2000. ISSN 1088-467X.

[171] C. D. Manning, P. Raghavan, and H. Schütze. *Introduction to Information Retrieval*. Cambridge University Press, 2008.

[172] Christopher D. Manning and Hinrich Schütze. *Foundations of statistical natural language processing*. MIT Press, Cambridge, MA, USA, 1999. ISBN 0-262-13360-1.

[173] Alireza Mansouri, Lilly Suriani Affendy, and Ali Mamat. A new fuzzy support vector machine method for named entity recognition. In *ICCSIT '08: Proceedings of the 2008 International Conference on Computer Science and Information Technology*, pages 24–28, Washington, DC, USA, 2008. IEEE Computer Society. ISBN 978-0-7695-3308-7.

[174] Mitchell P. Marcus, Beatrice Santorini, and Mary A. Marcinkiewicz. Building a large annotated corpus of English: The Penn Treebank. *Computational Linguistics*, 19(2):313–330, 1993.

[175] Shaul Markovitch and Danny Rosenstein. Feature generation using general constructor functions. *Machine Learning*, 49:59–98, 2002.

[176] Lluís Màrquez, Lluís Padró, and Horacio Rodríguez. A machine learning approach to pos tagging. *Mach. Learn.*, 39(1):59–91, 2000. ISSN 0885-6125.

[177] David Martens, Bart Baesens, Tony Van Gestel, and Jan Vanthienen. Comprehensible credit scoring models using rule extraction from support vector machines. *European Journal of Operational Research*, 183 (3):1466–1476, December 2007.

[178] Adam Mathes. Folksonomies – cooperative classification and communication through shared metadata. *Computer Mediated Communication - LIS590CMC*, December 2004.

[179] Y. Matsuo and M. Ishizuka. Keyword extraction from a single document using word co-occurrence statistical information. *International Journal on Artificial Intelligence Tools*, 13(1):157–169, 2004.

[180] David D. McDonald. Internal and external evidence in the identification and semantic categorization of proper names. *Corpus processing for lexical acquisition*, pages 21–39, 1996.

[181] Alexander Mehler. Aspects of text semantics in hypertext. In Klaus Tochtermann, Jörg Westbomke, Uffe K. Wiil, and John J. Leggett, editors, *Returning to our Diverse Roots. Proceedings of the 10th ACM Conference on Hypertext and Hypermedia (Hypertext '99), February 21-25, 1999, Technische Universität Darmstadt*, pages 25–26, New York, 1999. ACM Press.

[182] Alexander Mehler. Hierarchical orderings of textual units. In *Proceedings of the 19th International Conference on Computational Linguistics, COLING'02, Taipei*, pages 646–652, San Francisco, 2002. Morgan Kaufmann.

[183] Alexander Mehler. Text linkage in the wiki medium — a comparative study. In Jussi Karlgren, editor, *Proceedings of the EACL Workshop on New Text — Wikis and blogs and other dynamic text sources, April 3-7, 2006, Trento, Italy*, pages 1–8, 2006.

[184] Alexander Mehler. A network perspective on intertextuality. In Peter Grzybek and Reinhard Köhler, editors, *Exact Methods in the Study of Language and Text*, Quantitative Linguistics, pages 437–446. De Gruyter, Berlin/New York, 2006.

[185] Alexander Mehler. Compositionality in quantitative semantics. A theoretical perspective on text mining. In Alexander Mehler and Reinhard Köhler, editors, *Aspects of Automatic Text Analysis*, Studies in Fuzziness and Soft Computing, pages 139–167. Springer, Berlin/New York, 2007.

[186] Alexander Mehler. Large text networks as an object of corpus linguistic studies. In Anke Lüdeling and Merja Kytö, editors, *Corpus Linguistics. An International Handbook of the Science of Language and Society*, pages 328–382. De Gruyter, Berlin/New York, 2008.

[187] Alexander Mehler. Structural similarities of complex networks: A computational model by example of wiki graphs. *Applied Artificial Intelligence*, 22(7–8):619–683, 2008.

[188] Alexander Mehler. On the impact of community structure on self-organizing lexical networks. In Andrew D. M. Smith, Kenny Smith,

and Ramon Ferrer i Cancho, editors, *Proceedings of the 7th Evolution of Language Conference (Evolang 2008), March 11-15, 2008, Barcelona*, pages 227–234. World Scientific, 2008.

[189] Alexander Mehler. A short note on social-semiotic networks from the point of view of quantitative semantics. In Harith Alani, Steffen Staab, and Gerd Stumme, editors, *Proceedings of the Dagstuhl Seminar on Social Web Communities, September 21-26, Dagstuhl.* 2008.

[190] Alexander Mehler. Structure formation in the web. A graph-theoretical model of hypertext types. In Andreas Witt and Dieter Metzing, editors, *Linguistic Modeling of Information and Markup Languages. Contributions to Language Technology*, Text, Speech and Language Technology. Springer, Dordrecht, 2009.

[191] Alexander Mehler. A quantitative graph model of social ontologies by example of Wikipedia. In Matthias Dehmer, Frank Emmert-Streib, and Alexander Mehler, editors, *Towards an Information Theory of Complex Networks: Statistical Methods and Applications*. Birkhäuser, Boston/Basel, 2009.

[192] Alexander Mehler and Rüdiger Gleim. Polymorphism in generic web units. A corpus linguistic study. In *Proceedings of Corpus Linguistics '05, July 14-17, 2005, University of Birmingham, Great Britian*, volume Corpus Linguistics Conference Series 1(1), 2005.

[193] Alexander Mehler and Rüdiger Gleim. The net for the graphs – towards webgenre representation for corpus linguistic studies. In Marco Baroni and Silvia Bernardini, editors, *WaCky! Working Papers on the Web as Corpus*, pages 191–224. Gedit, Bologna, 2006.

[194] Alexander Mehler and Reinhard Köhler. Machine learning in a semiotic perspective. In Alexander Mehler and Reinhard Köhler, editors, *Aspects of Automatic Text Analysis*, Studies in Fuzziness and Soft Computing, pages 1–29. Springer, Berlin/New York, 2007.

[195] Alexander Mehler and Angelika Storrer. What are ontologies good for? In Uwe Mönnich and Kai-Uwe Kühnberger, editors, *Proceedings*

of OTT'06 — Ontologies in Text Technology, pages 11–18, Osnabrück, 2007.

[196] Alexander Mehler and Ulli Waltinger. Enhancing document modeling by means of open topic models: Crossing the frontier of classification schemes in digital libraries by example of the DDC. *Library Hi Tech*, 2009.

[197] Alexander Mehler and Christian Wolff. Einleitung: Perspektiven und positionen des text mining. *Journal for Language Technology and Computational Linguistics (JLCL)*, 20(1):1–18, 2005.

[198] Alexander Mehler, Matthias Dehmer, and Rüdiger Gleim. Zur automatischen klassifikation von webgenres. In Bernhard Fisseni, Hans-Christina Schmitz, Bernhard Schröder, and Petra Wagner, editors, *Sprachtechnologie, mobile Kommunikation und linguistische Ressourcen. Beiträge zur GLDV-Frühjahrstagung '05, 10. März – 01. April 2005, Universität Bonn*, pages 158–174, Frankfurt a. M., 2005. Lang.

[199] Alexander Mehler, Matthias Dehmer, and Rüdiger Gleim. Towards logical hypertext structure – A graph-theoretic perspective. In Thomas Böhme and Gerhard Heyer, editors, *Proceedings of the Fourth International Workshop on Innovative Internet Computing Systems (I2CS '04)*, Lecture Notes in Computer Science 3473, pages 136–150, Berlin/New York, 2006. Springer.

[200] Alexander Mehler, Rüdiger Gleim, and Matthias Dehmer. Towards structure-sensitive hypertext categorization. In Myra Spiliopoulou, Rudolf Kruse, Christian Borgelt, Andreas Nürnberger, and Wolfgang Gaul, editors, *Proceedings of the 29th Annual Conference of the German Classification Society, March 9-11, 2005, Universität Magdeburg*, pages 406–413, Berlin/New York, 2006. Springer.

[201] Alexander Mehler, Peter Geibel, Rüdiger Gleim, Sebastian Herold, Brijnesh-Johannes Jain, and Olga Pustylnikov. Much ado about text content. Learning text types solely by structural differentiae. In Uwe Mönnich and Kai-Uwe Kühnberger, editors, *Proceedings of OTT'06 —*

Ontologies in Text Technology: Approaches to Extract Semantic Knowledge from Structured Information, Publications of the Institute of Cognitive Science (PICS), pages 63–71, Osnabrück, 2007.

[202] Alexander Mehler, Peter Geibel, and Olga Pustylnikov. Structural classifiers of text types: Towards a novel model of text representation. *Journal for Language Technology and Computational Linguistics (JLCL)*, 22(2): 51–66, 2007.

[203] Alexander Mehler, Rüdiger Gleim, and Armin Wegner. Structural uncertainty of hypertext types. An empirical study. In *Proceedings of the Workshop "Towards Genre-Enabled Search Engines: The Impact of NLP", September, 30, 2007, in conjunction with RANLP 2007, Borovets, Bulgaria*, pages 13–19, 2007.

[204] Alexander Mehler, Rüdiger Gleim, Alexandra Ernst, and Ulli Waltinger. WikiDB: Building interoperable wiki-based knowledge resources for semantic databases. *Sprache und Datenverarbeitung. International Journal for Language Data Processing*, 2008.

[205] Alexander Mehler, Rüdiger Gleim, Ulli Waltinger, Alexandra Ernst, Dietmar Esch, and Tobias Feith. ehumanities desktop — eine webbasierte arbeitsumgebung für die geisteswissenschaftliche fachinformatik. In *Proceedings of the Symposium "Sprachtechnologie und eHumanities", 26.–27. Februar, Duisburg-Essen University*. 2009.

[206] Sven Meyer zu Eißen. On Information Need and Categorizing Search. Feb 2007. URL http://ubdata.uni-paderborn.de/ediss/17/2007/meyer_zu/.

[207] Sven Meyer zu Eißen and Benno Stein. Genre Classification of Web Pages: User Study and Feasibility Analysis. In Susanne Biundo, Thom Frühwirth, and Günther Palm, editors, *KI 2004: Advances in Artificial Intelligence*, volume 3228 LNAI of *Lecture Notes in Artificial Intelligence*, pages 256–269, Berlin Heidelberg New York, September 2004. Springer. ISBN 0302-9743. URL http://www.springerlink.com/index/T50XXAMDEE88GCC7.

[208] Peter Mika. Social networks and the semantic web. In *WI '04: Proceedings of the 2004 IEEE/WIC/ACM International Conference on Web Intelligence*, pages 285–291, Washington, DC, USA, 2004. IEEE Computer Society. ISBN 0-7695-2100-2. doi: http://dx.doi.org/10.1109/WI.2004.128.

[209] Peter Mika. Ontologies are us: A unified model of social networks and semantics. In *Proceedings of the 4th International Semantic Web Conference (ISWC 2005)*, LNCS 3729, pages 1–18. Springer, 2005.

[210] Peter Mika and Aldo Gangemi. Descriptions of social relations. In *Proceedings of the 1st Workshop on Friend of a Friend, Social Networking and the (Semantic) Web*, 2004.

[211] Andrei Mikheev, Marc Moens, and Claire Grover. Named entity recognition without gazetteers. In *Proceedings of the Ninth Conference of the European Chapter of the Association for Computational Linguistics*, pages 1–8, 1999.

[212] Stanley Milgram. The small-world problem. *Psychology Today*, 2:60–67, 1967.

[213] George A. Miller and Walter G. Charles. Contextual correlates of semantic similiarity. *Language and Cognitive Processes*, 6(1):1–28, 1991.

[214] David Mills. What is the role of cloud computing, web 2.0, and web 3.0 semantic technologies in an era of connected governance? *Semantic Exchange - Semantic Community Workshop and Web Conference*, 2009.

[215] David Milne. Computing semantic relatedness using wikipedia link structure. In *Proc. of NZCSRSC07*, 2007.

[216] Tom M. Mitchell. *Machine Learning*. McGraw-Hill, New York, 1997.

[217] Ruslan Mitkov. *The Oxford Handbook of Computational Linguistics (Oxford Handbooks in Linguistics S.)*. Oxford University Press, 2003. ISBN 0198238827.

[218] Charles W. Morris. Foundations of the theory of signs. *International Encyclopedia of Unified Science*, 1938.

[219] Tony Mullen and Nigel Collier. Sentiment analysis using support vector machines with diverse information sources. In Dekang Lin and Dekai Wu, editors, *Proceedings of EMNLP 2004*, pages 412–418, Barcelona, Spain, July 2004. Association for Computational Linguistics.

[220] David Nadeau, Peter D. Turney, and Stan Matwin. Unsupervised named-entity recognition: Generating gazetteers and resolving ambiguity. In *In 19th Canadian Conference on Artificial Intelligence*, 2006.

[221] Mark E. J. Newman. Models of the small world. *Journal of Statistical Physics*, 101:819–841, 2000.

[222] Mark E. J. Newman and Juyong Park. Why social networks are different from other types of networks. *Physical Review E*, 68:036122, 2003.

[223] Hien T. Nguyen and Tru H. Cao. Named entity disambiguation: A hybrid statistical and rule-based incremental approach. In *ASWC '08: Proceedings of the 3rd Asian Semantic Web Conference on The Semantic Web*, pages 420–433, Berlin, Heidelberg, 2008. Springer-Verlag. ISBN 978-3-540-89703-3.

[224] Sergei Nirenburg and Victor Raskin. *Ontological Semantics*. MIT Press, Cambridge, MA, 2004. ISBN 978-0-262-14086-7.

[225] Winfried Noth. *Handbook of Semiotics (Advances in Semiotics)*. Indiana University Press, September 1995. ISBN 0253209595.

[226] OCLC. Dewey decimal classification summaries. A brief introduction to the dewey decimal classification. http://www.oclc.org/dewey/resources/summaries/default.htm [accessed January 10, 2010], 2008.

[227] C.K. Odgen and I.A. Richards. *The Meaning of Meaning A Study of the Influence of Language upon Thought and of the Science of Symbolism*. Routledge & Kegan Paul Ltd., London, 10 edition, 1923.

[228] O'Reilly. O'reilly – what is web 2.0. http://www.oreillynet.com/pub/a/oreilly/tim/news/2005/09/30/what-is-web-20.html [accessed May 25, 2010], 2005.

[229] Lawrence Page, Sergey Brin, Rajeev Motwani, and Terry Winograd. The pagerank citation ranking: Bringing order to the web. Technical Report 1999-66, Stanford InfoLab, November 1999. Previous number = SIDL-WP-1999-0120.

[230] David D. Palmer and Marti A. Hearst. Adaptive sentence boundary disambiguation. In *Proceedings of the fourth conference on Applied natural language processing*, pages 78–83, Morristown, NJ, USA, 1994. Association for Computational Linguistics.

[231] Pang and Lee. A sentimental education: Sentiment analysis using subjectivity summarization based on minimum cuts. In *In Proc. of the ACL*, pages 271–278, 2004.

[232] Bo Pang and Lillian Lee. Seeing stars: exploiting class relationships for sentiment categorization with respect to rating scales. In *ACL '05: Proc. of the 43rd Annual Meeting on Association for Computational Linguistics*, pages 115–124, Morristown, NJ, USA, 2005. Association for Computational Linguistics.

[233] Bo Pang and Lillian Lee. *Opinion Mining and Sentiment Analysis*. Now Publishers Inc, July 2008.

[234] Bo Pang, Lillian Lee, and Shivakumar Vaithyanathan. Thumbs up?: sentiment classification using machine learning techniques. In *Proc. of the ACL-02 EMNLP '02*, pages 79–86. ACL, 2002.

[235] Peter Patel-Schneider, Patrick Hayes, and Ian Horrocks. Daml+oil reference description. http://www.w3.org/TR/2001/NOTE-daml+oil-reference-20011218 [accessed May 25, 2010], 2001.

[236] Peter Patel-Schneider, Patrick Hayes, and Ian Horrocks. Owl web ontology language semantics and abstract syntax. http://www.w3.org/TR/owl-semantics/ [accessed May 25, 2010], 2004.

[237] Charles S. Peirce. *Collected Papers of Charles Sanders Peirce*. Belknap Press of Havard University Press, 1974. ISBN 1855065568.

[238] Charles Sanders Peirce. Peirce on signs. writings on the semiotic by charles sanders peirce. 1991.

[239] Viktor Pekar. Modeling semantic coherence from corpus data: The fact and the frequency of a co-occurrence. In Rachel Hayes, William D. Lewis, Erin L. O'Bryan, and Tania S. Zamuner, editors, *Language in Cognitive Science*, Coyote Papers 12. University of Arizona Linguistics Circle, Arizona, 2002.

[240] Fuchun Peng and Dale Schuurmans. Combining naive bayes and n-gram language models for text classification. In *In 25th European Conference on Information Retrieval Research (ECIR*, pages 335–350. Springer-Verlag, 2003.

[241] Hanchuan Peng, Fuhui Long, and Chris Ding. Feature selection based on mutual information: criteria of max-dependency, max-relevance, and min-redundancy. *IEEE Transactions on Pattern Analysis and Machine Intelligence*, 27:1226–1238, 2005.

[242] D. Pieper and F. Summann. Bielefeld academic search engine (base): An end-user oriented institutional repository search service. *Library Hi Tech*, 24(4):614–619, 2006.

[243] Ferran Pla and Antonio Molina. Improving part-of-speech tagging using lexicalized hmms. *Nat. Lang. Eng.*, 10(2):167–189, 2004. ISSN 1351-3249. doi: http://dx.doi.org/10.1017/S1351324904003353.

[244] Artem Polyvyanyy and Dominik Kuropka. *A quantitative evaluation of the enhanced topic-based vector space model*. Universitaetsverlag Potsdam, August 2007.

[245] Jan Pomikalek and Radim Radim Rehurek. The influence of preprocessing parameters on text categorization. *International Journal of Applied Science, Engineering and Technology*, 4(1):430–434, 2007.

[246] Simone Ponzetto and Michael Strube. Wikirelate! computing semantic relatedness using wikipedia. In *Proceedings of the Twenty-First National Conference on Artificial Intelligence*, July 2006.

[247] A. Popescul and L. Ungar. Automatic labeling of document clusters. http://www.cis.upenn.edu/~popescul/Publications/popescul00labeling.pdf [accessed May 25, 2010], 2000.

[248] M. F. Porter. An algorithm for suffix stripping. *Readings in information retrieval*, pages 313–316, 1997.

[249] Richard Power, Donia Scott, and Nadjet Bouayad-Agha. Document structure. *Computational Linguistics*, 29(2):211–260, 2003.

[250] Rudy Prabowo and Mike Thelwall. Sentiment analysis: A combined approach. *J. Informetrics*, 3(2):143–157, 2009.

[251] U. Quasthoff, M. Richter, and C. Biemann. Corpus portal for search in monolingual corpora. In *Proceedings of the LREC 2006*, Genoa, Italy, 2006.

[252] Uwe Quasthoff, Christian Biemann, and Christian Wolff. Named entity learning and verification: expectation maximization in large corpora. In *COLING-02: proceedings of the 6th conference on Natural language learning*, pages 1–7, Morristown, NJ, USA, 2002. Association for Computational Linguistics. doi: http://dx.doi.org/10.3115/1118853.1118876.

[253] Lawrence R. Rabiner. A tutorial on hidden markov models and selected applications in speech recognition. In *Proceedings of the IEEE*, pages 257–286, 1989.

[254] Sebastian Rahtz. Building tei dtds and schemas on demand. In *Paper presented at XML Europe 2003, London, March 2003*, Taganrog, Russia, 2003.

[255] Sharath Rao, Ian Lane, and Tanja Schultz. Optimizing sentence segmentation for spoken language translation. *INTERSPEECH-2007*, pages 2845–2848, 2007.

[256] Georg Rehm. Language-independent text parsing of arbitrary html-documents. towards a foundation for web genre identification. *Journal for Language Technology and Computational Linguistics (JLCL)*, 2005.

[257] Georg Rehm. *Hypertextsorten: Definition, Struktur, Klassifikation.* Phd thesis, Angewandte Sprachwissenschaft und Computerlinguistik, Justus-Liebig-Universität Gießen (JLU), 2007.

[258] Georg Rehm, Marina Santini, Alexander Mehler, Pavel Braslavski, Rüdiger Gleim, Andrea Stubbe, Svetlana Symonenko, Mirko Tavosanis, and Vedrana Vidulin. Towards a reference corpus of web genres for the evaluation of genre identification systems. In *Proceedings of the 6th Language Resources and Evaluation Conference (LREC 2008), Marrakech (Morocco)*, 2008.

[259] Robert Remus, Uwe Quasthoff, and Gerhard Heyer. Sentiws - a publicly available german-language resource for sentiment analysis. In Bente Maegaard Joseph Mariani Jan Odjik Stelios Piperidis Mike Rosner Daniel Tapias Nicoletta Calzolari (Conference Chair), Khalid Choukri, editor, *Proceedings of the Seventh conference on International Language Resources and Evaluation (LREC'10)*, Valletta, Malta, may 2010. European Language Resources Association (ELRA). ISBN 2-9517408-6-7.

[260] Philip Resnik. Using information content to evaluate semantic similarity in a taxonomy. In *Proceedings of the IJCAI 1995*, pages 448–453, 1995.

[261] Jeffrey C. Reynar and Adwait Ratnaparkhi. A maximum entropy approach to identifying sentence boundaries. In *Proceedings of the Fifth Conference on Applied Natural Language Processing*, pages 16–19, 1997.

[262] Burghard B. Rieger. *Unscharfe Semantik: die empirische Analyse, quantitative Beschreibung, formale Repr"asentation und prozedurale Modellierung vager Wortbedeutungen in Texten.* Verlag Peter Lang GmbH, Frankfurt am Main, 1989.

[263] Ellen Riloff and Rosie Jones. Learning dictionaries for information extraction by multi-level bootstrapping. In *AAAI '99/IAAI '99: Proceedings of the sixteenth national conference on Artificial intelligence and the eleventh Innovative applications of artificial intelligence conference innovative applications of artificial intelligence*, pages 474–479, Menlo Park, CA, USA, 1999. American Association for Artificial Intelligence. ISBN 0-262-51106-1.

[264] S. E. Robertson. The probability ranking principle in ir. *Readings in information retrieval*, pages 281–286, 1997.

[265] Stefphen Robertson. Understanding inverse document frequency: On theoretical arguments for idf. *Journal of Documentation*, 60(5):503–520, 2004.

[266] J. Rocchio. Relevance feedback in information retrieval. *The SMART Retrieval System*, pages 313–323, 1971.

[267] Jason B. Rosenberg and Christine L. Borgman. Extending the dewey decimal classification via keyword clustering: the science library catalog project. In *ASIS '92: Proceedings of the 55th annual meeting on Celebrating change : information management on the move*, pages 171–184, Silver Springs, MD, USA, 1992. American Society for Information Science. ISBN 0-938734-69-5.

[268] D. Roussinov, K. Crowston, M. Nilan, B. Kwasnik, J. Cai, and X. Liu. Genre based navigation on the web. In *HICSS '01: Proceedings of the 34th Annual Hawaii International Conference on System Sciences (HICSS-34)-Volume 4*, page 4013, Washington, DC, USA, 2001. IEEE Computer Society. ISBN 0-7695-0981-9.

[269] Herbert Rubenstein and John B. Goodenough. Contextual correlates of synonymy. *Communications of the ACM*, 8(10):627–633, 1965.

[270] Carl Sable, Kathleen Mckeown, and Kenneth W. Church. NLP found helpful (at least for one text categorization task). In *In Proceedings of the 2002 Conference on Empirical Methods in Natural Language Processing (EMNLP-02*, pages 172–179, 2002.

[271] Magnus Sahlgren. *The Word-Space Model: using distributional analysis to represent syntagmatic and paradigmatic relations between words in high-dimensional vector spaces*. PhD thesis, 2006.

[272] G. Salton and M. McGill. *Introduction to Modern Information Retrieval*. McGraw-Hill, New York, 1983.

[273] G. Salton, A. Wong, and C. S. Yang. A vector space model for automatic indexing. *Readings in information retrieval*, pages 273–280, 1997.

[274] Gerard Salton. *Automatic Information Organization and Retrieval*. Computer Science Series. McGraw-Hill, New York, 1968.

[275] Gerard Salton. *Automatic text processing. The transformation, analysis, and retrieval of information by computer*. Addison-Wesley Publishing, Reading Mass., 1989.

[276] Gerard Salton and Christopher Buckley. Term-weighting approaches in automatic text retrieval. *Information Processing and Management*, 24(5):513–523, 1988.

[277] Gerard Salton, A. Wong, and C. S. Yang. A vector space model for automatic indexing. *Communications of the Association for Computing Machinery*, 18(11):613–620, November 1975.

[278] Christer Samuelsson. Morphological tagging based entirely on bayesian inference. In R. Eklund, editor, *9th Scandinavian Conference on Computational Linguistics*, pages 225–238, Stockholm, Sweden, 1994.

[279] Marina Santini. Identifying genres of web pages. In *Proc. of TALN 2006*, 2006.

[280] Marina Santini. Some issues in automatic genre classification of web pages. In *8emes Journees Internationales d'Analyse statistique des Donnees Textuelles (JADT 2006)*, 2006.

[281] Marina Santini, Richard Power, and Roger Evans. Implementing a characterization of genre for automatic genre identification of web pages. In *Proceedings of the COLING/ACL on Main conference poster sessions*, pages 699–706, Morristown, NJ, USA, 2006. Association for Computational Linguistics.

[282] Marina Santini, Alexander Mehler, and Serge Sharoff. Genres on the web: Computational models and empirical studies. Submitted to Springer, Berlin/New York, 2009.

[283] Marina Santini, Alexander Mehler, and Serge Sharoff. Riding the rough waves of genre on the web: Concepts and research questions. In Alexander Mehler, Serge Sharoff, and Marina Santini, editors, *Genres on the Web: Computational Models and Empirical Studies*, pages 3–32. Submitted to Springer, Berlin/New York, 2009.

[284] Sebastian Schaffert, François Bry, Joachim Baumeister, and Malte Kiesel. Semantic wikis. *IEEE Software*, 25(4):8–11, 2008.

[285] I. Scharlau, U. Ansorge, and O. Neumann. Reaktionszeitmessung: Grundlagen und anwendungen. *Psycholinguistik - Psycholinguistics. Reihe Handbuecher zur Sprach- und Kommunikationswissenschaft*, pages 190–202, 2003.

[286] Helmut Schmid. Improvements in part-of-speech tagging with an application to german. In *In Proceedings of the ACL SIGDAT-Workshop*, pages 47–50, 1995.

[287] Hinrich Schütze. Automatic word sense discrimination. *Comput. Linguist.*, 24(1):97–123, 1998. ISSN 0891-2017.

[288] Fabrizio Sebastiani and Consiglio Nazionale Delle Ricerche. Machine learning in automated text categorization. *ACM Computing Surveys*, 34:1–47, 2002.

[289] Gregory Shakhnarovich, Trevor Darrell, and Piotr Indyk. *Nearest-Neighbor Methods in Learning and Vision: Theory and Practice (Neural Information Processing)*. The MIT Press, 2006.

[290] Shady Shehata, Fakhri Karray, and Mohamed Kamel. A concept-based model for enhancing text categorization. In *KDD '07: Proceedings of the 13th ACM SIGKDD international conference on Knowledge discovery and data mining*, pages 629–637, New York, NY, USA, 2007. ACM. ISBN 978-1-59593-609-7.

[291] Alexander Sigel. Content intelligence durch verknüpfung semantischer wissensdienste am beispiel von semblogging. *Vortrag auf dem 2. Kongress Semantic Web und Wissenstechnologien: Semantic Webservices*, 2005.

[292] C. Silva and B. Ribeiro. The importance of stop word removal on recall values in text categorization. In *Neural Networks, 2003. Proceedings of the International Joint Conference on*, volume 3, pages 1661–1666 vol.3, july 2003. doi: 10.1109/IJCNN.2003.1223656.

[293] Munindar P. Singh. A social semantics for agent communication languages. Technical report, Raleigh, NC, USA, 1999.

[294] John Sowa. *Conceptual structures: information processing in mind and machine*. Addison-Wesley Longman Publishing Co., Inc., Boston, MA, USA, 1984. ISBN 0-201-14472-7.

[295] John Sowa. Ontology, metadata, and semiotics. *Conceptual Structures: Logical, Linguistic, and Computational Issues*, pages 55–81, 2000. URL http://dx.doi.org/10.1007/10722280_5.

[296] Lucia Specia and Enrico Motta. Integrating folksonomies with the semantic web. In *ESWC '07: Proceedings of the 4th European conference on The Semantic Web*, pages 624–639, Berlin, Heidelberg, 2007. Springer-Verlag. ISBN 978-3-540-72666-1. doi: http://dx.doi.org/10.1007/978-3-540-72667-8_44.

[297] Steffen Staab and Rudi Studer, editors. *Handbook on Ontologies*. International Handbooks on Information Systems. Springer, 2004. ISBN 3-540-40834-7.

[298] Steffen Staab, Pedro Domingos, Peter Mika, Jennifer Golbeck, Li Ding, Tim Finin, Anupam Joshi, Andrzej Nowak, and Robin R. Vallacher. Social networks applied. *IEEE Intelligent Systems*, 20(1):80–93, 2005. ISSN 1541-1672. doi: http://dx.doi.org/10.1109/MIS.2005.16.

[299] Steffen Staab, Thomas Franz, Hans-Peter Schnurr, and Daniel Hansch. Semantische systeme für das wissensmanagement. *IM 8211*, IMC(2), 2008.

[300] Benno Stein and Sven Meyer zu Eißen. Topic Identification: Framework and Application. In Klaus Tochtermann and Hermann Maurer, editors, *Proceedings of the 4th International Conference on Knowledge*

Management (I-KNOW 04), Graz, Austria, Journal of Universal Computer Science, pages 353–360, Graz, Austria, July 2004. Know-Center.

[301] Benno Stein and Sven Meyer zu Eißen. Topic-Identifikation: Formalisierung, Analyse und neue Verfahren. *KI – Künstliche Intelligenz*, 3: 16–22, July 2007. ISSN 0933-1875.

[302] M. Steinbach, G. Karypis, and V. Kumar. A comparison of document clustering techniques. In *Proc. KDD Workshop on Text Mining*, 2000.

[303] Wolfgang G. Stock. Folksonomies and science communication: A mashup of professional science databases and web 2.0 services. *Inf. Serv. Use*, 27(3):97–103, 2007. ISSN 0167-5265.

[304] C. Strapparava and A. Valitutti. WordNet-Affect: an affective extension of WordNet. In *Proc. of LREC*, volume 4, pages 1083–1086, 2004.

[305] Russell C. Swan and James Allan. Extracting significant time varying features from text. In *CIKM*, pages 38–45, 1999.

[306] Russell C. Swan and James Allan. Automatic generation of overview timelines. In *SIGIR*, pages 49–56, 2000.

[307] Maite Taboada, Julian Brooke, and Manfred Stede. Genre-based paragraph classification for sentiment analysis. In *Proc. of the SIGDIAL 2009 Conference*, pages 62–70, London, UK, September 2009. Association for Computational Linguistics.

[308] Hirotoshi Taira and Masahiko Haruno. Feature selection in svm text categorization. In *AAAI '99/IAAI '99: Proceedings of the 6.th national conference on AI*, pages 480–486, Menlo Park, CA, USA, 1999. American Association for Artificial Intelligence.

[309] Hiroya Takamura, Takashi Inui, and Manabu Okumura. Extracting semantic orientations of words using spin model. In *Proc. of ACL '05*, pages 133–140. ACL, 2005.

[310] Hironori Takeuchi, L. Venkata Subramaniam, Shourya Roy, Diwakar Punjani, and Tetsuya Nasukawa. Sentence boundary detection in conversational speech transcripts using noisily labeled examples. *Int. J.*

Doc. Anal. Recognit., 10(3):147–155, 2007. ISSN 1433-2833. doi: http://dx.doi.org/10.1007/s10032-007-0056-y.

[311] Songbo Tan. Binary k-nearest neighbor for text categorization. *Online Information Review*, 29(4):391–399, 2005.

[312] Songbo Tan and Jin Zhang. An empirical study of sentiment analysis for chinese documents. *Expert Syst. Appl.*, 34(4):2622–2629, 2008.

[313] TEI Consortium. The text encoding initiative. http://www.tei-c.org/.

[314] Egidio Terra and C. L. A. Clarke. Frequency estimates for statistical word similarity measures. In *NAACL '03: Proceedings of the 2003 Conference of the North American Chapter of the Association for Computational Linguistics on Human Language Technology*, pages 165–172, Morristown, NJ, USA, 2003. Association for Computational Linguistics. doi: http://dx.doi.org/10.3115/1073445.1073477.

[315] Pucktada Treeratpituk and Jamie Callan. Automatically labeling hierarchical clusters. In *dg.o '06: Proceedings of the 2006 international conference on Digital government research*, pages 167–176, New York, NY, USA, 2006. ACM. doi: http://doi.acm.org/10.1145/1146598.1146650.

[316] Yuen-Hsien Tseng. Multilingual keyword extraction for term suggestion. In *SIGIR '98: Proceedings of the 21st annual international ACM SIGIR conference on Research and development in information retrieval*, pages 377–378, New York, NY, USA, 1998. ACM. ISBN 1-58113-015-5.

[317] Peter Turney. Coherent keyphrase extraction via web mining. In *In Proceedings of IJCAI*, pages 434–439, 2003.

[318] Peter D. Turney. Thumbs up or thumbs down?: semantic orientation applied to unsupervised classification of reviews. In *ACL '02: Proc. of the 40th Annual Meeting on Association for Computational Linguistics*, pages 417–424, Morristown, NJ, USA, 2001. Association for Computational Linguistics.

[319] Peter D. Turney and Michael L. Littman. Unsupervised learning of semantic orientation from a hundred-billion-word corpus. *CoRR*, cs.LG/0212012, 2002.

[320] Hans Uszkoreit, Thorsten Brants, Sabine Brants, and Christine Foeldesi. NEGRA Corpus. http://www.coli.uni-saarland.de/projects/sfb378/negra-corpus/ [accessed May 25, 2010], 2006.

[321] C. J. van Rijsbergen. *Information Retrieval*. Butterworths, London, 1979. URL http://www.dcs.gla.ac.uk/Keith/Preface.html.

[322] C. J. van Rijsbergen. A non-classical logic for information retrieval. *Readings in information retrieval*, pages 268–272, 1997.

[323] Vladimir N. Vapnik. *The nature of statistical learning theory*. Springer-Verlag New York, Inc., New York, NY, USA, 1995. ISBN 0-387-94559-8.

[324] Olga Vechtomova. Query expansion for information retrieval. In *Encyclopedia of Database Systems*, pages 2254–2257. 2009.

[325] Olga Vechtomova and Murat Karamuftuoglu. Query expansion with terms selected using lexical cohesion analysis of documents. *Inf. Process. Manage.*, 43(4):849–865, 2007.

[326] Remco C. Veltkamp and Michiel Hagedoorn. Shape similarity measures, properties, and constructions. In *In Advances in Visual Information Systems, 4th International Conference, VISUAL 2000*, pages 467–476. Springer, 2000.

[327] David Vilar, Hermann Ney, Alfons Juan, and Enrique Vidal. Effect of feature smoothing methods in text classification tasks. In *Pattern Recognition in Information Systems, Proceedings of the 4th International Workshop on Pattern Recognition in Information Systems, PRIS 2004, In conjunction with ICEIS 2004, Porto, Portugal, April 2004*, 2004.

[328] Martin Volk and Gerold Scheider. Comparing a statistical and a rule-based tagger for german. In *Computers, Linguistics, and Phonetics between Language and Speech. Proc. of the 4th Conference on Natural Language Processing - KONVENS-98*, pages 125–137, 1998.

[329] U. von Luxburg. *Statistical Learning with Similarity and Dissimilarity Functions*. PhD thesis, Berlin, Germany, 2004.

[330] Ellen M. Voorhees. Query expansion using lexical-semantic relations. In *SIGIR '94: Proceedings of the 17th annual international ACM SIGIR conference on Research and development in information retrieval*, pages 61–69, New York, NY, USA, 1994. Springer-Verlag New York, Inc. ISBN 0-387-19889-X.

[331] Ellen M. Voorhees and Donna Harman. Overview of the fifth text retrieval conference (trec-5). In *TREC*, 1996.

[332] Piek Vossen, editor. *EuroWordNet: a multilingual database with lexical semantic networks*. Kluwer Academic Publishers, Norwell, MA, USA, 1998. ISBN 0-7923-5295-5.

[333] Ipke Wachsmuth. 'I, Max' - Communicating with an Artificial Agent. In Ipke Wachsmuth and Günther Knoblich, editors, *ZiF Workshop*, volume 4930 of *Lecture Notes in Computer Science*, pages 279–295. Springer, 2006. ISBN 978-3-540-79036-5.

[334] Ipke Wachsmuth and Barbara Gängler. Knowledge packets and knowledge packet structure. In *Text Understanding in LILOG, Integrating Computational Linguistics and Artificial Intelligence, Final Report on the IBM Germany LILOG-Project*, pages 380–393, London, UK, 1991. Springer-Verlag. ISBN 3-540-54594-8.

[335] Ipke Wachsmuth and Günther Knoblich. Embodied communication in humans and machines — a research agenda. *Artif. Intell. Rev.*, 24(3-4): 517–522, 2005. ISSN 0269-2821.

[336] Thomas Vander Wal. Folksonomy coinage and definition. http://vanderwal.net/folksonomy.html [accessed May 25, 2010], 2004.

[337] Ulli Waltinger. Polarity reinforcement: Sentiment polarity identification by means of social semantics. In *Proceedings of the IEEE Africon 2009, September 23-25, Nairobi, Kenya*, 2009.

[338] Ulli Waltinger. GermanPolarityClues: A lexical resource for german sentiment analysis. In Bente Maegaard Joseph Mariani Jan Odjik Stelios Piperidis Mike Rosner Daniel Tapias Nicoletta Calzolari (Conference Chair), Khalid Choukri, editor, *Proceedings of the Seventh conference on International Language Resources and Evaluation (LREC'10)*, Valletta, Malta, may 2010. European Language Resources Association (ELRA). ISBN 2-9517408-6-7.

[339] Ulli Waltinger. Sentiment analysis reloaded: A comparative study on sentiment polarity identification combining machine learning and subjectivity features. In *Proceedings of the 6th International Conference on Web Information Systems and Technologies (WEBIST 2010), Valencia*, 2010.

[340] Ulli Waltinger and Alexander Mehler. Who is it? context sensitive named entity and instance recognition by means of Wikipedia. In *Proceedings of the 2008 IEEE/WIC/ACM International Conference on Web Intelligence (WI-2008)*. 2008.

[341] Ulli Waltinger and Alexander Mehler. Social semantics and its evaluation by means of semantic relatedness and open topic models. In *Proceedings of the 2009 IEEE/WIC/ACM International Conference on Web Intelligence*, 2009.

[342] Ulli Waltinger and Alexander Mehler. The feature difference coefficient: Classification by means of feature distributions. In *Proceedings of Text Mining Services (TMS), March 23-25, Leipzig, Germany*, 2009.

[343] Ulli Waltinger, Alexander Mehler, and Gerhard Heyer. Towards automatic content tagging: Enhanced web services in digital libraries using lexical chaining. In *4rd International Conference on Web Information Systems and Technologies (WEBIST '08), 4-7 May, Funchal, Portugal*. Barcelona, 2008.

[344] Ulli Waltinger, Alexander Mehler, and Maik Stührenberg. An integrated model of lexical chaining: Application, resources and its format. In *Proceedings of KONVENS 2008*, 2008.

[345] Ulli Waltinger, Irene Cramer, and Tonio Wandmacher. From social networks to distributional properties: A comparative study on computing semantic relatedness. In *Proceedings of the Annual Meeting of the Cognitive Science Society - CogSci 2009, Amsterdam (NL), 2009*, 2009.

[346] Ulli Waltinger, Alexander Mehler, and Rüdiger Gleim. Social semantics and its evaluation by means of closed topic models: An svm-classification approach using semantic feature replacement by topic generalization. In *Proceedings of the GSCL-Conference, Potsdam (DE), 2009.*, 2009.

[347] Ulli Waltinger, Alexander Mehler, and Armin Wegner. A two-level approach to web genre classification. In *Proceedings of the 5th International Conference on Web Information Systems and Technologies (WEBIST '09), March 23-26, 2007, Lisboa*, 2009.

[348] T. Wandmacher. How semantic is Latent Semantic Analysis? In *Proceedings of TALN/RECITAL'05*, Dourdan, France, 2005.

[349] Pu Wang and Carlotta Domeniconi. Building semantic kernels for text classification using wikipedia. In *KDD08: Proceeding of the 14th ACM SIGKDD international conference on Knowledge discovery and data mining*, pages 713–721, New York, NY, USA, 2008. ACM.

[350] Christian Wartena and Rogier Brussee. Topic detection by clustering keywords. In *DEXA '08: Proceedings of the 2008 19th International Conference on Database and Expert Systems Application*, pages 54–58, Washington, DC, USA, 2008. IEEE Computer Society. ISBN 978-0-7695-3299-8.

[351] Duncan J. Watts and Steven H. Strogatz. Collective dynamics of 'small-world' networks. *Nature*, 393:440–442, 1998.

[352] Armin Wegner. *Nachbarschaften im semantischen Raum*. PhD thesis, Universität Trier, 2006.

[353] Xing Wei. *Topic models in information retrieval*. PhD thesis, 2007.

[354] Dawid Weiss. *Descriptive Clustering as a Method for Exploring Text Collections*. PhD thesis, Poznan University of Technology, 2006.

[355] Dominic Widdows. *Geometry and Meaning*. Center for the Study of Language and Inf, November 2004. ISBN 1575864487.

[356] Dominic Widdows and Kathleen Ferraro. Semantic vectors: a scalable open source package and online technology management application. In European Language Resources Association (ELRA), editor, *Proceedings of the Sixth International Language Resources and Evaluation (LREC'08)*, Marrakech, Morocco, May 2008.

[357] Janyce Wiebe and Ellen Riloff. Creating subjective and objective sentence classifiers from unannotated texts. In *Proc. of CICLing-05*, volume 3406, pages 475–486, Mexico City, MX, 2005. Springer-Verlag.

[358] Janyce Wiebe, Theresa Wilson, and Claire Cardie. Annotating expressions of opinions and emotions in language. *Language Resources and Evaluation*, 1(2):0, 2005.

[359] Michael Wiegand and Dietrich Klakow. The role of knowledge-based features in polarity classification at sentence level. In *Proc. of the 22nd Int. FLAIRS Conference (FLAIRS-2009)*, Athens, Greece, 2009.

[360] Theresa Wilson, Janyce Wiebe, and Paul Hoffmann. Recognizing contextual polarity in phrase-level sentiment analysis. In *Proc. of the HLT '05*, pages 347–354. ACL, 2005.

[361] René Witte and Jutta Mülle, editors. *Text Mining: Wissensgewinnung aus natürlichsprachigen Dokumenten*, Interner Bericht 2006-5, 2006. Universität Karlsruhe, Fakultät für Informatik, Institut für Programmstrukturen und Datenorganisation (IPD).

[362] Ian H. Witten, Gordon Paynter, Eibe Frank, Carl Gutwin, and Craig G. Nevill-Manning. Kea: Practical automatic keyphrase extraction. In *Proceedings of Digital Libraries 99 (DL'99*, pages 254–255, 1999.

[363] S. K. M. Wong, Wojciech Ziarko, and Patrick C. N. Wong. Generalized vector spaces model in information retrieval. In *SIGIR '85: Proceedings of the 8th annual international ACM SIGIR conference on Research and development in information retrieval*, pages 18–25, New York, NY, USA, 1985. ACM. ISBN 0-89791-159-8.

[364] Zhibiao Wu and Martha Palmer. Verb semantics and lexical selection. In *Proceedings of the 32nd Annual Meeting of the Association for Computational Linguistics*, pages 133–138, 1994.

[365] Jinxi Xu and W. Bruce Croft. Improving the effectiveness of information retrieval with local context analysis. *ACM Trans. Inf. Syst.*, 18(1):79–112, January 2000.

[366] Yiming Yang. An evaluation of statistical approaches to text categorization. *Journal of Information Retrieval*, 1:67–88, 1999.

[367] Yiming Yang and Jan O. Pedersen. A comparative study on feature selection in text categorization. In *ICML '97: Proceedings of the Fourteenth International Conference on Machine Learning*, pages 412–420, San Francisco, CA, USA, 1997. Morgan Kaufmann Publishers Inc. ISBN 1-55860-486-3.

[368] Kwan Yi and Jamshid Beheshti. A hidden markov model-based text classification of medical documents. *J. Inf. Sci.*, 35(1):67–81, 2009. ISSN 0165-5515. doi: http://dx.doi.org/10.1177/0165551508092257.

[369] Hong Yu and Vasileios Hatzivassiloglou. Towards answering opinion questions: Separating facts from opinions and identifying the polarity of opinion sentences. In *Proc. of EMNLP'03*, 2003.

[370] Lehel Csato. Zalan Bodo, Zsolt Minier. Text categorization experiments using wikipedia. In *Proceedings of the 1st Knowledge Engineering: Principles and Techniques, Cluj-Napoca, Romania, 2007*, pages 66–72, 2007.

[371] Torsten Zesch, Iryna Gurevych, and Max Mühlhäuser. Comparing wikipedia and german wordnet by evaluating semantic relatedness on multiple datasets. In *In Proc. of NAACL-HLT*, 2007.

[372] Torsten Zesch, Christof Müller, and Iryna Gurevych. Extracting lexical semantic knowledge from wikipedia and wiktionary. In *Proceedings of the Conference on Language Resources and Evaluation (LREC), electronic proceedings*, Mai 2008.

[373] GuoDong Zhou and Jian Su. Named entity recognition using an hmm-based chunk tagger. In *ACL '02: Proceedings of the 40th Annual Meeting on Association for Computational Linguistics*, pages 473–480, Morristown, NJ, USA, 2002. Association for Computational Linguistics.

[374] Xiaojin Zhu. Semi-supervised learning literature survey. Technical Report 1530, Computer Sciences, University of Wisconsin-Madison, 2005.

[375] V. Zlatic, M. Bozicevic, H. Stefancic, and M. Domazet. Wikipedias: Collaborative web-based encyclopedias as complex networks. *Physical Review E 74*, Jul 2006.

Die VDM Verlagsservicegesellschaft sucht für wissenschaftliche Verlage abgeschlossene und herausragende

Dissertationen, Habilitationen, Diplomarbeiten, Master Theses, Magisterarbeiten usw.

für die kostenlose Publikation als Fachbuch.

Sie verfügen über eine Arbeit, die hohen inhaltlichen und formalen Ansprüchen genügt, und haben Interesse an einer honorarvergüteten Publikation?

Dann senden Sie bitte erste Informationen über sich und Ihre Arbeit per Email an *info@vdm-vsg.de*.

Sie erhalten kurzfristig unser Feedback!

VDM Verlagsservicegesellschaft mbH
Dudweiler Landstr. 99   Telefon +49 681 3720 174
D - 66123 Saarbrücken   Fax   +49 681 3720 1749
www.vdm-vsg.de

Die VDM Verlagsservicegesellschaft mbH vertritt

Printed by Books on Demand GmbH, Norderstedt / Germany